NEW INTERNATIONAL BIBLICAL COMMENTARY

Old Testament Editors,
Robert L. Hubbard Jr.
Robert K. Johnston

PROVERBS, ECCLESIASTES, SONG OF SONGS

Old Testament Series

NEW INTERNATIONAL BIBLICAL COMMENTARY

PROVERBS, ECCLESIASTES, SONG OF SONGS

ROLAND E. MURPHY, O. Carm.
ELIZABETH HUWILER

Based on the New International Version

© 1999 by Hendrickson Publishers, Inc.
P. O. Box 3473
Peabody, Massachusetts 01961–3473

First published jointly, June 1999, in the United States by Hendrickson
Publishers and in the United Kingdom by the Paternoster Press, P. O.
Box 300, Carlisle, Cumbria CA3 0QS.

Printed in the United States of America

ISBN 1–56563–221–4

First printing — June 1999

Library of Congress Cataloging-in-Publication Data

Murphy, Roland Edmund, 1917–
    Proverbs, Ecclesiastes, Song of Songs / Roland E.
Murphy, Elizabeth Huwiler; Old Testament editors, Robert L.
Hubbard, Jr., Robert K. Johnston.
        (New International biblical commentary; 12)
    Includes bibliographical references and index.
    ISBN 1–56563–221–4 (pbk.)
        1. Bible. O.T. Proverbs—Commentaries. 2. Bible. O.T.
Ecclesiastes—Commentaries. 3. Bible. O.T. Song of
Solomon—Commentaries. I. Huwiler, Elizabeth, 1952–   .
II. Hubbard, Robert L., 1943–   . III. Johnston, Robert K.,
1945–   . IV. Title. V. Series.
    BS1465.3.M87   1999
223'.07—dc21   98-54757
                                                                                      CIP

British Library Cataloguing in Publication Data
A catalogue record for this book is available
from the British Library.

ISBN 0–85364–733–X

Dedicated to the Catholic and Lutheran communities we serve

Table of Contents

Foreword
New International Biblical Commentary

As an ancient document, the Old Testament often seems something quite foreign to modern men and women. Opening its pages may feel, to the modern reader, like traversing a kind of literary time warp into a whole other world. In that world sisters and brothers marry, long hair mysteriously makes men super-human, and temple altars daily smell of savory burning flesh and sweet incense. There, desert bushes burn but leave no ashes, water gushes from rocks, and cities fall because people march around them. A different world, indeed!

Even God, the Old Testament's main character, seems a stranger compared to his more familiar New Testament counter-part. Sometimes the divine is portrayed as a loving father and faithful friend, someone who rescues people from their greatest dangers or generously rewards them for heroic deeds. At other times, however, God resembles more a cruel despot, one furious at human failures, raving against enemies, and bloodthirsty for revenge. Thus, skittish about the Old Testament's diverse por-trayal of God, some readers carefully select which portions of the text to study, or they avoid the Old Testament altogether.

The purpose of this commentary series is to help readers navigate this strange and sometimes forbidding literary and spiritual terrain. Its goal is to break down the barriers between the ancient and modern worlds so that the power and meaning of these biblical texts become transparent to contemporary readers. How is this to be done? And what sets this series apart from oth-ers currently on the market?

This commentary series will bypass several popular ap-proaches to biblical interpretation. It will not follow a *precritical* approach that interprets the text without reference to recent scholarly conversations. Such a commentary contents itself with offering little more than a paraphrase of the text with occasional supplements from archaeology, word studies, and classical theol-ogy. It mistakenly believes that there have been few insights into the Bible since Calvin or Luther. Nor will this series pursue an *anticritical* approach whose preoccupation is to defend the Bible against its detractors, especially scholarly ones. Such a commentary has little space left to move beyond showing why the Bible's critics are wrong to explaining what the biblical text means. The result is a paucity of vibrant biblical theology. Again, this series finds inadequate a *critical* approach that seeks to understand the text apart from belief in the meaning it conveys. Though modern readers have been taught to be discerning, they do not want to live in the "desert of criticism" either.

Instead, as its editors, we have sought to align this series with what has been labeled *believing criticism*. This approach marries probing, reflective interpretation of the text to loyal biblical devotion and warm Christian affection. Our contributors tackle the task of interpretation using the full range of critical methodologies and practices. Yet they do so as people of faith who hold the text in the highest regard. The commentators in this series use criticism to bring the message of the biblical texts vividly to life so the minds of modern readers may be illumined and their faith deepened.

The authors in this series combine a firm commitment to modern scholarship with a similar commitment to the Bible's full authority for Christians. They bring to the task the highest technical skills, warm theological commitment, and rich insight from their various communities. In so doing, they hope to enrich the life of the academy as well as the life of the church.

Part of the richness of this commentary series derives from its authors' breadth of experience and ecclesial background. As editors, we have consciously brought together a diverse group of scholars in terms of age, gender, denominational affiliation, and race. We make no claim that they represent the full expression of the people of God, but they do bring fresh, broad perspectives to the interpretive task. But though this series has sought out diversity among its contributors, they also reflect a commitment to a common center. These commentators write as "believing critics"—scholars who desire to speak for church and academy, for academy and church. As editors, we offer this series in devotion to God and for the enrichment of God's people.

ROBERT L. HUBBARD JR.
ROBERT K. JOHNSTON
Editors

Abbreviations

AB	Anchor Bible
AEL	*Ancient Egyptian Literature.* M. Lichtheim. 3 vols. Berkeley, 1971–1980
ANET	J. B. Pritchard, ed. *Ancient Near Eastern Texts*
Aram.	Aramaic
ATD	*Das Alte Testament Deutsch*
Bar.	Baruch
BASP	*Bulletin of the American Society of Papyrologists*
BETL	Bibliotheca Ephemeridum theologicarum lovaniensium
BHS	*Biblia Hebraica Stuttgartensia*
BKAT	Biblischer Kommentar, Altes Testament. Ed. M. Noth and H. W. Wolff
BLS	Bible and Literature Series
BZAW	Beihefte zur Zeitschrift für die alttestamentliche Wissenschaft
CBQ	*Catholic Biblical Quarterly*
CBQMS	Catholic Biblical Quarterly Monograph Series
CBSC	Cambridge Bible for Schools and Colleges
CC	Continental Commentaries
ComC	Communicator's Commentary (= Mastering the Old Testament)
cf.	confer, compare
ch(s).	chapter(s)
CurRBS	*Currents in Research: Biblical Studies*
DSB	Daily Study Bible
EBC	*The Expositor's Biblical Commentary*
e.g.	*exempli gratia,* for example
esp.	especially
etc.	*et cetera,* and the rest
f(f).	and following

FCB	Feminist Companion to the Bible
Gk.	Greek, referring to lexical forms
HAT	Handbuch zum Alten Testament
Hb.	Hebrew
HBC	*Harper's Bible Commentary*. Ed. J. L. Mays et al. San Francisco, 1988
HBIS	History of Biblical Interpretation Series
ICC	International Critical Commentary
i.e.	*id est*, that is
Int	*Interpretation*
JBL	*Journal of Biblical Literature*
JSOT	*Journal for the Study of the Old Testament*
JSOTSup	Journal for the Study of the Old Testament: Supplement Series
JTS	*Journal of Theological Studies*
KBW	Katholisches Bibelwerk
KPG	Knox Publishing Guides
LBC	Layman's Bible Commentary
lit.	literally
LXX	Septuagint
MT	Masoretic Text
n(n).	note(s)
NAB	New American Bible
NAC	The New American Commentary
NCBC	New Century Bible Commentary
NIV	New International Version
NJB	New Jerusalem Bible
NJBC	*The New Jerome Biblical Commentary*. Ed. R. E. Brown et al.; Englewood Cliffs, 1990
NJPS	Tanakh, The Holy Scriptures
NRSV	New Revised Standard Version
OBO	Orbis biblicus et orientalis
OBT	Overtures to Biblical Theology
OT	Old Testament
OTG	Old Testament Guides
OTL	Old Testament Library
OTM	Old Testament Message
p(p).	page(s)
RB	*Revue biblique*
REB	Revised English Bible
rev.	revised (by)
RSV	Revised Standard Version

RV	Revised Version
SB	Sources bibliques
SBLDS	Society of Biblical Literature Dissertation Series
SBS	Stuttgarter Bibelstudien
Sir.	Sirach (Ecclesiasticus)
TBC	Torch Bible Commentaries
TDOT	*Theological Dictionary of the Old Testament*
TLZ	*Theologische Literaturzeitung*
Tob.	Tobit
TOTC	Tyndale Old Testament Commentaries
UF	*Ugarit-Forschungen*
v(v).	verse(s)
VT	*Vetus Testamentum*
VTSup	Vetus Testamentum Supplements
WBC	Word Biblical Commentary
WC	Westminster Commentaries
Wis.	Wisdom of Solomon
WMANT	Wissenschaftliche Monographien zum Alten und Neuen Testament
ZAW	*Zeitschrift für die alttestamentliche Wissenschaft*
ZBk	Zürcher Bibelkommentare

Proverbs

Roland E. Murphy, O. Carm.

Introduction: Proverbs

Wisdom Literature

At the outset it is necessary to discuss some features of the so-called Wisdom literature to which Proverbs, along with two other books in the Hebrew Bible, Job and Ecclesiastes (Qoheleth), belongs. The Roman Catholic and Greek Orthodox Churches would also include Sirach (Ecclesiasticus) and the Wisdom of Solomon in the body of canonical Wisdom literature. First, the age and the character of these writings should be noted. For the most part, they date from the postexilic period (Prov. 10–31 is probably largely preexilic; Job is difficult to date). While there is an oral stage to be presumed in the handing down of the collections that came to be assembled in the book of Proverbs, the rest of the works are literary compositions. This does not mean, for instance, that Ben Sira (writer of Sirach) composed the many sayings in his work off the top of his head in a scriptorium. It means, rather, that his book is the repository of a written and unwritten tradition that he controlled and expanded. The second characteristic of this wisdom tradition—and this has been a conundrum for biblical scholars—is the almost complete absence of the other traditions that figure explicitly and largely in the Torah and the Prophets. These other traditions include the promises to the patriarchs, the exodus, Sinai and covenant, and so forth. Only late in the wisdom movement is there any sign of these conventions—in Sirach 44–50 and Wisdom 10–19. The absence of these traditions is further underscored by the international character of wisdom: the wisdom of Israel is similar to that of her neighbors (e.g., Prov. 22:17–23:11 has similarities with the teaching of the Egyptian author Amenemope, who wrote a document of teachings on civil service).

How then is one to appraise the Wisdom literature? It is useful to distinguish between content and method. The content has to do mainly with human conduct in society before God. Wisdom literature is therefore cut from the same cloth as the material found in the Decalogue, but it is not put forth in terms of covenant obligations. The goal is to mold the character of an individual. The style is both demanding and experiential. Thus it may at times command or prohibit, but more often it will attempt to slyly persuade. Certain ideals emerge: fear of the Lord, prudent action, attitude to one's family and neighbor, self-control, the art of sensible speaking, wisdom as a means to the fuller life, etc. It is the experiential style that constitutes perhaps the most endearing aspect of wisdom. It observes and puts forth the situation "as it really is." It appreciates ambiguities that cannot be solved in a one-sided manner. It approaches God in a calm and yet often disputatious fashion (Job). It is beset with its own particular problems, especially that of retribution. This issue appears in every book from Proverbs to the Wisdom of Solomon without ever arriving at a full answer—only insights. In other words, these books of wisdom describe a long and fascinating journey in the life of Israel.[1]

Who are the teachers or sages to whom we owe the origins and transmission of these works? Scholars come down on opposing sides on this issue. Some maintain that it comes from the sphere of the family in the home and reflects tribal wisdom. Others believe wisdom is the product of the cultivated sages of the school, especially the court school in Jerusalem. Neither answer is a clear winner, and perhaps that is the way it should be. Both answers contain some truth. One may combine them by recognizing that the family would have been the natural setting for training the young. Then, as time passed, the court would have needed disciplined and educated courtiers, much as we see in Egypt, for instance. In the scholarly writings of the twentieth century there was a tendency to exaggerate the influence of Egypt and Mesopotamia upon Israelite wisdom. Scholars are gradually forming a more balanced judgment, although one must affirm the undeniable influence of such works as those of Ahiqar (Mesopotamia) and Amenemope (Egypt).[2]

In recent times much has been written about wisdom influence on other parts of the Bible. This influence is to be expected, but it should not be exaggerated. There are only five wisdom books, it would appear. But one can recognize some influence of wisdom in such Psalms as 37 and 73, for example. Perhaps "influence" is not the proper way of stating the question. Some parts of the Bible are simply written from the point of view of human experience, a primary characteristic of what we call Wisdom literature.[3]

Proverbs: Structure and Style

One cannot mistake the basic structure of Proverbs. It is a collection of collections that were formed over many centuries. This compilation is indicated by the titles that mark off certain parts:

1:1, "the proverbs of Solomon" (for chs. 1–9, and also 10–31?)

10:1, "the proverbs of Solomon" (10:1–22:16; there is probably more than one collection in this group)

22:17, "the sayings of the wise" (emended text)

24:23, "these also (belong) to the wise"

25:1, "the proverbs of Solomon" (the work of the men of King Hezekiah)

30:1, "the sayings of Agur"

31:1, "the sayings of Lemuel"

31:10–31, there is no title here, but an acrostic poem about an ideal wife begins at verse 10

A prominent feature of the book's structure is the difference between the intense didactic tone of the wisdom poems in chapters 1–9 and the various kinds of discrete sayings in chapters 10–31. It has been said with some justification that 1–9 is the hermeneutical key to what follows—that these chapters were composed to serve as an introduction (see esp. 1:1–7) to the rest of the book that had more or less received its final form. This "introduction" is commonly dated to the postexilic period.

The styles of writing found in Proverbs are quite varied, even if all reflect a wisdom background. Proverbs 2 can serve as an example of a full poem. It has twenty-two lines (the number of letters in the Hebrew alphabet). It is not, however, an obvious acrostic poem where each line begins with a successive letter of the Hebrew alphabet, as in Proverbs 31:10–31. The commentary below will point out some of the alphabetical tricks the writers employ. The twenty-two-line poem is particularly in evidence in the book of Sirach (e.g., 1:11–30; 5:1–6:4, etc.).

However, the more common literary expressions found in Proverbs are the short staccato sayings that are marked by the various kinds of parallelism which characterize biblical poetry. This commentary adopts the convenient and traditional classification of parallelism proposed by Bishop R. Lowth: *synonymous, antithetic,* and (for want of a better term), *synthetic.* Usually two short lines agree in presenting roughly similar meanings. But the second line is not simply repetitious; it usually specifies or intensifies the notion in the first line (synonymous parallelism). In antithetical parallelism, the subsequent line contrasts the thought of the first. It can also expand the meaning to effect a progression or further development in the saying (synthetic parallelism).[4]

The reader will also quite often meet five more technical terms that identify literary devices found throughout the book. *Chiasm* is a poetic structure whereby parallel words or themes of a verse or unit are arranged to form an inverted sequence, resembling the pattern a-b, b-a (e.g., 3:11–12). *Inclusio,* or inclusion, is a literary technique in which the opening word, phrase, or idea is repeated or restated at the end of the unit (e.g., 3:13–18). A *casus pendens* refers to a grammatical element, especially the subject of a verb, isolated outside a clause (usually at the beginning), but tied into the line by some connective, such as a pronoun (e.g., 17:13, 15). The terms *Qere* (what is read) and *Kethib* (what is written) are terms employed by the Masoretes, who handed down the text, to designate variant readings in the tradition. Qere was written in the margin, as opposed to Kethib, which is written within the text itself; cf. Prov. 20:16.

Another feature of the proverb is the frequent juxtaposition (without a connective, such as is/are) of subject and predicate. Thus, Proverbs 12:1, "A lover of discipline—a lover of knowledge."[5] This style is more impressive in Hebrew than in English, where it can hardly be duplicated. The Hebrew term *māšāl,* commonly but inadequately rendered as "proverb," has a root meaning of "compare." This meaning is adequate for most of the biblical sayings.

The sayings can be of the following kinds: sheer observations, value judgments, "better" sayings, comparisons, numerical sayings, beatitudes ("happy the one who . . ."), "abomination" sayings, and so forth. In addition to these various forms, the style is replete with such literary tricks as assonance, alliteration, and plays on words. Again, it is practically impossible to carry these over into another language. Thus, "when pride comes, then comes disgrace" (11:2a) does not capture the rhythmic sound of the Hebrew *bā'-zādôn wayyābô' qālôn*. As English speakers we are well aware of the power of alliteration in the formation of a saying. Thus, we say, "look before you leap" (note: lk/lp) or "the one who hesitates is lost" (note: st/ts/st). To treat these characteristics adequately would require another book.[6]

The two English sayings in the preceding paragraph also exemplify the partial and incomplete nature of a proverbial saying. In a sense, they are in conflict: one cannot wait too long, on the one hand, but on the other, one should not act precipitously. It is important to recognize the partial truth that is intrinsic to a proverb or saying. These insights reveal only a small piece of reality, and that piece is often to be balanced by a slice that another saying can provide. The modern reader must be prepared to avoid generalization and to read a proverb carefully. One who is also religiously inclined must be ready to recognize that not every proverb is a moral saying. The book is not a primer of social ethics or moral theology. Many of the sayings are merely observational and so contribute to the wisdom of the youth to whom the proverbs are addressed. Many are directive of conduct. One may conclude, then, that wisdom is manifold. We already distinguished above between content and method. Can we now define proverbial wisdom more closely? It is both knowledge and conduct (right living), with particular emphasis on the conduct. The knowledge is emphasized by the way in which the sayings induce the youth to think and to weigh personal actions. This kind of knowledge is not theoretical; it is practical, directed toward action. Yet it also constitutes a body of sayings for the youth to absorb and to be convinced of, in order to live by them.

How can one best approach the book of Proverbs? What has already been said about structure and style is helpful, but perhaps more thought should be given to the nature of these concise sayings. We might mention two of their many characteristics. First, the saying looks like a platitude, but upon deeper consideration it turns out to be complex and various levels of meaning appear. Thus, "ill-gotten treasures profit nothing, but virtue saves from death" (10:2). The interpretation of this saying will depend upon differing notions of profit and virtue and death. Or one might consider the transformation of an original setting. Thus, "one can bring a donkey to feed, but one cannot make it eat"—a saying that is applied to (human) stubbornness. Second, the saying may be paradoxical in nature, something totally unexpected, such as a soft answer that will break a bone (25:15), or what is bitter turns out really to be sweet (27:7). One is not expecting this kind of a reversal of what is normal, and therefore the saying packs more power.

The Range of Wisdom (Sapiential) Thought

This subject is suggested by Claus Westermann's statement that we cannot be satisfied with the traditional form of a commentary on Proverbs. Two approaches should be taken: the usual commentary form of chapter and verse and a synthesis of the style and viewpoints reflected in the work. His view is correct, but it cannot be realized within the format of this series.[7] Synthesis is not to be taken as a handy summary of the teaching of the book. That is really not possible in view of the many and various situations that underlie the sayings. The appeal and the pedagogical value of the proverbs would be flattened out and the singularity of the sayings lost if the work were reduced to a handbook of moral platitudes. Rather, we must enter into the world of thought of the Hebrew sages. Thus, in an analysis of the comparisons found in Proverbs, Westermann has described the wide range of items in heaven and earth: clouds, wind, rain, depths, fire, smoke, and minerals. In the countryside one meets paths, thorns, stones, and dew upon the grass. There are many kinds of plants and animals: trees, grass, foliage, birds, lions, bears, and serpents. It is the world of the farmer, of those who work the land. This is the everyday world of little people, not the world of courtiers. The most frequent contrast in the book is between the righteous and the wicked, or the just and the unjust (Hb. *ṣaddîq* and *rāšāᶜ*). This type of generalized saying occurs throughout the work, but is most frequent in chapters 10–15—providing a contrast that is reminiscent of Psalm 1. Westermann claims, perhaps too extravagantly, that they all fall together into what may be classified as one saying: the wise/righteous prosper and the foolish/wicked self-destruct—the perennial choice between life and death (Deut. 30:15–20).

This polarity of thought calls for consideration. The polarity itself suggests over-simplification. Can reality be so neatly summarized in positive and negative terms? Proverbial sayings carry a gray area with them. They enter into a narrow slice of life and particularize what is often a baffling aspect of reality. The original context fades with usage, but the sayings grow in meaning and in authority. One of the most frequent and puzzling dichotomies is the almost automatic division of humanity into the wise and the foolish. There may be some pedagogical reason behind this, for it seems to emphasize the disaster that folly brings. In writing these proverbs, the sages show little sympathy for the fools or for their conversion. It is almost as if it were taken for granted that they are incorrigible. Fools are described in such a bad light as though to underscore the value of wisdom and its characteristics.

This polarity has another troublesome effect. In the light of experience can one steadily maintain that prosperity awaits the wise and that adversity is the lot of the foolish? There is more than enough evidence to show that the sages were not simpletons. Their own standards called for listening to experience, but on the question of retribution, or reward and punishment, the corpus of proverbial sayings does not reflect a real awareness of the problem. There is a bold claim in Proverbs 3:11–12 (cf. Deut. 8:5) that adversity and discipline are signs of divine paternal love, but there is no sign of a struggle to maintain this equilibrium. The author of the book of Job and Qoheleth meet the problem squarely. They do not solve it, but neither do they avoid it. It should be pointed out that this mentality is not restricted to the Wisdom literature. Throughout the OT the standards of human justice are applied to the Lord. Even if the Lord of the covenant was "totally other," and mysterious, there were certain expectations; cf. Exod. 34:6–7.

While this mentality may be difficult to understand, it should not be allowed to distort the thought of the sages. After all, they ultimately succeeded in breaking through this "certain" and over-confident view of divine retribution. Some scholars (notably K. Koch) have argued that OT thinkers recognized a certain order in nature that embraced the fate of human beings and their actions.[8] The God who created the world set up an intrinsic connection between a good action and its reward, and a bad action and its punishment. They viewed as automatic a fixed pattern between a moral action and its result. God does not "intervene." Rather, "whoever digs a pit (for another) falls into it" (cf. Prov. 26:27; Ps. 7:16; Eccl. 10:8, etc.). This sort of saying is supposed to show the rigid mentality of the sage on the issue of retribution. A bad action will inevitably have a boomerang effect. In several passages one can detect a correspondence between an action and its (good/bad) result, but even more often is the Lord portrayed as intervening directly to reward or punish. An analysis of the Psalms indicates that Israel at prayer knew who was to be blamed for troubles—it was the Lord. There was no problem when the troubles were seen, as usual, to be the result of sin. But when the innocent suffered Israel complained to the Lord, not to some abstract correlation of deed and consequence.

Symbolism in Proverbs

Wisdom language is highly symbolical. Even on the level of basic teaching or observation, straightforward terms become suggestive. The parts of the body are used metaphorically: the ears and the eyes, the heart and the hand, the feet and the way/path that is trod. Of course these can be meant in a relatively literal sense, but often they indicate a deeper meaning, as when the heart becomes a "listening heart," the gift that the wise Solomon received from the Lord (1 Kgs. 3:9, 12). Indeed, almost anything physical takes on an extended meaning; there is rarely question of a sheer physical action. Sight means following the path that is sighted. Walking means hewing to the way that the sage has outlined for the youth. N. Habel has explored the doubling of these symbols: the two ways, the two hearts, the two companions, and the two houses. He rightly concludes that in Proverbs 1–9 "the way is a a nuclear symbol within a satellite system of images, which may be expanded or modified in different contexts."[9] He also points out that of all the symbols, wisdom continued to live its own life in the later Wisdom literature (e.g., Sir. 24).

Just as Habel has singled out the symbol of way/path as primary, one might also choose the elusive symbol of Wisdom herself. But before we can discuss her, we must also examine the levels of meaning in the images of the "stranger" (feminine, Hb. *zārâ*) and the "alien" (feminine, Hb. *nokriyyâ*). The NIV translations, "adulteress" and "wayward wife," do not leave enough room to appreciate the symbolism that is at work in these female figures. It will be up to the reader to judge the nuances when these terms occur in the commentary: 2:16; 5:3, 20; 7:5, *zārâ*; and 2:16; 5:20; 6:24; 7:5, *nokriyyâ*. The two terms are in parallel constructions in 2:16 and 5:20, and at least here they certainly seem to refer to sexual activity with a woman other than one's wife. Another level of meaning that has been suggested is that the stranger is described as being a goddess: she frequents the high places (7:12; 9:14); she has a house with bedding (2:18; 5:8; 7:16–17, 27; 9:14); and she is mentioned in the context of death (2:18; 9:18). Already this stranger has become the personification of evil who is pitted against Woman Wisdom. They are both women who attract youth, for life or for death. Their approach is markedly similar: speaking in public places and inviting to a private home. The emphasis on proper sexual conduct in chapters 5–7 is unmistakable. At the same time it raises questions. There is relatively little notice taken of this topic in the rest of the work: 31:3 is quite general; there are warnings in 2:16–19; 22:14; and 23:27. But the effect of chapters 5–7 is overwhelming. The language is clearly erotic.[10] While the sphere of physical sex is quite explicit, there appear to be higher stakes. Woman Wisdom and Woman Folly are locked in a battle for the possession of the youth, and this is a matter of life and death. The primary source for information about Woman Wisdom is chapter 8, but see also 1:20–33 and 9:1–6.[11]

What is one to make of this personification (not hypostasis, a philosophical term with more than one meaning)? Personification, a literary device that attributes personal characteristics to an entity that is not a person is no stranger to the Bible. Within Proverbs one can point to 23:31 where wine has "eyes" and thus gives "sparkle" to a cup. In 20:1 wine impersonates the effects that it produces. But the personification of Woman Wisdom is unique in the Bible; there is no other personification to rival it. Much has been written about the background to this figure, and her origins have been sought in Assyrian and Egyptian goddesses (Ishtar, Maʿat, Isis, etc.) without any consensus being reached.[12] The most astonishing claim that the Bible makes for her is divine origin before creation and a commission of some kind (see the comment on 8:22–36). Equally as important as the life of Woman Wisdom in this book is the full and rich description presented in several parts of Sirach (esp. ch. 24) and the Wisdom of Solomon (chs. 7–9). One may safely say that no other symbol in the Bible has received more attention—and its meaning seems to expand constantly. There is a definite *sophia* or wisdom background to the Johannine *logos,* and the role of Wisdom is prominent in the gnostic writings. It has been said that Woman Wisdom is really an aspect of the Lord involved with creation. She speaks with divine accents and, in the course of her long career, she assumes more than one form of revelation (e.g., the Law in Sir. 24). In Proverbs she is a divine call to life, to share in life more fully: "Whoever finds me finds life" (8:35).

Theology and Anthropology

The book of Proverbs involves both theology and anthropology, but it is the anthropological aspect that emerges most prominently. This is true at least in the sayings of chapters 10–31, which are usually considered to be preexilic and hence belong to "early wisdom." This emphasis can be seen most clearly by looking at the work of Jutta Hausmann.[13] In her study, she illustrates the large space given to human beings. She divides her investigation into the following parts: (1) groups of persons as types (wise/foolish; just/wicked; diligent/lazy; rich/poor), (2) groups that have specific functions (father/mother/son, friend/neighbor, king, and woman), and (3) contexts that influence life (education, the heart, speech, sorrow, evil, the individual and the community, the future and hope, and the relationship of human beings to God), and (4) the ideals of the wise (wisdom and righteousness, self-control, life as opposed to death, and human joy and well-being). It is well to keep in mind this wide range of topics that appears in the teachings.

We may conclude our introduction with a discussion of a topic that is indicated in the above list. It is both theological and anthropological. Further, it is frequent, practical, and revealing for the understanding of the sages: their ambiguous position on riches. The OT emphasis on this life, as opposed to the next, is obvious. When the sages wrote about the tree of life, or the fountain of life, they envisaged blessings from God such as riches, good health, many years ("gray hair is a crown of glory," 16:31), a large family, and prestige in the community. Job describes the happiness of the "days when God watched over me" (Job 29:2–25). These blessings were a sign of divine approval, but when they were absent the disorientation of the faithful was great, as the psalms of lament, in particular, illustrate. We have seen that the book of Proverbs takes a very optimistic view of retribution: wisdom/virtue succeeds, but folly/wickedness fails (e.g., 10:16; 11:18, etc.). Hence every effort is made to encourage diligence as opposed to laziness (10:4; 12:24). Such self-discipline and self-control is bound to bring success and divine blessings. By the same token, it would seem that failure, poverty, and other ills should point to personal shortcomings or perhaps inexplicable twists of fate ("One may plan one's course, but the Lord directs the way," 16:9). But the fact is that the views on riches and poverty are quite varied, as doubtless befits the realities of life upon which the sages reflected.

The ambiguity of riches is manifested especially in the "better" sayings. The poor who pursue a path of integrity are better than the rich who are perverse (28:6), and "better is a little with fear of the Lord than great wealth and anxiety with it" (15:16). Hence, riches are not everything. It is true that riches make a difference: the rich are treated accordingly, while the poor are despised (14:20); the poor have to beseech, while the rich can afford to be harsh (18:23). But the rich must remember a central fact: the Lord made both the rich and the poor (22:2). The Lord gives light to the eyes of both (29:13). Therefore let the rich beware of insulting or oppressing them because all have the same Maker (14:31; 17:5). The teaching is positive, not negative. One should give to the poor (28:27), for through this one is really lending to the Lord (19:17; see also 14:21). Chapter 22 has a number of varied statements assembled at the beginning. A good name or reputation is preferable to riches (v. 1); the Lord, who made both rich and poor (v. 2), pays no attention to such distinctions. Verse 4 picks up "riches" from verse 1 and associates them with fear of the Lord. Verse 7 returns to the rich/poor contrast and recognizes this inevitable stratification of society (the borrower becomes the slave of the lender). Finally, blessings come from sharing with the poor (v. 9).

Riches are far from being an unmixed blessing. Caution is necessary. So many sayings are tilted in favor of the poor (a "preferential option?") that one must be constantly aware of other aspects of the situation. Thus, Proverbs 10:15 seems to be a straightforward statement about possessions or lack of them. It is a sheer observation: "The wealth of the rich is a strong city, but the ruin of the poor is their poverty." Money makes a difference! However, there is an interesting variant of 10:15 in 18:11 that seems to suggest that one cannot rely too much on the "strong city" of wealth. Moreover, 18:11 is definitely colored by 18:10 in which the name of the Lord (not riches!) is said to be a strong tower that provides safety. Another apparently innocuous observation has to do with the effect of riches and poverty. The rich person acquires a circle of friends, in contrast to the poor whose "friends" desert them (14:20; 19:4, 7). Still, there is an ambiguity lurking in this situation. What kind of friends are these, who rally to the rich and abandon the poor? Are they worth having? The point is developed more explicitly, and in favor of the poor, in Sirach 13:2–25. The sages also raise the question as to how one has become rich. It may be due simply to the Lord, no matter how much personal effort is involved (adopting the NRSV marginal rendering of 10:22). As we have seen, riches may also be the reward of diligence (10:4). But the manner of acquisition stands under judgment. Anything acquired in haste raises suspicion: was evildoing involved? "One in haste to grow rich will not go unpunished" (28:20b). The origins of riches are thus a matter of concern: "ill-gotten treasures are of no value" (10:2a).[14]

This rich variety of aphorisms on a single topic, and a very serious one, illustrates several aspects about a proverb. First, the saying expresses a view that proceeds from a very particular situation and it is not to be universalized. Rather, it is to be balanced against other sayings on the same general topic. Second, the very multiplicity of these sayings is a warning that we must read proverbs carefully and not superficially. This is difficult to do, especially when they are gathered into a collection. It has been said that a proverb in a collection is "dead." That is really not so; we may not be able to attain the original context, but proverbs do not seem to lose their individuality. They may even acquire new applicability. Third, they must be read with the expectation that the meaning that seems "obvious" to us may be merely a superficial reaction on our part. Then we will not simply go on to the next verse; we will allow ourselves to be "caught" by mystery and questioning. In the commentary that follows, the aim is to explain what needs to be explained, to avoid mere paraphrase, to point out associations between the sayings, and, at the same time, to leave some questions for the reader to ponder.

Outline

Notes

1. This journey is best described by W. P. Brown in *Character in Crisis: A Fresh Approach to the Wisdom Literature of the Old Testament* (Grand Rapids: Eerdmans, 1996).

2. See J. Gammie and L. Perdue, eds., *The Sage in Israel and the Ancient Near East* (Winona Lake, Ind.: Eisenbrauns, 1990), pp. 19–65, 95–107.

3. For further details, see R. E. Murphy, *The Tree of Life: An Exploration of Biblical Wisdom Literature* (2d rev. ed.; Grand Rapids: Eerdmans, 1996), pp. 97–110.

4. There has been considerable discussion of the phenomenon of parallelism. M. P. O'Connor has proposed a syntactic approach, as opposed to merely lexical; see his *Hebrew Verse Structure* (Winona Lake, Ind.: Eisenbrauns, 1997), esp. pp. 611–61. For a short treatment of the varieties of parallelism, see A. Berlin, *The Dynamics of Biblical Parallelism* (Bloomington: Indiana University Press, 1985), esp. pp. 127–41.

5. This translation is the author's own, as are any subsequent translations that are neither NIV nor marked otherwise.

6. *Biblical Sound and Sense: Poetic Sound Patterns in Proverbs 10–29* (JSOTSup 128; Sheffield: JSOT Press, 1991) by T. P. McCreesh will help the interested reader to pursue this vein.

7. C. Westermann's *Roots of Wisdom* (Louisville, Ky.: Westminster John Knox, 1995) is a study that provides a helpful and enlightening synthesis.

8. See K. Koch, "Is There a Doctrine of Retribution in the Old Testament?" in *Theodicy in the Old Testament* (ed. J. L. Crenshaw; Philadelphia: Fortress, 1983), pp. 57–87.

9. N. C. Habel, "Symbolism of Wisdom in Proverbs 1–9," *Int* 26 (1972), pp. 131–57.

10. For more discussion, see R. E. Murphy, "Wisdom and Eros in Proverbs 1–9," *CBQ* 50 (1988), pp. 600–603.

11. Her function in the book is well described by R. J. Clifford, *The Book of Proverbs and Our Search for Wisdom* (Milwaukee: Marquette University Press, 1995).

12. See B. Lang, *Wisdom and the Book of Proverbs: A Hebrew Goddess Redefined* (New York: Pilgrim, 1986).

13. *Studien zum Menschenbild der älteren Weisheit* (Tübingen: J. C. B. Mohr [Paul Siebeck], 1995).

14. For further details, see R. N. Whybray, *Wealth and Poverty in the Book of Proverbs* (JSOTSup 99; Sheffield: JSOT Press, 1990).

Introductory Instructions (Prov. 1:1–9:18)

The contrast between the wisdom poems (chs. 1–9) and the discrete sayings (chs. 10–31) is striking. The former are strongly hortatory and didactic, leaving little to be verified by personal experience. At the most, it is the teacher's experience that is verified (e.g., 7:6–27). These instructions are presented with utmost confidence and promise, but also with no little cajoling, even threats. They are to be read as an introduction to the way in which one hears the sayings that follow. Some scholars (see R. N. Whybray, *Composition*) recognize ten didactic instructions in chapters 1–7, mainly on the basis of the occurrence of "my son," and the command to hear/obey the teaching that follows. But there is little agreement on the length of these instructions, and several other divisions have been proposed. It seems better to recognize these as simply repeated apostrophes to "my son." The NIV pays little attention to such divisions, and provides italicized headings at appropriate points which are based more or less on content (e.g., 2:1; 3:1). In chapters 10–31 the NIV headings are based on the titles provided at specific points within the text itself (10:1; 22:17, etc.).

§1 Proverbs 1:1–33

1:1–6 / This is one sentence in Hebrew, containing the title (for the book rather than just chs. 1–9) and purpose. Each verse begins with the preposition "to" (the exception in v. 5 is wisely taken by the NIV as a parenthetical remark). Typical wisdom terminology is used: **discipline, understanding, prudence, proverbs**, and **sayings and riddles of the wise.** There is no point in distinguishing nuances between these. The rest of the book fills out the proclamation contained in these verses. See the introduction on dating and theology.

1:7 / The theme or motto of the book is expressed in a classic statement that is echoed often: 9:10; 15:33; Job 28:28; Psalm 111:10. Wisdom is practical, aimed at conduct, but one must know the teachings of the sage and be guided by **the fear of the LORD.** The contrast between the wise and fools is primarily in conduct; **fools** refuse to listen, that is, obey. The obtuseness of fools spills over into their wicked behavior (1:10–19). Hence, the frequent opposition between the righteous (or the wise) and the wicked (or the fool) throughout the book.

1:8–19 / This is a typical lesson given by a sage with a customary introduction in verse 8 that reflects the original family situation. **My son** can be a stereotypical phrase used by the sages in the **instruction** of youth. Wisdom and virtue are frequently portrayed in terms of precious ornaments and clothing (cf. 3:3, 22; 4:9). An admonition follows in verses 10–19: one is not to yield to the enticements that **sinners** will offer to youth. Their proposition is to rob and slay someone in order to **share a common purse.** They will **waylay some harmless soul** (v. 11) only to **waylay themselves** (v. 18). Verse 16 seems to be a quotation from Isaiah 59:7, and is perhaps a gloss (a comment or interpretation). The meaning of verse 17 is ambiguous in context. The NIV takes it to mean that the **net** will fail because the **birds** have seen it laid out. If this is the meaning, then in verse 18 the wicked plunge ahead in their deeds, despite any warning. If, however, the saying in verse 17 is aimed at the innocent (which is less probable), then it would appear that the trap is set in vain for them since they are forewarned.

1:20–33 / The exhortation of the sage is strengthened by the personification of **Wisdom** as a woman. She makes the rounds of the town and threatens disaster if her words are not heard, but whoever **listens** to her **will live in safety** (v. 33). She positions herself where she can speak to a crowd (v. 21), especially to the **simple** (morally weak and in need of wisdom; cf. vv. 22, 32; 7:7; 8:5). The meaning of **my heart, my thoughts** (v. 23) is made clear in the denunciation in verses 24–33.

The tone of her message is entirely condemnatory. Contrary to many translations, such as the NRSV, v. 23 is not an invitation to repent. Because her **advice** is **ignored,** she **will laugh** at the **disaster** of these **fools** (cf. Ps. 2:4; 37:13 for divine laughter). Verse 28 echoes instances in the prophets where the Lord refuses to listen in the face of ignored advice (cf. Isa. 1:15; 59:2; Jer. 11:11; Mic. 3:4). The speech ends with a contrast between the fate of **fools** (vv. 31–32) and those who **listen** (i.e., obey, v. 33).

Additional Notes §1

There are no serious textual problems in ch. 1. The marginal NIV footnote at v. 21 indicates the LXX rendering. In v. 20 Hb. *ḥokmôt,* "wisdom," is an abstract plural, the plural of intensity, or perhaps a feminine singular form influenced by Phoenician. The same form occurs again in 9:1 and 24:7; cf. Ps. 49:4; Sir. 4:11; 32:16. For the structure of 1:20–33, see P. Trible, "Wisdom Builds a House: The Architecture of Proverbs 1:20–33," *JBL* 94 (1975), pp. 509–19, and J. A. Emerton, "Note on the Hebrew Text of Proverbs 1:22–3," *JTS* 19 (1968), pp. 609–14.

1:20–33 / For further discussion, see R. E. Murphy, "Wisdom's Song: Proverbs 1:20–33," *CBQ* 48 (1986), pp. 456–60.

§2 Proverbs 2:1–22

This chapter is a parade example of a wisdom poem, an instruction in 22 verses (the number of letters in the Hebrew alphabet). Moreover, it is tightly structured with six strophes: 4, 4, 3 and 4, 4, 3 verses. Each strophe has opening words that are flags, or signs. ʾAlep (the first Hebrew letter) opens verse 1 (after the customary "my son") and closes verse 4. This conditional strophe (or structural division) is followed by two other strophes (beginning at vv. 5, 9) indicating what will happen. Both are introduced in the same way: "then you will understand" (beginning with ʾālep: ʾāz). The second half of the alphabet begins with lāmed ("to"). In a similar fashion as ʾālep, lāmed opens the two strophes at verses 12 and 16. Both begin "to save you" according to the MT— the NIV paraphrases and so loses the structure. An initial lāmed occurs again at verse 20 and begins the subordinate clause "in order that you may walk," according to the MT. This formal structure is in harmony with the sequence of the thought: If . . . then . . . then . . . to save you . . . to save you . . . in order that you may walk. . . . Verses 1–11 indicate the positive gains wisdom brings and verses 12–22 indicate the dangers from which wisdom preserves a person ("wicked men," v. 12; "the adulteress," v. 16). The final strophe describes the fate of the "righteous" and "wicked."

2:1–4 / The repetition of **my son** is for emphasis. Although the youth is to seek out wisdom (it is **hidden treasure,** like **silver**) and expend every effort to find it, wisdom remains paradoxically a divine gift (2:6). At times there is a kind of commingling of the voice of the teacher and the call of wisdom (e.g., 3:13–18 and 8:10–11, 32–35).

2:5–8 / The most important result of the pursuit of wisdom will be to **understand the fear of the LORD,** one of the central components of wisdom (cf. 1:7). It is devotion, obedience, and love (**knowledge of God,** v. 5b). **Wisdom** is a gift of God, who will care for the **faithful ones.**

2:9–11 / These verses describe more effects of wisdom: to know what is **right and just.** This knowledge will come from the inner person **(heart)**, where **wisdom** dwells and will protect the one who possesses her.

2:12–15 / In particular, **Wisdom** (which the NIV introduces into the text from v. 10) will save one from the **wicked,** whose **ways** are described as **evil.** It has already been suggested that "way" is a key symbol, which is often illustrated negatively as here in chapters 1–9 by the wicked way.

2:16–19 / Another particular deliverance of wisdom (NIV: **It** will save you) is in the case of the "strange woman," the "alien one" (rendered in the NIV as **adulteress, wayward wife**). Adultery is indicated in verse 17, where marriage is described as the **covenant of her God** (see NIV margin). But covenant (Hb. *bᵉrît*) in this context has nothing to do with the covenant between God and Israel. The only occurrence of "covenant" in Proverbs is here and it simply designates the marriage contract (cf. Mal. 2:14). Is *yhwh* meant by her God, or is the woman a foreigner who recognizes a different deity in her contract? The text remains ambiguous. It should be noted that she is described as speaking **seductive words.** The speech of the strange woman will appear again in 7:5, almost verbatim, and in 7:21. The reader may begin to think of another level of meaning, beyond sexual infidelity, especially because **her paths** (v. 18) lead to death (i.e., Sheol, or the place or condition in which the dead find themselves; cf. 7:27; 9:18). See Additional Notes. The **death** and **life** in verses 18–19 are more than merely physical.

2:20–22 / The final strophe begins with *lāmed*, "so that" (NIV, **Thus**), and the fate of **the upright** and **the wicked** are described in terms of **ways** and **land.** See the introduction and chapters 5–7 for further discussion of the strange woman.

Additional Notes §2

For further details on the structure and pedagogy of ch. 2, see P. W. Skehan, *Studies in Israelite Poetry and Wisdom* (Washington, D.C.:

Catholic Biblical Association, 1971), pp. 9–10, 16; cf. also M. V. Fox, "The Pedagogy of Proverbs 2," *JBL* 113 (1994), pp. 233–43.

2:7–8 / The NIV rightly follows the Qere *yiṣpōn* and *ḥᵃsîdāw*.

2:18 / The NIV paraphrases a difficult line in v. 18a; the lit. translation is perhaps "(he? she?) sinks to death, her house." It is not easy to conceive of a house sinking in that direction. Various suggestions have been made to improve the text; perhaps read Hb. *nᵉtîbātāh* (her way) for *bêtāh*, for the sake of parallelism with v. 18b; so the NAB.

3:1–2 / The NIV wisely prints verses 1–12 as couplets of two verses, with the second verse of each couplet providing some kind of motivation. Thus the command in verse 1 is followed by a promise of long **life** and **prosperity,** which is the ideal goal envisioned by the wise. It has been said that the kerygma of the book of Proverbs is life (cf. Murphy, "Kerygma"). The **teaching** of the sage is further expanded in verse 12, which refers to the Lord's **discipline.**

3:3–4 / Cf. 6:21 and 7:3. **Love and faithfulness** are famous covenantal terms (Hb. *ḥesed* and *ʾemet*). They are associated with royal rule (20:28) and also social relationship (14:22; 16:6). These ideals are to penetrate deeply, written **on the tablet of your heart** (cf. Jer. 31:33). The result will be **favor** and prestige before God and mortals.

3:5–6 / The command to **trust in the LORD** is expressed positively and negatively (it is foolish to trust in oneself; cf. 26:5, 12; 28:26a). The motive in 6b is the assurance of divine direction in life.

3:7–8 / The antithetic character of prohibition and command defines an aspect of **fear** of the Lord. Fearing the Lord results in health and well-being. For **body** the MT has "navel"; apparently the NIV regarded this as a part to designate the whole (or a synecdoche).

3:9–10 / The command to **honor** involves such cultic rites as Deuteronomy 26:2, or Leviticus 2:14. The command may be intended merely in a general sense here and the reward is appropriate to the action: full **barns** and overflowing **vats** (a sign of divine blessing). **New wine** is the juice of the grape before fermentation.

3:11–12 / Both the command and its reason are expressed in chiasm. In verse 12b, the NIV translates the Hebrew but notes the LXX (which is preferable; see Additional Notes) in the margin. These verses are unusual in that Proverbs never explicitly discusses the problem of adversity, but simply reflects the typical biblical view that suffering and sin go together. But here the paternal disciplining of a son is transferred to God and interpreted as a sign of love—a paradox. Commentators generally refer to 20.13 of Papyrus Insinger (*AEL,* vol. 3, pp. 184–217) as a parallel ("Whatever hardship comes, place yourself in the hand of God in it"), but this does not mention the fatherly love of God. See also Job 5:17; 33:15–30, and Hebrews 12:5–6.

3:13–18 / This is a hymn to personified Wisdom, introduced with the "blessed" formula (and see the *inclusio* in v. 18b where **blessed** is repeated). Her value is beyond any of the most **precious** metals (a frequent comparison; compare 8:18–19 with vv. 14–15). The description of wisdom in verse 16 echoes the standard portrayal of the Egyptian goddess Ma^{c}at, who has the *ankh* (life) in one hand and a sceptre (ruling power) in the other. Wisdom brings **riches,** but the great benefit is indicated in verse 17, **paths** of **peace. Tree of life** occurs elsewhere only in Genesis 2:9; 3:22, 24 where it has its own meaning, but it is a mythological symbol in the ancient Near East, evoking fertility and immortality. Here and in 11:30, 13:12, and 15:4, it is merely a figure of speech for a full life. The erotic language used of Wisdom is transferred here to the tree **(embrace).** On the eroticism in the description of Wisdom, see Murphy, "Wisdom and Eros." One should note that this poem opens with the question of "finding" wisdom (cf. Job 28:12) and verse 13 resembles Wisdom's own speech about herself in 8:32, 34 **(blessed).**

3:19–20 / Despite the compactness and inclusion in the hymn of verses 13–18, some commentators would add verses 19–20 to it. These verses are, as it were, an abbreviated form of 8:22–31, but they indicate more clearly that wisdom plays a role in creation (see comment on 8:30). The NIV rightly has **by wisdom,** rather than "in wisdom," as though wisdom were something *in* which God created the world (so G. von Rad, *Wisdom in Israel* [Nashville: Abingdon, 1972], p. 155). **Earth** and **heavens** are a merismus, or two representative components, standing for the totality of the world (Gen. 1:1). Verse 20 presupposes the division of the water below and the water above (Gen. 1:6–7). **Dew** is a special gift during the rainless summer.

3:21–26 / In verse 21, the NIV transposes lines a and b, disguising the fact that **them** has no antecedent; it could be anticipatory of what is to follow in line b. The results of obeying the command are described in verses 22–25: a secure and prosperous **life** (v. 22; cf. 1:9; 3:3). This is conveyed by the metaphors of walking and sleeping (vv. 23–24; cf. 6:22). The admonition not to **fear** (v. 25) is motivated by the divine protection (v. 26; cf. 2:7–8).

3:27–28 / The NIV indicates by format that the style reverts to the couplets that marked verses 1–12. The admonitions specify doing **good** to those who have a valid claim (a decision is called for here), provided one has the resources. Verse 28 sharpens this advice by prohibiting delay in helping the **neighbor.**

3:29–30 / In contrast to verses 27–28, where sins of omission were envisioned, these commands forbid sins of commission (malice and quarreling) against a **neighbor** who **has done you no harm.**

3:31–32 / The prohibition against **envy** is probably due to the success of the violent person (cf. Ps. 37:1; 73:3). The reaction of the **LORD** reaction is expressed antithetically and chiastically.

3:33–35 / The portrayal of the direct intervention of the Lord continues: cursing and blessing (v. 33, with chiasm). God reciprocates in dealings with **mockers** and **the humble.** The final verse gives a wise/foolish orientation to the divine retribution. See Additional Notes.

Additional Notes §3

3:12 / One should read Hb. *wᵉyakʾib* for the *ûkᵉʾāb* of the MT.

3:21 / Lit. v. 21 is "let them not depart(?) from your eyes." The verb, Hb. *lûz*, is difficult. It is used in the Hiphil in the same general sense in 4:21, and the Niphal participle, *nālôz* **(perverse)** occurs in 3:32.

3:35 / The grammar of v. 35b is not clear. The verse is chiastic, **shame** and **honor** are opposed to each other. The NIV understands God as the subject and inserts **to** before shame in order to derive its translation, but this is doubtful. Lit. the text seems to say: "but fools hold up (Hb. *mērîm*, each one?) shame." The subject is in the plural, and the participle is in the singular. The NAB (and perhaps NJPS?) conjectures Hb. *môrīšîm*, "inherit."

§4 Proverbs 4:1–27

4:1–9 / This section is noteworthy because the sage repeats verbatim (vv. 4–9) his own father's exhortation which personifies Wisdom as a woman to be possessed and embraced (the erotic language of 3:18 is intensified in 4:5–8). **My sons** (not "my son") are addressed, as in 5:7; 7:24; 8:32. The call for attention is motivated by the promise of **sound learning** in verse 2 and the urgency is increased by the personal tone of the father who opens his instruction in a typical way (v. 4; cf. 7:2a for repetition of the last line). The intensity is suggested by the fourfold repetition to **get wisdom** and **understanding.** In return for loving and embracing wisdom, she will **protect, exalt,** and bestow **honor.** Verse 9 should most likely be taken in a metaphorical sense, but it does suggest wedding ornaments (cf. Song 3:11). Verse 7a is literally: "best is Wisdom," or "the beginning of Wisdom is": get Wisdom. The literal rendition of verse 7b is: "with all your getting, get understanding."

4:10–19 / After the customary invitation to **my son,** the sage picks up the recurring theme of the **way** and illustrates it both positively and negatively (see the comment on 2:12–15). He will guide him **in the way of wisdom (paths, steps);** there will be no stumbling. This is in lively contrast to **the path of the wicked** against which the youth is warned (vv. 14–15; note the intensity of the prohibitions and imperatives). The very life of such people (**eat, drink,** v. 17) depends upon their evildoing. This contrast is continued in the **light** and **darkness** metaphors of the two ways in verses 18–19.

4:20–27 / Another appeal to **my son** calls for strict attention and obedience to the **words.** It is noteworthy that the commands and admonitions center on the **heart, mouth, lips, eyes** and eyelids (v. 25b, **gaze**), and **feet.** If all these parts of the body are regulated, **life** (v. 22) is secured. The twisted mouth and perverse lips (v. 24) reflect a conduct that was described (vv. 14, 19) as walking in the path of the wicked—paths to which one must not **swerve** (v. 27). The emphasis on the eyes anticipates straightforward conduct—walking on **level** and **firm ways** (v. 26).

Additional Note §4

There are no textual difficulties. The NIV wisely reads the Qere in v. 16b and notes another possible meaning of Hb. *pls* in v. 26.

§5 Proverbs 5:1–23

This chapter picks up the theme of sex and adultery (mentioned briefly in 2:16–19) and, except for the puzzling interruption in 6:1–19, this topic continues into chapter 7. Such emphasis is striking in view of the fact that there are only very few sayings concerning this subject in chapters 10–31. Is there another level of meaning indicated here? Is the "strange woman" also a symbol?

5:1–6 / The teacher addresses a reassuring appeal to **my son** (vv. 1–2), which is suddenly followed by the theme of the "strange woman" (see introduction). Her threat seems to lie in her seductive **speech** (v. 3). Her **lips** contrast with the knowledgeable **lips** of the youth (v. 2). Her speech turns out to be as **bitter** as the wormwood plant (NIV, **gall**). Even more serious, her **steps** (recall 4:14–27 and the emphasis on **feet** and **path**) lead down to death/Sheol (see 2:18; 7:27; 9:9–18). On the translation of verse 6, see Additional Notes.

5:7–14 / With renewed insistence that **my sons** obey (v. 7), the teacher warns against the path that leads to **the door of her house** (cf. the house of Woman Folly in 9:14). The admonition is motivated by the considerations in verses 9–10 and the regrets in verses 11–14. Verses 9–10 are rather indefinite, perhaps deliberately: the danger of losing one's **strength** (v. 9, youthfulness? sexual prowess?) and one's best **years to one who is cruel** (Hb. ʾakzārî, man or woman?). One might lose one's "strength" (NIV, **wealth**) to strange men (Hb. zārîm, v. 10a) and work in the house of another stranger (masculine, Hb. nokrî, v. 10b). These threats are more vivid due to the end-of-life regrets voiced in the first person in verses 11–14. The presumption is that the youth who would fail to heed these warnings can have only bitter feelings about the **end** to which he has come. The implication of verse 14 is that he escapes with his life, but loses everything else, especially his standing in the community. O. Plöger (*Sprüche Salomos [Proverbia]* [Neukirchen-Vluyn: Neukirchener, 1981–84]) thinks that the "strange woman" is deliberately left indefinite. She can be simply unknown, the wife of another, a foreigner, or a cultic prostitute.

5:15–20 / In contrast to verses 7–14, the sage now offers positive recommendations. A. Meinhold (*Die Sprüche* [Zürich: Theologischer Verlag, 1991]) regards verses 15–18a as an allegory. According to Meinhold, the allegory is explained in verses 18b with an expansion in verse 19, and ends with a rhetorical question in verse 20. One may regard **water** as the dominant symbol that governs the passage: **cistern, springs,** and **fountain.** The animals in verse 19 are also symbolic and refer to one's wife (regardless of whether the youth was already married or not). The commands recommend fidelity (v. 15). Verse 16 is ambiguous; the springs could refer to the infidelity of the woman or of the man. The NIV interprets the verse as a rhetorical question although the interrogative particle is not present. This suggests that the verse refers to the man. The emphasis in verse 17 is on fidelity to the woman; she will reciprocate and bring him joy. The animal images (v. 19) compare with Song 2:17 and 4:1–2. A rhetorical question in verse 20 rounds off the recommendation of the sage.

5:21–23 / These verses seem to have no connection with the vivid exhortations that preceded, although Hb. *šāgâ* (vv. 19–20: "captivated," v. 23: **led astray**) may be a catchword for verses 19–20, 23. However, the verses are very general. The Lord sees **all paths** (cf. the emphasis on "ways" in ch. 4). The **wicked** are caught in their own **evil deeds** and this leads to death. Plöger *(Sprüche)* recognizes the strangeness of these verses here and associates them with the interruptive character of 6:1–19, into which they lead. In 6:20, the text returns to the topic of women. On verse 22, see Additional Notes.

Additional Notes §5

5:6 / The Hb. is ambiguous. The subjects of the verbs can be either "you" or "she." The sense of the NIV seems to be the indifference, even the ignorance, of the adulteress (an emendation of Hb. *pen* to *lōʾ*), but it is not likely that she is unaware that **her paths are crooked.** The MT can be translated with *pen* ("unless") and v. 6 is then interpreted as the purpose of the seduction—so that the youth does not consider **the way of life,** and does not really **know** where her **paths** wander.

5:22 / The translation of v. 22a is lit. "his evil deeds will take him, the wicked man. . . ." The last phrase, Hb. *ʾet-hārāšāʿ*, is missing in the LXX—this is perhaps a gloss.

The first 19 verses of chapter 6 have the appearance of an errant block of exhortations. They interrupt the theme of sex, and they seem to be a miscellany of proverbs.

6:1–5 / There is an almost frantic tone to this command against going surety for a **neighbor.** Such a warning against standing **pledge for another** is not rare (see 11:15; 17:18; 22:26–27, etc.). Ben Sira had a more relaxed and realistic attitude (cf. Sir. 29:14–20). The action is seen as a burden and **snare,** and every effort must be *made immediately* to **free** oneself from it, even to the abject humbling of oneself before the **neighbor.**

6:6–11 / Diligence is another frequent topos (traditional theme) in Proverbs (10:4–5; 12:14, etc.). These words reflect a certain sarcasm in holding up **the ant** as a model of industry. Without anyone urging on that tiny creature, it makes sure of its **provisions** for the future. The sarcastic question addressed to the **sluggard** in verse 9 seems to evoke an answer from him (**a little sleep,** etc.) as if he were to say, "just give me time." But the sage holds out the threat of fierce **poverty.** For the alternate readings provided for verse 11 in the NIV, see Additional Notes. Verses 10–11 are repeated practically verbatim in 24:33–34.

6:12–15 / Behind this instruction lies the presumption that exterior actions betray the inner attitude of a person. When the deportment is suspicious (even verging on magic?), one can suspect inner **deceit.** The fate of such a person will be sudden and disastrous, but it is left unspecified (sickness, death?). Verse 15b is found also in 29:1b. Several terms occur elsewhere: **scoundrel** (lit. a man of Belial, a term of uncertain etymology) in 16:27; **winks** in 10:10.

6:16–19 / This is a numerical saying in the style of X and X + 1 (here, 6/7). Several of these sayings occur in 30:11–31 (cf. Amos 1). The **detestable** things reflect some of the vices indicated in verses 12–15. Note how the sins are associated with the organs of the body singled out in verses 17–18, from **eyes** to **feet**—the whole person is pointed toward **evil**. After these verses the book returns to the former style of instruction that characterized chapters 1–5.

6:20–35 / This section is introduced in the NIV by the heading, "warning against adultery." Verse 20 continues the admonitions of chapter 5 with an opening reminiscent of 1:8. The command in verse 21 is found with variations in 1:9; 3:3, 22. The **forever** of the NIV is better rendered "continually." In verse 22, the NIV glosses over the third feminine singular, "she will guide you," by assuming that **commands** and **teaching** are understood as a collective. Another possibility is that personified wisdom is assumed as the subject, or that the verse has been misplaced and should follow 5:19; so the NAB. The three lines in verse 22 call for another line. **Awake** is the opposite parallel of **sleep**, but what would be the opposite of **walk**? In verse 23, the singular is used **(command)** and there is no demonstrative pronoun, **these,** in the Hebrew text as in the NIV. The verse is juxtapositional and chiastic; it is reminiscent of Psalm 119:105. In verse 24a, the MT has "evil woman" in parallelism with the stranger. A slight change would suggest "neighbor" for **immoral** (see Additional Notes) and lead into the topic of the "strange woman." The usual temptations (cf. 2:16; 5:3) are mentioned **(smooth tongue, eyes).** The translation of verse 26a is uncertain; literally: "for because (or on account) of a harlot (un)to a piece of bread." The paraphrase of the NIV intensifies the verse: action with a harlot impoverishes **(loaf of bread)** but the **adulteress** slays **(your very life).** Thus action with a **prostitute** is less harmful; it leads only to poverty. Others have interpreted the verse as indicating that wages for a prostitute are nothing, but terribly high for adultery (cf. vv. 34–35). The assumptions behind both kinds of advice are not pleasant. The worth of a woman is measured by her marital status, not by her own self; hence a prostitute is, as it were, expendable and dealing with her is not all that harmful.

The appropriate rhetorical "impossible" questions in verses 27–28 suggest perhaps the fire of sexual passion. These questions point out the danger and stupidity of such conduct. Verse 29 confirms that the adulterer will not **go unpunished.** Although it is not described, the following verses would seem to indicate that the injured (male) party will seek revenge. A **thief** may not suffer because of the mitigating circumstances of **hunger,** but **if he is caught,** there is no escape from punishment. If this is so for the thief, it will be even more for the adulterer. The **sevenfold** restitution to which the thief is bound (v. 31) is not to be found in the law codes. It is possibly an exaggeration, to emphasize the damage that will come from the **fury** of the injured husband. This comparison to a thief is odd. The threat seems to lie in being caught. Is the hungry thief, who is not caught, also an expendable member of society? Or is the thief a symbol of the adulterer? These verses are a reminder that the married woman was regarded as the property of the husband. The aggrieved **husband** will refuse to be won over, even by bribery (v. 35). Such a **bribe** will not be able to turn aside a physical beating (v. 33).

Additional Notes §6

6:11 / The comparisons are difficult, as indicated by the NIV marginal notes. For **bandit** the MT has literally "one who causes to go" (but in 24:34, it is Hitpael, "one who marches?"), and in v. 11b, "a man of shield," is taken to be **an armed man** (NIV). "Beggar" is alleged on the basis of a Ugaritic parallel and "vagrant" seems to be an interpretation of the Hb. verb *hlk.*

6:24 / The Gk. has *hypandrou,* "belonging to a man." This would suggest vocalizing Hb. r^c as *rēaʿ,* "neighbor," instead of *rāʿ,* "evil."

6:26 / The NIV relies upon the Gk. to interpret Hb. *bᵉʿad* as **price** (Gk. *timē*), but it occurs nowhere else in the Bible.

§7 Proverbs 7:1–27

The title given to chapter 7 in the NIV does not really differ from that which begins both 5:1 and 6:20. The present chapter, by its vivid description of the "adulteress," makes the admonition very concrete. The structure is quite symmetrical. In verses 1–5, the sage opens with the familiar exhortation to listen and obey (cf. 2:1; 3:1) and resumes this style at the end (v. 24) when he draws his conclusion from the episode related in verses 7–23. This episode is an example story that describes a typical event. Though based on experience, the conversation in verses 14–20 is also a literary creation.

7:1–5 / The opening exhortation of the sage is in the style of previous addresses to **my son.** The **apple of your eye** (cf. Deut. 32:10; Ps. 17:8) is the image of what appears in the pupil (lit. the little man in your eyes), the pupil itself. Verse 3 emphasizes the intensity of concentration demanded by the teacher. The metaphors of this verse are similar to those in 3:3 and 6:21, but the substitution of **fingers** for neck is striking. The intended meaning of verse 4a is a marriage with **wisdom** (**sister** means also bride; cf. Song 4:9–5:2). The parallelism calls for "kinswoman" (cf. NJPS). However, "kinsman" of the NIV is supported by the MT. Verse 5 again designates the woman as stranger. It is prejudgment and also misleading to speak of **adulteress** and **wayward wife** (see the discussion above on 2:17). The woman whose activities are about to be highlighted is described as **dressed** as a harlot (v. 10) and she is clearly married (v. 19). But the image of the "strange woman" is a symbol in all these chapters regardless of the details of the example story in 7:6–27.

7:6–27 / The sage launches into a rather dramatic description of a scene that is played out in public. We should not, however, bother to ask how he was able to see and hear all this through his **lattice,** or how he fastened his gaze on a particular **youth who lacked judgment.** The youth is described as nearing

her house (a deliberate omission of the particular antecedent to **her**). The time is right for it: **the dark of night.** On verse 6 see Additional Notes. A deft description of seduction follows, presenting concrete details (thus illuminating the general admonition of 5:3–7). The woman is bold and restless until she can settle upon her victim. She does that with an impudent kiss. Her speech is clearly aimed at seduction, but the details are puzzling. First there is the reference to her cultic **offerings** (v. 14). What is the point? Is she looking for someone to share a cultic meal with? Or is this simply religious blather to give some reassurance to the young man? In any case, she has prepared the **bed** daintily for their encounter. And everything is so timely since her **husband** is away apparently on a business trip that will last some time. So there is no danger, nothing to prevent drinking **deep of love till morning.** The successful maneuver of the woman could almost be foreseen. The sage refers (v. 21), as so often, to all this **smooth talk** and the inevitable fall of the man—conveyed with vivid comparisons to an **ox, a deer** (see Additional Notes), and a snared **bird.** The man, who is a fool, does not realize that his very **life** is at stake (vv. 22–23).

In verses 24–27, the sage resumes his teaching mode after the harrowing description of yielding to temptation. All the students **(my sons)** are addressed, although the prohibition in v. 25 is expressed in the singular. In vivid language, he describes the "stranger" as a warrior who has claimed many **victims,** whose **house** (recall v. 6) leads to Sheol (rather than the NIV **grave**). These words are reminiscent of the description of the "strange woman" in 2:18–19, and verse 27 anticipates the remarks concerning Woman Folly in 9:18.

Chapter 7 brings to a head the various discussions about the "strange woman" who first appears in 2:17. One cannot certainly determine from that verse whether she is a foreigner or the wife of another (or even both). In 5:3, 17, 20 where the strange woman appears, there is no certain identification of her as married, despite the tendentious translation in the NIV. She could be a foreigner. In chapter 7, it is clear that the woman is married, but she is not identified as a stranger or foreigner. Plöger *(Sprüche)* thinks that she is more likely a foreigner and he draws a parallel for this from the teaching of Ani, "Be on thy guard against a woman from abroad, who is not known in her [own] town . . . who is far away from her husband" *(ANET,* p. 420). But he is justified in concluding that we cannot make any definite decision.

She could be the wife of another man, or she could be a foreigner. The "stranger" is a kind of catchword that is loosely used, but there is no doubt about the death to which she invites the youth (2:18–19; 5:5; 7:27; 9:18).

Additional Notes §7

7:6–7 / The Gk. has as the subject of looking and seeing the "strange woman"—*parakuptousa:* she is peeking out the window. This theme of "the woman in the window" gave rise to theories about a fertility goddess. But the Gk. is simply mistaken, as v. 10 indicates.

7:22 / Verse 22b is rightly said to be of uncertain meaning in the NIV marginal footnote. The MT does not yield any sense: "like fetters (or anklet) to the disciplining of a fool." The text is hopelessly corrupt and the many reconstructions are quite uncertain. Probably there is another comparison parallel to that of the ox; hence the NIV reading.

§8 Proverbs 8:1–36

The personification of Wisdom reaches new heights in this chapter that is entitled "Wisdom's Call" in the NIV—an understatement, if one truly considers the claims Wisdom makes about herself. There is a superficial similarity between the opening verses and 1:20–21, but the tenor of Wisdom's proclamation in this chapter is unique. She appeals to all, including the simple and the fools. They are to listen to her because of her claims to truth and righteousness, which are far more valuable than material riches. Who is she? In verses 22–31, she launches a description of herself as begotten of God *before* creation, at God's side, but also delighting in human beings. The final words in verses 32–36 are spoken by her, and not by the sage, as might be expected (cf. 7:24–27).

8:1–3 / Presumably it is the sage who utters the rhetorical question calling attention to Woman Wisdom (in the grammatically singular Hebrew form, ḥokmâ, instead of ḥokmôt as in 1:20 and 9; see Additional Notes). She is described as stationing herself **beside the gates** of the **city** where she can reach a crowd of people. This open approach contrasts with the stealthy activity of the strange woman in chapter 7, who was covered by nightfall.

8:4–11 / The appeal is to **all,** but especially to the **simple** and **foolish** who most need **understanding.** Wisdom is prepared for this because truth and justice are the hallmarks of her speech, yielding an **instruction more precious** than **silver** or **gold.** On v. 11 see Additional Notes.

8:12–21 / A strong **I** (repeated in v. 14) initiates this part of the discourse and imparts to Woman Wisdom an authority greater than that of a sage who merely communicates wisdom. She *is* Wisdom and associates other aspects of wisdom with herself (vv. 12–14). Indeed she resembles the Lord in her detestation of evil. On verse 13 see Additional Notes. She possesses the qualities which are associated with the spirit of God in Isaiah 11:2 (cf. also Job 12:13–16) and by which one can truly **reign** and **govern** (vv. 14–16). On verse 16 see Additional Notes. The emphatic **I** (*ʾⁿnî*) in verse 17 introduces a new and unusual idea. Wisdom stands in a love relationship with **those who love** her (the NIV correctly follows the Qere). In Egyptian scarabs, this reciprocity formula has been found and is attributed to deities such as Isis: "Isis loves the one who loves her" (see Additional Notes). In contrast to the unsuccessful search for wisdom mentioned in 1:28b, her lovers will **seek** and **find** her. In her train come **riches** and prestige so that her value **surpasses** the treasures of **silver** and **gold**. The recurring motif of the **way** is echoed in verses 20–21. Those who follow her and **love** her will become wealthy themselves. One can detect a certain enlargement in the portrayal of Woman Wisdom; she approaches divine dimensions. But this is as nothing compared to the new development that takes place in verses 22–31.

8:22–31 / This famous passage enunciates several things about Woman Wisdom. She existed before God created the world, begotten apparently by *yhwh*. Her preexistence is affirmed several times and it is asserted that she was at the Lord's side as an *ʾmwn* (craftswoman? nursling?). She also found pleasure among human beings.

8:22 / The translation of the verb is disputed, as the text and margin of the NIV indicate. Other possibilities are: "create" (NJPS, NRSV) or "begot" (NAB). See Additional Notes. In any case, her existence **before** the creative activity of God is clearly affirmed in verse 22b and a birthing process is mentioned in verses 24a and 25b. **Works** is an acceptable rendering of "way" in MT, as the **deeds** in verse 22b suggest. "Dominion" in the marginal note is less likely.

8:23 / The NIV indicates in the margin another possible (and preferable) meaning for **appointed: fashioned;** see Additional Notes. The several verbs employed suggest a mystery surrounding Wisdom's origins from the creator, and the following verses go to great lengths to emphasize that she is preexistent to creation. About six times various idioms are used: "when there was no," "before," etc. This formulaic style is reminiscent of the description of the opening lines of the Mesopotamian creation epic, *Enuma Elish* (cf. *ANET*, pp. 60–61). The manner of phrasing throughout this passage emphasizes in an unusually exaggerated fashion Wisdom's priority to and presence at the works of creation. Her presence is affirmed at every point down to verse 30.

8:24–26 / The sequence of the description is upward, from the waters of the abyss, where the **fountains** (v. 28b) are and in which the pillars of the earth, or **mountains** are settled (cf. Ps. 104:6–8; Jon. 2:7), to the **earth** and eventually to the **heavens** (v. 27a).

8:27 / Again there is a strong repetition of **I** (v. 27a ends: there [was] I). The **horizon** is created by the arched firmament closing down on the surface of the **deep.**

8:28–29 / The reference is to all the **waters** that obey the divine command—both the **clouds** above and the **fountains of the deep** below. Once the waters were tamed, the fixing (in the abyss!) of **the foundations of the earth** was possible.

8:30–31 / **I was** is repeated (the same verb form, Hb. *ᵓehyê*, as occurs in the puzzling explanation of the divine name in Exod. 3:14) and it is Wisdom who says that she was posted at God's **side** as an *ᵓmwn*, a Hebrew term for which there is no certain translation (see Additional Notes). It is generally translated in two different ways, either as artisan, craftswoman, or as nursling, child. Verse 30a reads literally: "I was delight(s) every day." It is not clear whether she is **filled with delight** (so NIV) or gives delight to God (many follow the Gk. version and translate "his delight"). It can mean that wisdom is all delight, giving and taking. She is twice described as playing (perhaps dancing?): before God always and also on the face of the earth (a difficult phrase). Moreover, her delights are said to be with human beings. So much attention has been given to her mysterious and undetermined role at God's side, that her openness and joy to be with the human race is not sufficiently emphasized. The scene is reminiscent of the celebration of creation among the morning stars and the sons of God (Job 38:7). However, the mood and role of Wisdom is more than just celebratory. In view of all the characteristics of Woman Wisdom, her joyful relationship to earthly people is particularly meaningful, even if the details are not spelled out here.

8:32–36 / Instead of the sage speaking, Wisdom continues, employing the exhortatory style used by the sage (cf. 4:1; 5:7; 7:24). A threefold insistence upon listening (and that means obeying) culminates in the beatitude of verse 35 where the suitor of Woman Wisdom is portrayed as ardently pursuing her. The suitor is at her very **doors.** The doors of the strange woman in 5:8 and the door of Woman Folly in 9:14 make an interesting contrast. Verse 35 sums up the message of Wisdom: **life** comes as a **favor from the LORD** (or gift; cf. 2:6 and also see 3:13 on "finding" wisdom). In contrast to this vision, those who miss the mark and do not choose **(hate)** wisdom are in **love** with **death.** Gerhard von Rad once wrote that only the Lord can speak in the manner in which Woman Wisdom expresses herself, especially in verse 35 (*Old Testament Theology* [New York: Harper & Row, 1962], vol. 1, p. 444). Wisdom is an "I" not an "IT." However, von Rad went on to identify Wisdom as the "self-revelation of creation." But before trying to identify Wisdom more closely, one must examine chapter 9.

Plöger (*Sprüche*, pp. 91–93) has noted the possibility of the correlation of personified Wisdom with Egyptian ideas, but he has also pointed to a significant fact. The figure of biblical Wisdom, addressing human beings in both an inviting and threatening manner, is foreign to the Egyptian Maʿat. Any alleged influence must still deal with the unique presentation of Wisdom in these chapters. Perhaps the more important question is the suddenly prominent position of Wisdom in view of the traditional proclamation of the Lord as Israel's savior. As a further development of this theme, one should recall that, in the Wisdom of Solomon 10, Wisdom is hailed many times as savior. Yet the uniqueness of the Lord is not undone. Wisdom is subordinate to the Lord for she is born of the Lord. Yet, "seen from the point of view of creation, she is brought nearer to Yahweh, but seen from the point of view of Yahweh, she has a stronger affinity to creation" (p. 93). For more details on the personification of Wisdom, see Murphy, *The Tree of Life,* pp. 133–49.

Additional Notes §8

8:1 / The singular form for wisdom (Hb. *hokmâ*) is to be expected. The so-called plural form was explained in a note to 1:20 as an abstract plural, a plural of intensity, or as a feminine singular with an *wt* ending for the usual *t* (see *TDOT* 4:371).

8:11 / This verse repeats almost verbatim the evaluation of Wisdom in 3:15. Moreover, it is in the third person. In ch. 8, it is Wisdom who speaks about herself in the first person. The verse should be seen as interruptive, coming just before the emphatic "I" of v. 12.

8:13 / Contrary to the form in the rest of this poem (two lines), there are three lines. Although **fear of the LORD** is a genuine and frequent wisdom theme, it hardly belongs here with the first person discourse of Woman Wisdom. It is in the third person and has two words, **hate** and **evil**, that appear at the end of lines b and c. It looks like a gloss.

8:16 / The NIV adopts an alternate reading, "and all nobles who rule on earth," which is reflected in the Gk.; see also the marginal note. The MT can also be translated: "nobles, and all judges of the earth" on the basis of alternative readings of some Hb. manuscripts that read ʾāreṣ for ṣedeq.

8:17 / Other examples of the reciprocity formula are found in C. Kayatz, *Studien zu Proverbien 1–9* (WMANT 22; Neukirchen-Vluyn: Neukirchener, 1966), pp. 101–102.

8:22 / There is some variation in the rendering of the root *qnh* (NIV "brought forth"): (1) possess or acquire (perhaps implying that the Lord got wisdom from some unknown source?); (2) create (the ancient Gk., although the Latin Vulgate has *possedit;* see also the verbs in the following verses which indicate creation or begetting); and (3) beget (cf. Gen. 4:1).

8:23 / The NIV prefers **appointed** to fashioned, which it relegates to the marginal note. The translators seem to have derived this from the Hb. *nsk; skk* seems to convey the sense better.

8:30 / There are arguments for "artisan" and for "nursling" as the meaning of the difficult Hb. word ʾmwn. The range of opinions and their arguments are well surveyed by H. P. Rüger, "ʾAmôn—Pflegekind: zur Auslegungsgeschichte von Prv 8:30a," in *Übersetzung und Deutung* (Nijkerk: Callenbach, 1977), pp. 154–63. Rüger himself opts for nursling *(Pflegekind),* but there is no consensus on the issue.

§9 Proverbs 9:1–18

The NIV entitles this chapter "Invitations of Wisdom and of Folly." This certainly captures the main points, but it neglects verses 7–12. The personification of the two women, Wisdom (vv. 1–6) and Folly (vv. 13–18) is the proper way to end these chapters (1–9) which have been so dualistic: wisdom/folly, life/death, and good/bad.

9:1–6 / The rendering of Woman Wisdom in verses 1–6 contains several new items (in contrast to the businesslike description of Folly in vv. 13–15). Thus, she has **her house** of **seven pillars,** which she has **built.** It is reasonable to presume that this narrative is uttered by the sage (as in 1:20–21 and 8:1–3). It is difficult to fit in the significance of the house. But there is no lack of hypotheses: is it a house, a palace, or a temple? Are the pillars physical, associated with the building, or are they symbolic? Similarly, does the fact that there are seven pillars suggest that the house is symbolical? No definite answers can be provided. According to 1 Kings 7:17 (but not 2 Chron. 4:12), Solomon's temple had seven pillars. Commentators give many other necessarily tentative answers to identify this construction. At the very least it is an imposing and hence attractive building, in contrast to the mere statement about Folly's house in verse 14.

9:2 / Like the woman of chapter 31:10–31, she has been busy, and an apparently attractive meal has been **prepared** and set on a **table,** no less. No such activity has been attributed to Wisdom thus far.

9:3 / Another surprising feature is the **maids** at her disposal, whom she sends out to issue the invitation that follows. Although the MT has the singular (NIV, **she calls**), the sense must be that it is her message that the maids make public. The mention of **the highest point of the city** is perhaps natural but puzzling. It is natural since it suggests a commanding and imposing position. It is puzzling because Folly has a seat by her house that is also at the highest point of the city (v. 14). Perhaps the puzzle can be dissipated by recognizing that these positions are merely to suggest rivalry between the two women in announcing their invitations.

9:4 / Those who are targeted are the **simple** (as in 1:4), those "who lack heart (understanding)." The latter are usually regarded as opposed to wisdom, those for whom there is not much hope (e.g., 10:13, 21).

9:5–6 / The invitation is straightforward. The symbolism of bread (NIV, **food**), **wine** (contrast water—stolen at that—in v. 14) is indicated by the moral exhortation of verse 6. This is a common symbol for spiritual sustenance (Isa. 55:1–3; Sir. 15:3). Life and **way**, two great symbols of chapters 1–9, appear in verse 6.

9:7–12 / The interruptive character of these verses has already been indicated. Even if one calls them "complementary commentary" (Plöger, *Sprüche*), they are not a neat fit. However, Plöger points out rightly that there is certain unity to verses 7–9. The NIV recognizes this by starting a separate paragraph. Verse 10 picks up the motto of 1:7 about the **fear of the LORD** and in verse 11 the **me** is presumably the sage (perhaps personified Wisdom), who proclaims the promise of **life** as in 3:2. The final verse (12) seems to leave open the choice to be a **mocker** (thus returning to the thought of vv. 7–9) or a **wise** person. The hypothetical placement of these verses elsewhere in chapters 1–9 brings no improvement to the reading of the text. Meinhold *(Sprüche)* has pointed out the opposition between **mocker/wise** and **righteous/wicked**. These opposites indicate the two types that go to the respective residences of Woman Wisdom and Woman Folly. At the same time, the reprise of "fear of the Lord" is appropriate to a final chapter of this section. On this score Meinhold describes verses 7–12 as an insert.

9:7 / The parallelism between the mocker and the wicked is found also in Psalm 1:1. These terms occur frequently in these first nine chapters. The statement is in synonymous parallelism and points up the futility (even personal hurt) of dealing with these types.

9:8 / This is an antithetic saying, similar to Proverbs 15:12a.

9:9 / This command reflects the identity of the wise and righteous, and it is in the spirit of 1:5.

9:10 / Verse 10 is a key statement for understanding verses 7–12. **Holy One** is literally the plural (of majesty) as in 30:3b. **Knowledge of the Holy One** is a definition of **fear of the LORD**. As always, knowledge is practical, active, and reverent.

9:11–12 / The unexpected **me** can only be Wisdom; cf. **live** in verse 6. Verse 12 provides a link with verses 7–8 and thus returns to the contrast between the wise and the mocker.

9:13–17 / The description of Woman Folly's house, as well as the invitation to passersby, are couched in appropriately disdainful style in comparison to the portrayal of Woman Wisdom in 9:1–6. Folly is merely a common temptress who has nothing of value to offer.

9:13 / She is said to be literally "a woman of folly" (cf. 14:1). This phrase might seem to eliminate the personification and opposition to 9:1. Plöger *(Sprüche)* regards Folly as a "typifying" of the strange woman of chapter 7; as it were, she is a type of a temptress. It is better to see her as a personified rival to Woman Wisdom incorporating all the ugly features of the strange woman who appeared earlier. She is **loud** and stormy (cf. 7:11); she is reckless and ignorant.

9:14–15 / The writer deliberately describes **her house** in such a way that she must be close to the house of Woman Wisdom (v. 4). But there is no other resemblance. A certain cheapness is suggested by her **calling out** to those who pass by. These passersby are described as going **straight**—a deliberate ambiguity to indicate both physical and moral status?

9:16–17 / Contrary to the NIV, it is better to understand verse 16a as Folly's general invitation to passersby. Then verse 16b specifies that she speaks to those who **lack judgment** (lit. "lack heart"). Verse 16 deliberately repeats 9:4 as Folly apes Wisdom in an ironic fashion. There should be a colon after **way** in 15 and after **judgment** in 16. Verse 17 is the seductive prospect that Folly offers and it is a deliberate play on the true and rich food offered in verse 5. See 4:17 for the **food** of the wicked. The seductive tone of the invitation is obvious and it almost succeeds by being so blunt. This is the intention of the writer who wants to paint Woman Folly at her best/worst.

9:18 / This verse is a reflection of the sage author; it reaches back to the house of death indicated in 2:19 and 7:27. How appropriate to close on the note of Sheol!

§10 Excursus: Role and Significance

It will repay the reader to look back at chapters 1–9 and try to assess their role and also their intrinsic significance. We have already pointed to the widely accepted view that the purpose of these chapters structurally is to serve as an introduction to the collections of individual sayings that follow. Moreover, the role played by Woman Wisdom (already in ch. 1) seems to be matched by the description of the industrious woman in 31:10–31. A more important issue is the orientation given to the rest of the book by this "introduction." The discrete sayings beginning in chapter 10, no matter how non-religious they may appear to be, no matter how experiential and homespun, are presented as the nourishing food that Woman Wisdom offers (e.g., 9:2). It is imperative that we recognize our standards of sacred and profane, secular and spiritual, and other such distinctions as largely due to our cultural conditioning. Israel measured by different standards and was able to embrace a wide span of conduct under the umbrella of wisdom. It is true that wisdom has many faces, but the whole is a pattern of integration, not disintegration. One must surely admit that the contents span a broad range of time—centuries, in fact. But the sages accepted the sayings as in keeping with their piety. It is futile to try to distinguish between religious and non-religious in the collections that were handed down. Whatever validity one or another distinction in meaning is claimed for a saying (e.g., religious or non-religious), this may be a distinction imposed by us. We must not neglect the biblical nuance given to the book of Proverbs by these introductory chapters. Moreover, the recognition of various levels of meaning (e.g., God-talk as opposed to shared experience), while possible and interesting, remains speculative. The exegesis in this style does not yield the *biblical* sense, as shaped by the sages who handed down the tradition.

In an epilogue to his treatment of these chapters, Plöger (*Sprüche*, p. 110) points to three important aspects: the first two are the warning against the wicked person and the warning against the strange woman. These two emphases are surely obvious and not to be disputed. The first warning is echoed many times throughout the collections that follow. However, the second warning is reflected hardly at all. The third theme is the association of the Lord and Wisdom in terms of what Plöger calls Yahwist piety and the pursuit of wisdom. There are many echoes of this in the following collections, but in chapters 1–9 the topics are singled out for their own sake. The personification of Wisdom is an important factor in this development. There is hardly a hint of such a personification in the collections that follow. Plöger sees this figure as an illustration of a close personal relationship between the Lord and Wisdom. I would like to put it in the following way. No matter what theories may be devised to explain the origin and development of the growth of the figure of Woman Wisdom, there is no denying that she is a communication of God and that she finds joy among human beings (8:31). She is inextricably involved with them and their observations about life. Their ways are to become her ways. God's gift and human experience are the two levels of Wisdom explored in the book. The life of Woman Wisdom is extended even more and her contours made sharper in the books of the Apocrypha (esp. Sir. 1:1–10; 24:1–22, and identified by Ben Sira with the Torah in Sir. 24:23; Bar. 3:9–4:4; and Wis. 7:1–9:18). For a succinct portrayal of the growth of the figure of Woman Wisdom in later literature, see Murphy, *The Tree of Life*, pp. 133–49.

The Proverbs of Solomon (Prov. 10:1–22:16)

The MT includes the title ("the proverbs of Solomon") as part of 10:1 and it applies to the collection in 10:1–22:16 a total of 375 proverbs (375 is the numerical equivalent of the Hebrew name *šlmh,* or Solomon). The breadth and meaning of *mᵉšālîm,* or proverbs, is illustrated particularly in the following collections that are mainly one-line sayings. This is in contrast to the lengthy wisdom poems that characterize chapters 1–9. On the nature and style of the proverbial sayings, see the introduction above. Antithetic parallelism is conspicuous in chapters 10–15, and the most prominent theme is the contrast between the just (wise) and the wicked (fool)—their conduct and reward. Claus Westermann has suggested that such sayings are really the development of that single theme (*Roots of Wisdom: A Survey of Modern Study* [Leiden: Brill, 1995], pp. 75–81).

10:1 / The opening verse highlights a frequent theme; cf. 13:1; 17:21, 25; 23:24–25, and verse 1a is identical to 15:20a. These sayings provide support for home and family as a setting, if not the origin, for wisdom teaching in Israel. It is noteworthy that the first saying deals with the **son** after so many references to "my son" in chapters 1–9. As C. R. Fontaine remarks, "the proverbs of chap. 10 restate the vocabulary and themes present in 1–9" ("Proverbs," in *HBC*, p. 509).

10:2 / Here, as in many other sayings, one sees the law of retribution at work. Wrongdoing cannot profit and virtue is to be rewarded. Long life (cf. the patriarchs) was a divine blessing reserved for the virtuous. The justice of God, as Israel measured it, demanded a distinction in the treatment of good and evil; otherwise the problem of theodicy arose (cf. Job). **Righteousness delivers from death,** namely, from an early or unpleasant death that is supposedly the fate of wrongdoers. Such a fate deprives them of the riches they strove for. At a later period, righteousness came to be understood particularly as almsgiving (cf. Tob. 4:7–11) and death was also seen as no obstacle to immortality (Wis. 1:15).

10:3 / Antithetic and chiastic, this saying is an application of the principle enunciated in verse 2. Divine justice distinguishes between the just and unjust.

10:4–5 / Exhibiting antithetic parallelism, verse 5 is a concrete application of the teaching in verse 4. See 12:24 and 19:15. Diligence/laziness is a common topic. But poverty is not always due to laziness, although this is a "main cause" (Whybray, *Wealth*, p. 114). Sometimes a loose context is provided for the grouping of sayings. Thus, verses 1–5 begin and end with **a wise son** and serve as an envelope for sayings about the righteous (vv. 2–3) and the diligence (vv. 4–5) that the wise demonstrate. The context does not greatly influence the interpretation of a given saying, but the grouping of the sayings is certainly not haphazard. The topic, or sometimes merely a catchword, can serve to unify them, as the attentive reader can discover. However, these markers will not always be obvious in English translation.

10:6 / The NIV paraphrases verse 6b. The alternative in the marginal footnote is a more literal translation, but the precise contrast between lines a and b is not clear. One would expect curses to be paired with **blessings**. The text is probably corrupt (v. 6b is repeated in v. 11b) and commentaries offer various solutions, without much success.

10:7 / The meaning is that the **righteous** (because of their good name, or reputation; cf. 3:4 and 22:1) are remembered after death, but not the **wicked**. **Blessing** is the catchword for verses 6–7.

10:8 / Although the verse is antithetic, the parallelism is deficient (v. 8b occurs again in v. 10b). In verse 8b, one would expect the foolish (lit. "a fool as to lips") not to heed advice, but perhaps it is presumed that a garrulous person is not one who listens. The **commands** are the recommendations of the sages (or other responsible characters).

10:9 / Antithetic. It is presumed that the wicked will be **found out** by others, or certainly by the Lord, and hence they will fare ill. The assonance of verse 9a in the MT is striking.

10:10 / The text is uncertain. Though verse 10b repeats verse 8b, it does not provide a satisfactory parallel to verse 10a. Winking an eye is usually interpreted in a bad sense (cf. 6:13; 16:30). Many versions (NAB; NRSV) and commentators prefer to follow the LXX and render verse 10b: "the one who frankly reproves creates peace." See Additional Notes.

10:11 / Antithetic. Verse 11b repeats verse 6b (see comment). The alternative translation provided in the NIV footnote should be disregarded. However, **overwhelms** is too strong; the MT has simply "covers" or "hides." The meaning seems to be that ultimately wrongdoing and harm come from the mouth of the wicked, in contrast to the **life** given by the words of the **righteous**. **Fountain of life** is a frequent phrase for wisdom (cf. 13:14; 14:27; 16:22; see the comment on 3:4). Note that speech is a frequent topic in chapter 10; see verses 13–14, 19–21, 31–32.

10:12 / Antithetic. **Hatred** refuses to forgive, and so prolongs quarrels, but **love** shows forgiveness for the faults of others. For verse 12b, compare 17:9a. In James 5:20 the concealment refers to God's forgiveness of sins (cf. also 1 Pet. 4:8).

10:13 / Verse 13a is similar in meaning to verse 11a and also 14:33. The importance of correct (wise) speech is a constant topos in this literature. The parallelism (antithetic in the NIV) with verse 13b is not obvious. Perhaps the sense is that while the sages increase in **wisdom,** fools learn only from corporal punishment (cf. 26:3b; also 19:25), if then. Verses 13–14 are associated by **lips** and **mouth.**

10:14 / Antithetic. It is characteristic of the **wise** to be careful in speech (17:27). They know when to speak and what to say. But the foolish invite **ruin** by their thoughtless talking.

10:15 / Antithetic. This saying is a matter of fact, without any moral edge. Of themselves, riches are helpful and **poverty** means **ruin.** But this is not the last word, as 18:11 indicates: the **fortified city** may be overrated by the **rich** person. The attitude toward **wealth** and poverty is ambivalent in Proverbs. Wealth can be a divine blessing, or the fruit of silence, but it has several drawbacks, as indicated in 11:4 and 28:11. In certain cases, poverty is even preferable (19:22b; 28:6). This verse illustrates the frequent (and chiastic) juxtapositional style of the proverb: wealth of rich . . . strong city; ruin of poor . . . their poverty.

10:16 / Antithetic. Juxtapositional style: "**wages** . . . to **life; income** . . . to sin." In verse 16, the NIV presupposes that "sin" (Hb. *lᵉḥaṭṭā'ṭ*) here really means **punishment** for sin, hence possibly death. If so, then the parallelism with "life" is assured. Similarly, the NRSV assumes the same (see 11:19 and 12:28).

10:17 / Antithetic. The sense of the NIV is that one who **heeds** instruction helps others **(shows the way to life);** the opposite type **leads** them **astray.** This follows the causative meaning of the verb in verse 17b. The NRSV and others read, "go astray."

10:18 / Juxtapositional style: a concealer of **hatred—lying lips;** and a spreader of **slander—a fool.** This is perhaps a rare example of synthetic parallelism in this collection: the dissembler hides hatred by lies; a slanderer is a fool. The parallelism lacks any bite; the text may be corrupt.

10:19 / Antithetic. Careful speech is an ideal in all cultures. The value of careful speech and appropriate silence is delineated in Ecclesiastes 9:13–18 and Sirach 20:1–7. Verses 19–21 are unified by the topic of speech. Human nature being what it is, garrulousness leads to all kinds of blunders.

10:20 / Antithetic. This has a moral edge to it. One trusts whatever the **righteous** say, but it is the (perverted) **heart** of the **wicked** that renders their words worthless.

10:21 / Antithetic. This saying applies the truth of verse 20: the **righteous** "shepherd" or **nourish** others by their advice, whereas the foolish, far from helping others, **die**. Here, as often, death is used as a symbol for any adversity, anything that is "non-life." Death is the antithesis to the fullness of "life" that wisdom brings (cf. 10:11, 16, 17, 27).

10:22 / The meaning depends on 22b. The NIV, with many others (e.g., the NRSV), understands the lines in synonymous (or perhaps synthetic) parallelism: the Lord's **blessing** accounts for all human prosperity. Others, with the NRSV footnote, consider verse 22b in antithetic parallelism: Without the divine blessing, human toil will not be enough for success.

10:23 / Antithetic. Wrongdoing is the delight of the foolish, whereas **wisdom** satisfies the sensible.

10:24–25 / These verses deal with retribution. The **wicked** will receive what they fear, while the **righteous** achieve their **desire** (v. 24). However, the fear is not specified; perhaps it is the fear that they inspire or with which they are threatened. In any case, they will be appropriately punished (v. 25), blown away by tempest, whereas the **righteous** remain unmoved.

10:26 / Two vivid similes, smarting to the senses, convey the trouble that a lazy messenger causes. On the **sluggard,** compare 24:23–24 and 26:13–16; and for the trustworthy messenger, see 25:13.

10:27–28 / Antithetic. Long **life** (v. 27) and happiness (v. 28; cf. 11:7) are in store for the **righteous,** those who **fear the LORD** (see 1:7 for comment on this phrase). It will be just the opposite for the **wicked**. This is typical of the view of retribution in this book. See verse 21 for the comment on life.

10:29 / Antithetic. The NIV (and the NRSV) replaces righteousness with **righteous.** But **the way of the LORD** conceived as a **refuge/ruin** is a strange expression. Without changing the consonantal text, others (the NAB and commentators) prefer to read *yhwh* (the Lord) as subject. Therefore the Lord is the stronghold for the virtuous (lit. "to the upright of way") and destruction for evildoers. See Additional Notes.

10:30 / Antithetic. See Psalm 37:9–11 for inhabiting **the land.** Although dwelling in the land is also meant physically, it comes to have a metaphorical meaning (cf. 2:21–22; Matt. 5:5) to designate security and peace.

10:31–32 / Antithetic. The organs of speech are the topic, but they stand for what issues from them. As always, it is the speech of **the righteous** and **the wicked** which characterizes them; one is constructive, the other destructive. The **perverse** speech of the wicked is opposed to the **wisdom** of the righteous. The image in verse 31 is that of a tree and its fruit; hence the **tongue** is **cut out.** The sense of verse 32a is that **the righteous** know what to say and how to say it so as to gain assent (so Meinhold, *Sprüche;* cf. the NAB).

Additional Notes §11

10:3 / The NIV would show the Hb. chiasm if it rendered v. 3b: "the craving of the wicked he thwarts."

10:4 / The NIV presupposes a revocalization: *rēʾš ʿōśâ.*

10:10 / The repetition of v. 8b in v. 10b is suspicious. The LXX rendering presupposes the following Hb. text: *ûmôkîaḥ ʿal pānîm yašlîm,* "But he who rebukes openly (lit. to the face) makes peace." The Gk. reads *ho de elegchōn meta parrēsias eirēnopoiei,* "But he who rebukes with frankness makes peace."

10:11–12 / The NIV does not bring out the chiasm in these verses; the catchword is Hb. *ksh* (to cover, conceal).

10:13–15 / **Wisdom** and **wise** are catchwords for vv. 13–14, and vv. 14–15 are associated by the word **ruin.** Thus in v. 15 four words or phrases are simply juxtaposed without a verb. It is hardly possible to convey this in suitable English translation.

10:16–17 / **Life** is the catchword binding these verses together. In v. 17 the Hiphil of the Hb. verb to stray, *tʿh*, is both transitive and intransitive.

10:18–21 / Since proper speech is a prime value in wisdom doctrine, there are frequent references to the organs of speech, as in vv. 18–21, **lips** and **tongue**, and in vv. 31–32.

10:24–31 / The catchwords **righteous** and **wicked** dominate these verses. They are, in the view of the usage in this book, more or less synonymous with wise and foolish.

10:29 / The Hb. revocalization suggested for v. 29a is *lᵉtom-derek*.

11:1 / Antithetic. Honesty in business transactions is emphasized by the sages (cf. 16:11; 20:10, 23; see also Deut. 25:15).

11:2 / Antithetic. This is a popular proverb in many cultures (cf. 15:33; 16:18; 18:12). It is an observation drawn from experience with many applications. The meaning of **humility** here is an honest evaluation of oneself, the avoidance of arrogance. For the assonance in verse 2a, see Additional Notes.

11:3 / Antithetic. The contrast is between **integrity** and **duplicity** and their effects upon human beings.

11:4–6 / **Righteousness** unites these sayings, all of which are antithetic. In verse 4, **the day of wrath** stands for any serious reversal, especially death. A proper use of **wealth** is implied, though not spelled out; but verse 4a means more than "you can't take it with you." **Righteousness** in verse 4b (=10:2) can be understood as almsgiving. In verse 5 the basic orientation of a person (cf. v. 3) has an effect on the way he or she turns out. This point is made also in verse 6.

11:7 / The Hebrew is uncertain. The NIV supplies **his** in 7a. **Hope** might refer to his good name or his progeny. But verse 7b does not provide a satisfactory parallel; literally, "and the hope of strength perishes." The NIV interprets this as further comment on the hope of the evil person. See Additional Notes. Compare 10:28.

11:8 / Antithetic. This is an example of the law of retribution at work. The **trouble** that the **righteous** (sometimes) has, will be (and must be) transferred to **the wicked** who deserve it! Compare 21:18.

11:9 / Antithetic. Despite the calumny by the wicked, the wisdom of the **righteous** will save them. Such is the advantage of **knowledge** (= wisdom).

11:10–11 / Antithetic. Both sayings deal with the **city**. As C. H. Toy (*A Critical and Exegetical Commentary on the Book of Proverbs* [Edinburgh: T & T Clark, 1899], p. 226) remarks concisely, "the first couplet states the fact, the second the reason."

11:12 / Antithetic. Control of the **tongue** is a cardinal aspect of wisdom. Derision of one's **neighbor** (see also 14:21a) is unwise; although no reason is given, many can be presupposed (harm to oneself, etc.).

11:13 / Antithetic and juxtapositional. Verse 13a is repeated in 20:19a. Like verse 12, this saying underscores control of the tongue. The ability to **keep a secret** is highly prized (cf. 25:8–10; Sir. 27:16–21).

11:14 / Antithetic and chiastic. The importance of several **advisers** is stressed also in 15:22. Verse 14b is repeated in 24:6b. "Two heads are better than one," as we say.

11:15 / Antithetic and chiastic. The practice of making a surety for another is a very frequent topic. What is meant is lending/borrowing without interest. The general attitude is against the practice (e.g., 6:1–5; 17:18; 22:26–27), but Ben Sira is much more open to it as an act of charity (Sir. 29:15–20). However, he does recognizes its dangers.

11:16 / Antithetic. A contrast between men and women is unique in this book and the parallelism is wanting: the good should gain, but the **ruthless** should lose (**only,** in the NIV, is not present in the Hebrew, but it is employed also in the REB to convey the sense). The text is disturbed, as the four lines in the LXX suggest (see Additional Notes). Others think that the **kind-hearted woman** wins **respect** without effort, in contrast to a man's ruthless pursuit of **wealth.**

11:17 / Antithetic and juxtapositional. The contrast is between the happy and sad results that **kind** and **cruel** conduct achieves for a person.

11:18–21 / Antithetic. These verses (note the juxtaposition) characterize the **righteous** and the **wicked**. According to verse 18, only virtue brings a true reward (cf. 10:16). Verse 19 (in the NIV, but see the Additional Notes) repeats the idea of verse 18 in the ultimate terms of **life/death;** of course, the perspective is this world. In verse 20, **detests** is literally "abomination," probably derived from cultic language (e.g., see also 12:22, 15:9). Literally, verse 21a reads, "Hand to hand! The wicked . . ." The certainty of divine retribution is affirmed.

11:22 / Lines a and b bring out the incongruity between beauty and lack of wisdom in a woman. The qualities are juxtaposed, without any "like." Womanly character cannot be replaced by (exterior) decoration.

11:23 / Antithetic and juxtapositional. **Good** or **wrath** (cf. 11:4) are the results awaiting the **righteous** and the **wicked** (cf. 10:23).

11:24 / Antithetic. This may be merely the recording of a paradox: the spender somehow prospers, but the miser loses what he has. This is a fact of life. The NIV insinuates a moral observation by translating, **unduly,** but the Hebrew can mean simply "too sparing" (cf. NAB). Meinhold (*Sprüche*, p. 198) suggests that the image of sowing seed is appropriate: a generous sowing leads to growth, but an unwise thriftiness leads to disaster. The saying is general enough to also be understood with a moral edge (stinginess toward others as opposed to hoarding).

11:25 / Synonymous (this kind of parallelism is rare in chs. 10–15). See verses 17–19 for the idea.

11:26 / Antithetic. This verse does not have the same meaning as did verse 24. Here, the issue is a wrongful **hoarding** of **grain,** a speculation about price or value.

11:27 / Antithetic. The **goodwill** can be that of God or society; in any case, **evil** rebounds upon the one who pursues it (cf. 10:24a).

11:28 / Antithetic. It is the *trust* in **riches** that is harmful (cf. Sir. 5:1). By implication, such a person is not **righteous.** See 10:2 and 11:4.

11:29 / The two lines are hardly parallel (perhaps synonymous). A home-wrecker can look forward to nothing (the **wind** is the only inheritance; see the usage in Hos. 8:7). Folly leads to low estate (v. 29b).

11:30 / The text is corrupt; see Additional Notes. The NIV proclaims the benefits of the **wise/righteous.** For the association of wisdom with the **tree of life** (but not as the fruit of the righteous person!), see 3:18; righteousness or wisdom brings life. **Wins souls** could be understood as the effect of wisdom, but the translation is doubtful.

11:31 / An *a fortiori* argument that the **ungodly** will *certainly* be punished (since v. 31a indicates that even the **righteous** receive punishment).

Additional Notes §12

11:1 / The NIV translates by "abhors" or "detests" the Hb. "abomination," which seems to be derived from cultic usage; cf. 11:20. In both lines, subjects and predicates are simply juxtaposed.

11:2 / There is alliteration in the Hb. v. 2a: *bāʾ-zādôn wayyābôʾ qālôn* that is almost impossible to produce in English. The REB has, "When pride comes in, in comes contempt."

11:3 / Read the Qere in v. 3b, "[it] destroys them."

11:7 / The LXX translates: "When the righteous person dies, hope does not vanish / and the presumption of the wicked is destroyed." Any translation of v. 7 remains uncertain.

11:15 / There is a noteworthy alliteration in v. 15a: the Hb. letters *rêš* (four times) and *ʿayin* (three times). In v. 15b, subject and predicate are juxtaposed participles.

11:16 / Evidence for the uncertainty of the text can be seen from the LXX: "A gracious woman acquires honor for her husband, but a woman who hates righteousness is a throne of dishonor. Sluggards end up lacking in wealth, but the courageous acquire riches."

11:19 / The Hb. is difficult: "Thus righteousness (is) to life / but whoever pursues evil (is) to his death." W. McKane (*Proverbs: A New Approach* [Philadelphia: Westminster, 1970], p. 435) renders the Hb. thus: "He who is steadfast in righteousness is destined for life, but he who pursues evil suffers death for it." This presupposes a minor change in the vocalization of *kn* ("thus") and takes the abstract for the concrete (the righteous one) in v. 19a. **"Righteous(ness)"** is the catchword for vv. 18–21.

11:25–26 / **Blessing** (in v. 25a, "a person of blessing") is a catchword uniting these verses.

11:30b / The meaning of this line is uncertain. Besides the NIV rendition, one could also translate, "and a wise person takes lives." "Take souls" is the problem. *lqḥ* cannot really mean **win**; it suggests taking lives, destroying—which makes no sense. The LXX would suggest that **wise** should be changed to "violence." Perhaps the best solution is a different vocalization for "takes" (Hb. *leqaḥ* could mean what is taken in by instruction): "the wise person [communicates] the instruction of others" (so Plöger, *Sprüche*, p. 143).

12:1 / Antithetic and juxtapositional. The sages are emphatic in teaching the need for discipline and openness to reproof. **Discipline** *(mûsār)* is a mark of love (13:24), but it is also parallel to corporal punishment. It has a wide range of meaning, such as "instruction" or **correction** (as the word pair in this verse suggests). **Stupid** is, literally, "brutish, like an animal."

12:2–3 / Antithetic. These verses are an affirmation of traditional retribution theory.

12:4 / Antithetic and chiastic. **Noble character** is literally "power" and indicates strong men (as warriors). It also connotes able and good women and is used in this way here and in 31:10, where a full description follows. The judgment is made from the viewpoint of the **husband**. The frequent reference to wives shows how much Israelite men were dependent upon them (cf. 11:16; 19:14; 30:23, and the unfavorable comparisons in 21:9, 12; 25:24).

12:5–7 / All of the verses are antithetic and verse 7 is a chiasmus. The contrast in all three is between the **righteous** and the **wicked**. Plöger (*Sprüche*, p. 149) detects a certain "heightening" in the statements: **plans, words,** and results.

12:8 / Antithetic. It should be recalled that these sayings are not to be taken only on the intellectual plane; action and conduct are included.

12:9 / Antithetic "better" saying. The NIV suggests that honesty and integrity in one's state in life is to be upheld. However, a change in the vocalization (with the LXX) gives better sense in verse 9a: **Better to be a nobody,** "but self-supporting." Hypocrisy is a frequent target of the sayings.

12:10–11 / Both of these antithetic sayings would be at home in a peasant culture. The point of verse 10 is to contrast the universal consideration that the **righteous** have for others, even for an **animal,** in contrast to the "tender mercies" (as the RV puts it) of the **wicked** who have no regard for any one. Verse 11 finds a close parallel in 28:19. Diligence and serious farmwork is urged in verse 11a, as opposed to stupid activity that has no goal.

12:12 / The text is corrupt. The NIV can be taken to mean that the **wicked** seek spoil that is gotten wickedly (v. 12a). But the translation, **plunder,** is questionable and **the plunder of evil men** is hardly meaningful in context. In verse 12b, **flourishes** is a wishful translation for the simple word "gives" (that calls for an object) and the sense bears little if any relationship to verse 12a. See the Additional Notes.

12:13–14 / Antithetic and synonymous. Both sayings deal with the effects of speech, a topic that emerges frequently in verses 17–23. The point of verse 13 is that the **righteous** do not have to suffer from the sorry effects that **sinful talk** (lit. "sin of the lips") causes for the wicked. In verse 14, both the speech and action of a person have certain consequences, even good ones, unless **good things** is a later addition. This raises the question: why should these good things be mentioned when verse 14b simply expresses recompense for actions? **As surely** of the NIV is not in the MT. **Rewards** follows the Qere, but the sense is "returns to."

12:15 / Antithetic and juxtapositional. **Right to him** (lit. "right in one's own eyes") indicates a lethal blindness (cf. 3:7; and esp. 26:12; cf. also Judg. 17:6). It is contrasted here with the openness of the wise person to what others have to say.

12:16 / Antithetic and chiastic. The contrast is between mindless and spontaneous reaction of anger and a calm, deliberate response. Self-control is a common topos of the sages.

12:17–19 / The topic of these antithetic sayings is proper speech. Verse 17 is not an admonition to general truthfulness; it refers specifically to a legal situation where perjury would be committed by a **false witness.** Verse 18 contrasts the beneficent effects of wise speech with the lethal effects of rash, ill-considered **words.** For the comparison with **sword** thrusts, see Sirach 28:18. Verse 19 enunciates the permanence of truth over (evanescent) falsehood. A good illustration of this proverb is the story of Darius's bodyguards in 1 Esdras 3–4: "Great is truth and strongest of all" (4:41).

12:20 / Antithetic and chiastic. **Deceit** and **joy** are not an exact word pair, but they are adequate here, especially if they are understood in both a subjective and objective sense (i.e., deceit consists of both self-deception and the deception of others).

12:21 / Antithetic. This is a typical statement of retribution (in this life); compare also Sirach 33:1.

12:22 / Antithetic and chiastic. This verse resembles 11:20. Truthfulness is a very frequent topic (e.g., cf. 12:19) and there is a similar saying in Amenemope (ch. 10; 13.15ff.; *ANET*, p. 423; *AEL*, vol. 2., p. 154).

12:23 / Antithetic. Control of the tongue is another frequent topic. The wise know how to keep their own counsel, but the foolish speak out of their ignorance (cf. 12:16, 22). Again, there is similar advice in Amenemope (ch. 21; 22.10–15, *ANET*, p. 424; *AEL*, vol. 2, p. 159).

12:24 / Antithetic. The saying favors diligence which will lead a person to authority and power—unlike the slavery that is the lot of the lazy person.

12:25 / Antithetic. A psychological observation about the effects of both anxiety and encouragement; see also the awareness displayed in 13:12, 15:13, and 17:22.

12:26 / The Hebrew text is corrupt (see Additional Notes). The NIV provides two translations of verse 26a, and the parallelism with verse 26b is not clear in either case. Caution in **friendship** is a frequent motif (cf. 18:24; 19:4, 6–7; Sir. 6:5–17) but is it to be found in verse 26a? The footnote follows the RV, but **guide** is a doubtful translation. As for verse 26b, Toy (*Proverbs*, p. 257) points out that it is never said that the way itself causes one to stray. Rather, one goes astray in the wrong way. But the NIV translates what the MT has. The NJPS silently emends to "leads astray," omitting **them.**

12:27 / The text is quite uncertain. There is a contrast between the **lazy** and the **diligent,** but the point eludes us. The NIV notes that **roast** is a doubtful translation; the meaning would seem to be that the lazy one fails to profit from hunting. In verse 27b, the NIV seems to transpose two words; the MT has, literally: "the possessions of a man (are) precious (when?) diligent."

In other words, the riches are precious to the diligent. See the Additional Notes.

12:28 / Verse 28a is clear: the association of **righteousness** (wisdom) with **life** is found in 3:1–2; 8:35; and 14:27. In 28b, the NIV glosses over a text that is not translatable (lit. "a way of a path, not [or 'to'] death"; see Additional Notes). In any case, **immortality** cannot be understood here as life with God beyond death. Sheol is the consistent perspective in this book.

Additional Notes §13

12:1 / The succinct effect of the participles and the juxtaposition of the words cannot be captured in translation: "One who loves discipline—one who loves knowledge / but (and) one who hates correction—stupid."

12:2 / The word **LORD** occurs only in v. 2a, but it is to be understood in v. 2b. The root *rš*ᶜ, "condemn," is a key word uniting vv. 2–3.

12:9 / The suggested change in vocalization is ᶜōbēd. The "better" saying is an expression typical of the wisdom literary style. See also Sir. 10:27. In v. 9a a change in vocalization yields better sense: "and be self-supporting" (Hb. *weᶜōbēd lô*).

12:12 / The LXX reads, "Desires of the wicked are evil, but the roots of the just are in strongholds (i.e., endure?)." The ancient versions and modern conjectures are not much help. The NJPS translation remarks simply that the meaning of the Hb. is uncertain.

12:13 / The LXX has an added couplet: "The one who looks calmly will be pitied, the one who opposes in the gates will afflict souls."

12:14 / The NIV reads the Kethib; the Qere suggests that the Lord is the one who **rewards**.

12:16 / The MT is, lit. "the fool, on the (very) day, his anger becomes known."

12:19 / The verse is cleverly constructed by the use of chiasm and the repetition of Hb. ᶜad ("until").

12:25 / Despite the disagreements in gender between subject and verb in v. 25a, and between the suffixes of the verbs and the antecedent (*lēb* is masculine), there can be no doubt about the sense of the entire verse.

12:26 / V. 26a cannot really be translated. Perhaps the MT says: "A just person explores [causes to explore?] his friend." If the Hiphil of *tûr* (which the MT puts in the jussive!) can mean "show the way" (so André Barucq, *Le Livre des Proverbes* [Paris: Librairie Lecoffre, 1964]), then the footnote in the NIV can be justified. It is not clear how the NIV obtains **cautious** from *ytr*. A common emendation (changing the vowels in *mr'hw*) yields "pasture," and this can be taken in a metaphorical sense (well-being): "looks out for his own well-being" (Plöger, *Sprüche*). Perhaps the most reasonable conjecture is that of J. A. Emerton ("Note on Proverbs 12:26,"*ZAW* 76 [1964], pp. 191–93): "The righteous is delivered (from *ntr*, Hophal) from harm *(mērā'â)*, but the way of the wicked leads them (i.e., the wicked) astray."

12:27 / Hb. *ḥrk* (**roast?**) is a *hapax legomenon* (occurs only once in the Hb. Bible); hence the uncertain translation. If one adopts the transposition of two words (with the LXX and Syriac), v. 27b reads, lit. "the possessions of an industrious person—precious." The NIV seems to derive **prizes** from this reading.

12:28 / V. 28b cannot be rendered as in the NIV. In addition, the word "not" is the particle used with verbs, and not with nouns; "not-death" is the doubtful Hb. that is made to yield **immortality**. Perhaps the original was "to death" (*'el* for *'al*), as the LXX and Vulgate suggest. **Along that path** of the NIV is also problematic. The ancient versions suggest a contrast—something like "a path of wickedness/abomination (?) is to death." The REB reads, "but there is a well-worn path to death."

§14 Proverbs 13:1–25

13:1 / Antithetic. Literally, verse 1a exhibits juxtaposition: "a wise son—a father's discipline" (see the Additional Notes). In any case, the emphasis is on docility and openness to learning.

13:2 / See 12:14a and 18:20. The MT reads: "From the fruit of his mouth a man eats good (things)," that is, there is profit from his words. This presumes that the speech of a (good) person will be rewarded. The parallelism with verse 2b, where the soul (or "life," "desire," or **craving**) of the deceivers is **violence,** is quite obscure. There seems to be a contrast between the fruitless greed of the **unfaithful** and the one who uses speech effectively and profitably. The text is uncertain; see Additional Notes.

13:3 / Antithetic and juxtapositional. Control of one's tongue is a common topic (e.g., 20:19 and 21:23). The Hebrew catchword for verses 2–4 is *nepeš,* "soul," **life,** "desire," (it occurs four times).

13:4 / Antithetic and chiastic. The condemnation of laziness, as opposed to diligence, also occurs frequently (cf. 6:6–11; 10:4–5).

13:5 / Antithetic and chiastic. The contrast is between the honesty of the **righteous** and the harm wrought (both to self and to others) by the **wicked.**

13:6 / Antithetic. Abstract virtue and vice are personified in their corresponding activities—one **guards** and the other **overthrows.** See the Additional Notes.

13:7 / Antithetic. See 11:4 and 12:9. Verse 7 seems to present a kind of paradox and to affirm that looks can be deceptive (hence this is not a moral judgment; contra Toy, *Proverbs*). The Hitpael form of the verbs can connote "pretense," but the saying is not a condemnation of false pretense; it merely registers a fact of human conduct.

13:8 / Antithetic. This saying points out the ambiguities of **riches**. The rich can buy their way out of a difficulty, whereas the **poor**, having no riches that would entice an enemy, do not even receive a **threat**. There is a certain ironic tone here; the poor person has nothing to fear (because they have nothing valuable to offer), in contrast to the rich.

13:9 / Antithetic. Another **righteous/wicked** contrast (cf. vv. 5–6). **Light** is a symbol of life and good fortune (e.g., cf. Job 3:20). **Shines brightly** is literally "rejoices." A spent **lamp** is a sign of non-life, misfortune, and death. See 4:18–19.

13:10 / Antithetic. Literally, verse 10a has "only by pride one gives quarrels"—slightly different from the NIV. **Quarrels** arise due to various reasons, not only **pride**. And pride is not quite an antithesis to **those who take advice.** Hence changes have been suggested; see Additional Notes. Verse 10b seems obvious; the NJPS marks 10a as "meaning uncertain."

13:11 / Antithetic, but the precise antithesis is not clear. **Dishonest money** is literally "money from vanity" (Hb. *hebel*, "breath" or "nothing"), which does not necessarily mean dishonest. Nor is it opposed to a gradual increase in money. The NIV (influenced by the LXX) makes this a very moral saying: honesty in verse 11a, saving of earnings in verse 11b. Probably one should read in verse 11a: "Money hastily gotten." Then the sense is that when money comes too easily (and perhaps unjustly) for a person, it will not last. See the Additional Notes.

13:12 / Antithetic and chiastic. Another psychological observation (cf. 12:25), expressed by juxtaposition: **hope** protracted—sickens **heart**/and (but) **tree of life**—desire having come. On the mythological background of the tree of life, see 3:18. No moral point is made here; contrast 13:19.

13:13 / Antithetic. In this context **instruction** and **command** are those of the sages, not the law code. This verse also exemplifies the working of (proper) retribution.

13:14 / As in verse 13, the torah or **teaching** of the sage is meant. **Fountain of life** is fresh, flowing water (cf. 10:11). **The snares of death** are wrongdoing, but the imagery is taken from the mythological concept of the Ugaritic god Mot (Death), who pursues every living thing, entrapping them. The parallelism is synthetic, in that verse 14b continues the thought of verse 14a, without duplicating it.

13:15 / Verse 15a is clear, but as the NIV marginal note would indicate, the parallel line in verse 15b is suspect; literally, "the way of deceivers is permanent (?)." See Additional Notes.

13:16 / Antithetic. The **knowledge** of the **prudent** derives from the observation and the teaching of the sages that guide conduct. The **fool** lacks depth.

13:17 / Antithetic. Reliable **messengers** were a concern (cf. 25:13; 26:6). The parallelism could be improved; see Additional Notes.

13:18 / Antithetic and chiastic. **Discipline** is a frequent topos (see also 15:5, 32).

13:19 / While this couplet is clear in itself, it is suspect because of the lack of parallelism. Verse 19a resembles 13:12b and verse 19b is similar to 29:27b. Attempts to improve the verse have not been successful.

13:20 / Antithetic. The recommendation to associate **with the wise** is a staple in wisdom teaching (cf. 15:31; Sir. 6:34–36; 8:8–9; 9:14–16). See Additional Notes.

13:21–22 / Antithetic. Both sayings illustrate the traditional doctrine of reward and punishment. According to verse 22, the **good** (must) prosper and can leave a legacy to descendants. Even if sinners acquire some **wealth,** this cannot remain with their progeny; it is bound to end up with the **righteous.** Catchwords for both verses are **righteous** and **sinner.**

13:23 / The Hebrew is difficult and probably corrupt. Literally: much food—tillage of the poor; and (but) property is swept away—without justice. See Additional Notes. The NIV seems to say that **injustice** (of whatever kind) deprives the **poor** of the fruits of their land.

13:24 / Antithetic and chiastic. There is a certain paradoxical aspect in this love/hate relationship (cf. 3:11–12). Corporal punishment is a frequent recommendation of the sages (cf. 19:18; 23:13–14; Sir. 30:1–13).

13:25 / Antithetic. This saying flows from the under-standing of divine retribution for the **righteous** and the **wicked** (cf. 10:3).

Additional Notes §14

13:1 / The LXX has "a diligent son heeds his father." B. Gemser (*Sprüche Salomos* [Tübingen: J. C. B. Mohr, 1963], p. 62) and others pro-pose "a wise son loves discipline."

13:6 / Lit., the MT has: "righteousness will guard upright con-duct, but evil will subvert sin." The abstract is used for the concrete, as the NIV indicates.

13:10 / In v. 10a some read "lightheaded" for **only** (*rēq* for *raq*). In v. 10b Toy (*Proverbs*, p. 267) and others obtain better parallelism by emending the text to read: "with the humble is wisdom" (cf. 11:2b).

13:11 / The word "hastily" (for **dishonest**) is gotten by read-ing the Hb. word *mbhl*, in place of *mhbl*. Then the antithesis to **little by little** is clear. In the doctrine of the sages, anything that is acquired hastily is suspect—it will not be appreciated, or else it may have been acquired wrongfully (cf. 20:21; 28:22).

13:15 / Neither the NIV nor its footnote for v. 15b is probable here. On the basis of the Gk. many suggest an emendation: Hb. *ʾêdām*, "their ruin" for Hb. *ʾêtān*, "permanent." So the NRSV and the NAB: "The way of the faithless is their ruin."

13:17 / A mere change in the vocalization produces "brings trouble" (so NRSV).

13:20 / The NIV reads the Qere in v. 20a. The paronomasia, or punning, in both a and b is striking.

§15 Proverbs 14:1–35

14:1 / Antithetic. The NIV has rendered the general sense, but see the Additional Notes. A real **house** might be meant, but more probably it is a metaphor for home—the family or even for one's own life; see 24:3 and 31:10–31.

14:2 / Antithetic and juxtapositional. Here is an obvious contrast between the just and the wicked in their relationships to the **LORD**.

14:3 / Antithetic. Here is another example of the effects of wise and foolish speech (cf. 10:21; 15:7; Eccl. 10:12–13). The **rod to his back** (cf. also the NRSV) is a silent correction. Literally, the MT has a "rod (or shoot) of pride"—this would seem to mean that a fool's pride is punished by foolish talk.

14:4 / Antithetic and juxtapositional: "When no oxen— manger empty (clean?); and (but) much produce—in strength of an ox." The point seems to be that there will be no food to eat if there are no animals to work the farm. See McKane (*Proverbs*, pp. 470–71) for a different interpretation.

14:5 / Antithetic and chiastic. This is another saying about public **witness** in a legal case. The condemnation is implicit (cf. 12:17; 14:25). Verse 5b repeats 6:19a.

14:6 / Antithetic and chiastic. The nuance of the **mocker** or scoffer (Hb. *lēṣ;* cf. 9:7–8; 21:24) is difficult to determine. His search for **wisdom** cannot be understood as truly serious.

14:7 / Avoiding the company of fools is recommended again here (cf. 13:20; 17:12; 26:4–5; 26:1, 8). Verse 7 seems to give the reason: one can learn nothing from them. The Hebrew is difficult; verse 7a is a command and there is no antithesis. The tense of verse 7b is unusual (lit. "and you do/did not know lips of knowledge"). The phrase, "lips of knowledge," is unique.

14:8 / Antithetic. The style is juxtapositional: "The wisdom of the clever—the understanding of their ways; the folly of fools—deception." The **prudent** see their way clearly, but **fools** deceive themselves (and others). Verse 8a = v. 15b.

14:9 / The Hebrew is difficult; literally, "fools scoff at a guilt offering(?), but among the upright is good will." "Scoff" is in the singular, contrary to the grammatical construction, and **amends for sin** is a doubtful translation. The meaning intended by the NIV is that **fools** ridicule the cult, but the **upright** receive its benefit (**goodwill** means, presumably, God's approval). But the text and ancient versions are uncertain. See Additional Notes.

14:10 / Antithetic and chiastic. The point is that there are certain feelings and attitudes so deep and personal that they cannot be shared with others.

14:11 / Antithetic. This verse exemplifies the traditional view of retribution. The reference is to the household and family, not just to the physical dwellings.

14:12–13 / Both sayings illustrate the fact that things are not always what they appear to be. Verse 12 is repeated in 16:25. It can be applied in a moral sense (which is probably intended here; cf. 11:5 and 12:15a), as well as to a simple sense of direction in travel. The MT has, literally, "there is a path straight before a person." The sages recognized that any path, and especially the path of life, can be a puzzle. Verse 13 is another psychological observation (cf. v. 10; 12:25). As against the pessimistic "is" of the NRSV, the NIV properly translates **may**. Verse 13b reads literally, "and its end, joy," which should be corrected to "the end of joy (is **grief**)," as the NIV presupposes. See Additional Notes. The verse alerts the reader to the mixture of joy and sorrow that the sages recognize in life's activities.

14:14 / Antithetic. This is another statement of traditional retribution for the good and the bad people. See the Additional Notes.

14:15–17 / Antithetic. In a broad sense, cautious action is the topic that binds these sayings together. In regard to verse 15, the **simple** person is gullible in contrast to the wise. Though in verse 16 the NIV supplies the term **LORD** and makes 16a equivalent to Job 1:1 (a description of Job himself), verse 16a should be taken as a description of the caution (reasonable fear) with which the **wise** person avoids **evil** (whether moral or physical), in contrast to the **fool** who is **reckless** and self-confident. Verse 17 shows little parallelism or antithesis. There seems to be a contrast between the **quick-tempered** and the **crafty** (cf. 12:2, but also 1:4), but the contrast breaks down with the verbs: acts foolishly/is hated. See Additional Notes.

14:18 / Antithetic. The NIV translates the MT literally. However, **folly** is not something that is inherited; rather it is acquired (so the RSV) by the **simple** unless they better themselves by the pursuit of wisdom. See the Additional Notes.

14:19 / Synonymous. This reflects the typical wisdom view of the way things *should* turn out.

14:20–24 / These sayings can be grouped under the theme of poverty and riches, and they are antithetic. Verse 20 states a fact of experience: money (or the lack of it) makes a difference in one's social relationships (cf. 19:4, 7; Sir. 6:10–12; 12:8–9; 13:21–23). Verse 21 is a criticism of the situation described in verse 20; one should not lord it over those who are less fortunate. The word pair is **neighbor** and **needy** (see v. 31). In verse 22, the **evil** and **good** envisioned is broader than care of the poor, but it fits into this context. The good can expect **love and faithfulness** (conspicuous divine attributes) from the poor especially, but also from God. Verse 23 reflects the familiar emphasis on **hard work** and diligence (cf. 10:4–5) and warns against self-inflicted **poverty.** Verse 24 is juxtapositional. While wisdom and **wealth** are generally associated (as in the MT and the NIV), the emphasis here is unusual. The NRSV follows the LXX and reads "wisdom" (instead of wealth) as the **crown.** Verse 24b is rather flat; literally, "the folly of fools—folly." See Additional Notes.

14:25 / Antithetic and juxtapositional. This is another saying about a **truthful witness** in a legal context (cf. 6:19; 12:17; 14:5). Verse 25b is literally, "the one who utters lies—deception!"

14:26–27 / The theme of **fear of the LORD** unites these verses. Verse 26 is literally "in the fear of the Lord—a strong fortress; and to his children there will be a refuge." The NIV silently corrects the MT which has no antecedent for **his.** Fear of the Lord is, of course, a key concept in OT wisdom (cf. 1:7) and here is shared in by the **children** of the God-fearer (cf. 20:7). Both verses 26–27 are in synthetic, not antithetic, parallelism. Verse 27 is almost identical with 13:14. It is important to notice identification between fear of the Lord and the teaching of the wise. Such a view did not distinguish between religious and "profane" wisdom (cf. Sir. 1:25–27).

14:28 / Antithetic. W. O. E. Oesterley (*The Book of Proverbs: With Introduction and Notes* [London: Methuen, 1929], p. 114) remarks that "this is the only instance in *Proverbs* of the king being mentioned in a purely secular connection." However, **a large population** is considered to be part of the blessing that a wise **king** receives. Oesterley also points out the many royal sayings that have an explicit religious cast (e.g., 16:12–13), and verse 28 should not be separated from these.

14:29 / Antithetic; cf. verse 17a. The **quick-tempered** (lit. short of wind/spirit), as opposed to the **patient,** is a frequent topos in the wisdom literature. Self-control is the ideal. In the teaching of Amenemope there is frequent warning about the "heated man" (e.g., chs. 2–4; *AEL,* vol. 2, p. 150).

14:30 / Antithetic. This psychosomatic observation is not unlike verse 29. **Envy** is too narrow a meaning; rather "passion" or "jealousy."

14:31 / Antithetic and chiastic. See also 17:5 and 19:7. The juxtapositional style is worth noting: "Whosoever oppresses the poor—condemns their Maker; one who honors God—one kind to the needy." Verse 21 is explicitly related to **God** in this saying. One's attitude to the **poor** is at the same time one's true attitude to God, and God is not influenced by the wealth or poverty of an individual. The saying is intended particularly for the wealthy (cf. 17:5; 22:2; 29:13).

14:32 / Antithetic. The MT clearly affirms that the downfall of the **wicked** is brought on by their own doing. Verse 32b reads, literally: "but (and) the righteous one has hope in his (own) death." The great majority of commentators and translators (cf. NRSV, NEB) adopt the LXX here: "in his integrity." This gives sharper parallelism and is in harmony with the OT view that there is no life (with God) after death. **The righteous have a refuge** in their integrity, that is, they avoid the **calamity** that death brings upon the evil (see 12:2a; 11:4).

14:33 / Antithetic. The NIV translation of verse 33b is doubtful, as the footnote suggests. The NIV translation mitigates the antithesis of verse 33b. Furthermore, the harmony of **wisdom**

and **fools** is contrary to wisdom teaching. The NRSV renders correctly: "but it is not known in the heart of fools." See the Additional Notes.

14:34 / Antithetic. **A nation** finds true glory in the **righteousness** that characterizes it, whereas **sin** is its **disgrace** (a relatively rare meaning for this word). The viewpoint is international.

14:35 / Antithetic. The viewpoint is intranational. Unless the **king** is strong in dealing with his administrators, the nation will suffer. Hence, this saying about the correct attitude of a king to his **servants**.

Additional Notes §15

14:1 / Lit., the first two Hb. words can be translated "wisdom of women" or "the wise(st?) among women." Many scholars bring this in line with 9:1 by omitting "women" (Hb. *nāšîm*) and making "wisdom" (Hb. *ḥkmwt*) the subject of the singular verb: "wisdom has built . . . "

14:3 / The preferred reading is Hb. *gēwōh* (= back); cf. 10:13.

14:9 / The LXX has "the houses of the godless will need purification, but the houses of the just are acceptable."

14:13 / The NIV reads the Hb. text as *weʾaḥᵃrît haśśimḥâ*, "and the end of joy."

14:14 / In v. 14b, the NIV glosses over a difficulty. The text reads lit. "and from him(self is sated) a good man." The NIV implies a correction of the MT that is widely adopted: "his deeds" (Hb. *mmᶜllw*) parallel to **ways.**

14:17 / **Quick-tempered** is lit. "short of face" (contrast "long of face" for "patient," v. 29). The contrast in the parallelism is better preserved in the LXX, which seems to be based on an original Hb. verb, *yiśśaʾ*, "bear, carry." Therefore v. 17a in the LXX reads, "the thoughtful person endures many things."

14:18 / If Hb. *nḥlw* in v. 18a is read as the Niphal of *ḥlh*, ("be adorned with"), the parallelism is strengthened. So the NRSV; cf. the NAB.

14:24 / The LXX has "the crown of the wise is prudence" in v. 24a, probably based on an alternate Hb. reading, *ᶜrmh* ("prudence"), rather than the MT reading, *ᶜšrm* ("their riches"). The tautology of v. 24a is perhaps to be kept; cf. the NJPS: "the stupidity of dullards is stupidity."

14:32 / The just could not trust in a joyful immortality (until the end of the OT period), but they could trust that their integrity would make a difference in this life. The LXX has: "the righteous (can) trust(s) in his integrity," reading the Hb. as *btmw* instead of the MT *bmtw*.

14:33 / The reading of the NRSV, NAB, and others follows the LXX in inserting the negative "not" in v. 33b.

§16 Proverbs 15:1–33

This chapter is marked by many antitheses between the wise and the foolish and the topic of speech occurs several times (vv. 1, 2, 4, 7, 14, 23, 26, 28). Notably frequent also are the *yhwh* sayings ("abomination," vv. 8, 9, 26; "fear of the Lord," vv. 16, 33). Their frequency in 14:26–16:15 has led some (Skehan, *Studies*, pp. 17–20) to ask if they were not added to provide a suture between the antithetical proverbs of chapters 10–15 and another group beginning in chapter 16.

15:1 / Antithetic. For the idea see 25:15, where **gentle** is used of a tongue "breaking" a bone. Speech is a basic topic in this book. Throughout, the reader is confronted with various assertions about speech: when to be gentle, silent, cautious, or to speak at the right time (cf. v. 23).

15:2 / Antithetic. The contrast between **wise** and foolish makes the general meaning of the verse obvious, but **commends** is a doubtful translation. See the Additional Notes.

15:3 / The parallelism is progressive and specifying. The point is that nothing escapes **the eyes of the LORD.** This is both consoling and threatening. Were the sages also aware of how often things escaped their own gaze and judgment?

15:4 / Antithetic; juxtaposition of subjects and predicates. Another saying about speech (cf. vv. 1–2). For the **healing** effect, cf. 16:24, and for the **tree of life,** cf. 3:18. See Additional Notes.

15:5 / Antithetic. The parallelism is not perfect (no mention of the mother; cf. 10:1), but the point is clear: the wise person is teachable, docile.

15:6 / Antithetic. The translation of the NIV is guided by the contrast between the just and the **wicked.** See the Additional Notes.

15:7 / Antithetic. The parallelism of **wise** and foolish determines the meaning (cf. 10:14). Knowledge is associated with the former, not with the latter. See the Additional Notes.

15:8 / Antithetic and chiasmic; there is a juxtaposition of subjects and predicates (also in v. 9a). **Detests** (lit. "abomination") serves as a catchword with verse 9. The evaluation of the cult (sacrifice) is in line with prophetic teaching. For other mentions of cult, see 21:3, 27.

15:9 / Antithetic and chiasmic. In contrast to verse 8, a broader view than just cultic observance is offered here. **Path** (v. 10) and **way** associate verses 9–10.

15:10 / Synonymous parallelism. This is a warning. Here **discipline** is equivalent to death (v. 10b), but normally it is considered positively as necessary for the conversion of a person. Similarly, **correction** is usually praised as something to heed.

15:11 / A succinct *a fortiori* saying about divine omniscience. The NIV supplies **lie open.** In Sheol (see the NIV margin) the dead are not beyond the power ("hand," Ps. 89:49; 139:3) of the Lord, but they lack a loving contact with God (none to praise him; cf. Ps. 6:5). *Abaddon* (NIV margin) is parallel to Sheol (see also 27:20; Job 26:6), and derived from the word, "perish."

15:12 / Synonymous parallelism. See also verses 5 and 10. **Correction** is always something to be heeded, but the foolish scoffer lives sealed in his own little world, apart from **the wise.**

15:13 / Antithetic. The point is that the inner feelings of a person will come to exterior expression, whether for joy or sadness. This is a purely experiential observation (cf. Sir. 13:25–26).

15:14 / Antithetic. Both parts of the line are similar to other sayings: verse 14a to 18:15a and 14:33a; verse 14b (reading the Qere, not the Kethib, "my face") resembles 15:2. The knowledge envisioned here is the teaching of the sages; note the contrast with verse 7.

15:15 / Antithetic; juxtaposition of subject and predicate. The idea is not unlike the observation in verse 13, but it emphasizes the corresponding lots of the **oppressed** and the **cheerful.**

15:16 / This is the first of two "better" sayings that modify conventional wisdom. Wealth is normally preferable to poverty—but not at any price. The saying calls for an attentive evaluation (everything has limitations) and favors **the fear of the LORD.**

15:17 / See also 17:1. More important than food at a **meal** is the spirit and comradeship among the participants. In the comparison meat is obviously more highly prized for a feast than **vegetables.**

15:18 / Antithetic. See 14:29 and Sirach 28:8–12. The contrast between the **hot-tempered** (cf. also 29:22) and the **patient** (cf. 16:32) is a topos also in Egyptian wisdom (e.g., see Amenemope, 6.1–12; *ANET,* p. 422; *AEL,* vol. 2, pp. 150–51).

15:19 / Contrary to the NIV, the MT says that the **way** is like a thorn hedge. The obstacles seem to reside within and without the **sluggard,** who will get nowhere. The contrast is suspect: the sluggard the opposite of the "diligent" (as in the LXX), not of the **upright.**

15:20 / Antithetic. Verse 20a is identical with 10:1a (see also 23:22). **Foolish man** is, literally, "a fool of a man" (cf. Gen. 16:12).

15:21 / Antithetic. The serious resolve of the wise contrasts with the light-headedness of the fool.

15:22 / Antithetic and chiastic. See 11:14. On all sides, public or private, the sages urge listening to advice.

15:23 / Synonymous and chiastic; verse 23b specifies and completes verse 23a. The emphasis is on the speaker, who not only gives good advice, but gives it at the right time (see also 25:11). The proper time (Gk. *kairos*) in speech is singled out in the Egyptian Anchsheshonq 12.24: "Do not say something when it is not the time for it" (*AEL,* vol. 3, p. 169).

15:24 / Antithetic in style, but the second line is a purpose clause. The adverbs **upward** and **down** are merely directional (cf. Deut. 28:13, 43). The saying refers to quality of life (or lack of it). There is no basis for claiming that these adverbs (absent from the LXX) were added to indicate **life** beyond death.

15:25 / Antithetic and chiastic. The **proud** may be also those who oppress the **widow**. See the remark about the boundary stone in 22:28. The prophets also indicated the greed of those who tried to add to their territorial possessions (Mic. 2:1; Isa. 5:8).

15:26 / The NIV does not translate the MT which reads, "pleasant words are pure."

15:27 / Antithetic and chiastic; note also the juxtaposition and alliteration in verse 27a. Bribery and greediness go together. See Additional Notes.

15:28 / Antithetic. Comparison with verse 2 shows the correspondence between **righteous**/wise and **wicked**/foolish. Because of the wise consideration given to speech, the words of the righteous will be honest, charitable, and prudent. This is in contrast to the **evil** talk. See Sirach 5:10–13.

15:29 / Antithetic and chiastic. Even if the **wicked** pray (cf. 28:9), God is too distant to hear them (cf. v. 8). The Hebrew root *šmᶜ* ("hear") occurs in verses 29–32. As always, there is a sharp division between the **righteous** and the wicked. Real life is going to raise problems for this either/or stance.

15:30 / Synonymous. Literally, "light of the eyes" (NIV, **cheerful look**) is to be found in the one who announces the **good news** as well as in the one who receives it.

15:31 / Synthetic. Verse 31 reads literally, "an ear that hears a reproof of life." This thought is continued in a single sentence in verse 31b. The point is that openness to correction secures wisdom and the company of the **wise** for such a person. The LXX does not have this verse.

15:32 / Antithetic and juxtapositional style. Again, the need for docility is underscored (cf. vv. 5, 10; 13:18).

15:33 / The parallelism, if any, is not clear. Disregard the NIV margin. Verse 33a is juxtapositional. **Teaches a man wisdom** is, literally, "discipline of wisdom," namely, leads to wisdom (cf. 1:7; 9:10). Verse 33b is repeated in 18:12b, where it fits. It may be a deliberate insertion here in order to emphasize the prerequisites: **fear of the LORD** and **humility**, which are united in 22:4a.

Additional Notes §16

15:2 / The Hb. for **commends** is, lit., "does well." A slight change of one Hb. letter yields *taṭṭîp* ("drips") for *têṭîb* ("commends"). This change preserves the parallelism.

15:4 / Some (Plöger, *Sprüche*) would derive Hb. *marpēʾ* from *rph*, and then the meaning would be "calm" instead of **healing**.

15:6 / **Contains** is not in the MT, but Hb. *bêt* can be understood as local, "in the house of." **Trouble** is an uncertain translation of the Niphal feminine participle of *ʿkr*.

15:7 / Doubt has been cast on the MT. It has "scatter," a strange verb for dispensing knowledge. The **not so** is rather abrupt and also an odd parallel to v. 7a; it can be translated as "not right" (so LXX and many moderns).

15:19 / The NIV, with other versions, omits the Hb. preposition *k-* ("like") before hedge (of thorns).

15:27 / From 15:27 to 16:9, the couplets in the LXX have been dislocated.

§17 Proverbs 16:1–33

There is a noticeable change here. The antithetic style of previous sayings starts to give way to synonymous and synthetic or progressive parallelism. More important, there are indications of a deliberate arrangement. The Lord is the subject of verses 1–7, 9, 11, 20, 33, and the king is the topic in verses 10, 12–15. Moreover, the Lord and the king seem to be meshed together (cf. 24:21): verse 11 interrupts 10–15. In addition, the decision (*mišpāṭ*; NIV "justice") of the king and of the Lord are spoken of in verses 10, 33. The "abomination" (NIV "detest") of wickedness is ascribed to the king in verse 12 and to the Lord in 15:9. The rest of the sayings do not betray such close connections, but this is enough to indicate that the collection is not haphazard. The entire chapter is further unified by alliteration, wordplays, "better" sayings, and smaller groups (words and wisdom in vv. 20–24; and "man" begins vv. 27–29). The Greek text of this chapter is problematic (e.g., vv. 1–3 are missing; v. 4 follows upon v. 9 of the MT, etc.).

16:1 / Antithetic. This verse has been variously interpreted. It seems to say that while humans make **plans** (and rightly so), **the LORD** determines the outward result **(the reply of the tongue)**. One is reminded of Balaam's oracles in Numbers 23–24. This is in agreement with the biblical emphasis on divine sovereignty and determinism. Between thought and action, God can intervene, but the decision comes from the Lord (cf. v. 9, an *inclusio*?). Such dependence upon the divinity is reflected in similar words in Ahiqar (viii, 115; *ANET,* p. 429). Less likely is the interpretation that sees the **reply** as a gift of God because plans stand in need of divine help in order that a reply be made. Others regard the lines as continuous: both plans and reply are from the Lord. The differing views are due to a selective emphasis. See also Amenemope 19.16–17 (*ANET,* p. 423); Anchsheshonq 26.14 (*AEL,* vol. 3, p. 179).

16:2 / Antithetic. Several sayings are similar: 3:7; 14:12; 21:2; see also Jer. 17:10. Human and divine judgment are contrasted. **All** (v. 2a) is either a deliberate exaggeration or should be understood as a concession: "even if all . . ." Self-deception is a possibility—but not with God.

16:3 / Synthetic and progressive. The distinction here is from action to **plans.** If the actions are done according to God, then the plans will succeed. In Hebrew the imperative form can be considered the equivalent of a conditional clause (cf. also Ps. 37:5). Trust in God is also urged in Amenemope 22.5–7=23.8–10 (*AEL*, vol. 2, p. 159).

16:4 / Synthetic and progressive. More than one translation is possible. **Ends** can also be rendered "to give an answer." However, to whom is the answer given: the **wicked** or God? Probably God—everyone must answer to God. The NIV, with many others, makes a sweeping claim for divine causality; nothing escapes God, even what seem to be an exception, the wicked. The **day of disaster** designates any catastrophe in this life, including death. Disaster should be understood in the sense of due retribution or punishment. See also Sirach 29:21, 34.

16:5 / Synthetic and progressive. **The LORD detests** is the usual NIV translation of "an abomination to the Lord." The spirit of this proverb is found throughout the OT (cf. 6:17, "haughty eyes"). Verse 5a is similar to 11:20, and verse 5b to 11:21. Literally, verse 5b is "hand to hand"—an idiom similar to a handshake or a hand on one's heart. In the LXX, two verses are inserted at this point that are not found in the MT.

16:6 / Synonymous? The proverb is ambiguous: **love** and **faithfulness** can be referred to God (cf. Ps. 51), so one should **fear** God, who forgives. Or the lines can be taken as strictly parallel and indicate how humans can attain forgiveness. Or the *ḥesed* and *ʾemet* are to be shown to one's neighbor (Mic. 6:6–9) and forgiveness will be granted. Many commentators understand the two lines to be in synonymous parallelism, with the NIV and NJPS.

16:7 / Synthetic. The point is that conduct **pleasing to** God will bring **peace**—even with one's **enemies** (e.g., Gen. 26:27–29). The subject of the verb in 7b could be either the human being (urged by McKane, *Proverbs*) or God. It is more likely the latter, although secondary causes are not to be ruled out.

16:8 / A "better" saying that is practically identical with 15:16 (see also 17:1; 28:6). Similar also is Amenemope 9.5–8; 16.11–14 (*ANET*, pp. 422–23). The attitude of the sages concerning poverty is ambiguous. It could be the result of laziness or diligence—but the key value is a right relationship to God.

16:9 / Antithetic. One has to reckon with the Lord between conceiving and carrying out an action. This emphasizes the gap between thought and deed. See the comment on verse 1 and also Jeremiah 10:23.

16:10 / Synonymous. The "king" sayings begin here. Verse 10a reads, literally, "an oracle is on the lips of the king." This is not a statement of fact, but rather an ideal picture (cf. the widow of Tekoa and David in 2 Sam. 14:17–20) that expresses the reverence with which the **king** was honored. Verse 10b should be rendered, "his mouth does not err in a decision *(mšpṭ)"*; see also "decision" in verse 33. While many sayings favor the king, others are critical (e.g., 28:15; 29:12; 31:3–5).

16:11 / Synonymous. The instruments of business **(scales, weights)** are concerns of **the LORD,** who will not tolerate injustice in these matters (cf. 11:1; 20:10).

16:12 / Synthetic, progressive. The royal ideal is continued (cf. 20:28; 25:5; 29:14). The association of the **throne** with **righteousness** seems to have been common to both Egypt and Jerusalem (Plöger, *Sprüche*, p. 192). The Pharaonic throne was formed in the sign of justice *(maʿat)*. Similarly, it may be inferred that the Solomonic throne (1 Kgs. 8), with its six steps, was founded on a pedestal or base designated "justice" (see esp. Ps. 89:14; 97:2).

16:13 / Synonymous. Honesty and integrity, particularly from courtiers, are necessary for a successful reign; see also 22:11.

16:14 / Synthetic and progressive. The threat of **a king's wrath** was a serious one, tantamount to **death** (cf. 14:35b; 19:12a; 20:22). It takes a **wise** person, indeed, to avoid it or escape from it. The wrathful king seems to have been a topos in Wisdom literature (cf. Ahiqar 103–104; *ANET*, p. 428; and also Eccl. 8:2–4).

16:15 / This is the opposite of verse 14. All signs are positive (cf. 15:30a; 19:12b), and the result is prosperity. The **rain cloud** is the spring rain (March–April) on which the harvest will depend.

16:16 / Literally, "Get wisdom! What can be better than gold?" (See the Additional Notes.) The comparisons repeat the ideas of 3:14–15 and 8:10–11; **get wisdom** is found as an imperative in 4:5, 7. Meinhold *(Sprüche)* see this as a "redactional verse" that looks back on the presentation of wisdom in chapters 1–9. It comes immediately before the middle verse (v. 17) of the book, as marked by the Masoretes, who worked on preserving and copying the Hebrew text of the OT between the sixth and tenth centuries A.D.

16:17 / Synonymous and juxtapositional, with alliteration. Verse 17b is, literally, "the one who guards his soul/the one who watches his path" (cf. 13:3; 19:16a). Here **evil** can stand for harm's way, and not necessarily wickedness.

16:18 / Synonymous and juxtapositional. The idea appears frequently (cf. 11:2; 15:33; 18:12). It can form an antithesis with the following verse. In context, it could have a bearing on the "king" sayings that precede it. The events it presupposes would have occurred often enough to give rise to the saying.

16:19 / A "better" saying, which forms an antithesis to verse 18. It gives strong support to the **lowly** (cf. also v. 8) against the haughty who have (probably unjust) spoil to divide. See Additional Notes.

16:20 / Synonymous. One can recognize a block of sayings in verses 20–24 dealing with speech. The NIV translates the Hebrew word, *dābār*, with **instruction**, which was presumably given by the sage. However, because the parallelism with verse 20b heightens verse 20a, one could understand the instruction as God's word. The NIV means that one should attend to the sage and trust **in the LORD.**

16:21 / Synonymous. For verse 21b see verse 23b. The NIV can be justified by the same phraseology in 1:5 and 9:9: **promote instruction.** But the alternative reading, although somewhat free, is in the right direction. Translate: "pleasing speech makes a person persuasive."

16:22 / Antithetic and juxtapositional. **Fountain of life** is a common metaphor (cf. 10:11; 13:14; 14:27) and indicates the blessings which wisdom brings. The meaning of verse 22b is that **folly** itself is the chastisement for **fools.** Any teaching simply compounds their innate folly (cf. 15:10).

16:23 / Synonymous. The alternative reading in the NIV is to be preferred (cf. v. 21). In verse 23a, **guides his mouth** refers to eloquent and intelligent speech.

16:24 / Synthetic and juxtapositional. See verse 21 for gracious speech, which is here compared to honey. The good effects on those who listen are described in verse 24b. The catchword in verses 21–24 is "lips."

16:25 / See 14:12 and comment.

16:26 / Synonymous. Line b gives the reason for line a. The paronomasia, or play on words, of the Hebrew can be preserved by substituting "labors" for **works.** There is a certain advantage to **hunger;** it can lead to more diligent labor. But the author of Ecclesiastes is not so optimistic (Eccl. 6:7).

16:27 / Synonymous? "Lips," "evil," and "perversity" are repeated in verses 27–30; and "man" begins verses 27–29 (cf. also 29:8–10). **Scoundrel** is, literally, "a man of Belial"; the etymology of Belial is uncertain (see also 6:12–15). **Plots evil** is an uncertain translation of "digs evil" (NRSV, "concocts evil"). Some think that one digs a pit of evil for others (cf. 26:27). The harm done by **speech** is compared to **fire.**

16:28 / Synonymous. **Perverse** is, literally, "(a man of) upsets—turning things upside down." This person intrigues and sows discord among friends. See also 17:9.

16:29 / Synthetic. The enticement of the **violent** leads one to (spiritual) death. In line with 1:10–11, this is an enticement to collaborate in evildoing; see also the "paths" in 4:11–15.

16:30 / Synonymous and juxtapositional. Outward appearances can betray the character of a person (cf. 6:13). See the Additional Notes.

16:31 / **Gray hair** implies longevity, which is a sign of virtue. The normal assumption (cf. 20:29) would be that the wicked should not be long-lived. See Sirach 25:3–6, but contrast Wisdom 4:8–9.

16:32 / Synonymous "better" sayings. Literally, **a patient man** is "long of nostrils/breath." The synonym is "one who rules the breath (spirit)." See comment on 14:29.

16:33 / Antithetic. The presupposition is that nothing escapes the divine will. Hence even the casting of lots, which seems so casual (they are thrown into the **lap**—i.e., the fold of the garment) is determined by God. Lots are referred to frequently in the OT (cf. Urim and Thummim, Num. 27:21).

Additional Notes §17

16:16 / The text is unsteady, but the general meaning is clear. The forms of the Hb. term *qnh* can be explained as unusual imperative forms, or vocalized as such. In the MT they appear to be infinitives (in v. 16b, following the analogy of *lamed-he* verbs) and translated as "the acquisition of . . ." Some delete *mah* ("what," rendered in NIV, **how**) as a dittography, or a scribal error in which a letter, word, or line is mistakenly repeated.

16:17 / The LXX inserts several lines in this verse, expanding it with typical wisdom teaching.

16:19 / The Qere reads "humble" instead of "poor" (NIV, **oppressed**).

16:21 / See 7:7 for the nuance of persuasiveness in the Hb. term *leqaḥ* (note the marginal reading in the NIV).

16:22 / The NIV presupposes a dative (preposition *lᵉ*) in v. 22a.

16:30 / Probably the Hb. word *ʿōṣēm* (cf. Isa. 33:15) should be read in v. 30a if one translates **wink** (NIV). The Hb. word *ʿōṣê* in the MT occurs nowhere else in the Hb. Bible. In 6:13 and 10:10 *qrṣ* (compress) is used with eyes; here it has the sense of "purse" (lips).

17:1 / Antithetic "better" saying, with lively assonance. See also 15:17. The margin of the NIV indicates the cultic nuance of the Hebrew term *zebaḥ* ("sacrifice"), but this may have been gradually lost. The contrast is extreme—sheer bread and sumptuous feast. (See also Amenemope 9.7–8=16.13–14; *ANET*, pp. 422–23.)

17:2 / Synthetic. Although there were rules for inheritance (Deut. 21:15–17), instances illustrated by this saying could occur. See 27:18, and also Ben Sira's advice about servants in Sirach 7:20–21.

17:3 / This verse is a "priamel," a poetic form in which all objects share a common concept. Here "testing" is common to all the objects mentioned, with the climax in verse 3b. Verse 3a is found again in 27:21a. For the Lord's dealing with the **heart**, see also 21:2 and 24:12. The theme is frequent in the Bible (cf. Jer. 9:6; Ps. 17:3). For detailed stylistic analysis, see McCreesh, *Sound*, pp. 109–12.

17:4 / Synonymous and juxtapositional. The point is that the evildoer takes in harmful gossip, presumably to do further harm. **Liar** is, literally, "falsehood."

17:5 / Synonymous. The juxtaposition of participles is noteworthy. In contrast to 14:31a, the emphasis here is upon disdain and mockery (which may include oppression). Care of the **poor** is a frequent topos. See Sirach 7:11. See also 19:17; and Amenemope 24.9–12 (*ANET*, p. 424).

17:6 / Synonymous and juxtapositional. On the striking sound pattern, see McCreesh, *Sound*, pp. 131–32. The issue is the relationship of **children** to their forebears, and vice versa. Each group brings honor, even inspiration, to the other. The presupposition is that both are virtuous and thus properly rewarded (cf. 13:22a; 20:7; Sir. 3:1–16).

17:7 / Antithetic; an *a fortiori* saying about speech. For the style, see 11:31; 26:1. Both **arrogant** and **eloquent** (NIV margin) are doubtful; see Additional Notes. The point of the NIV is that there is discord between subject and predicate, whatever the precise nuance may be.

17:8 / Synthetic. **Charm** is, literally, "stone of favor," something valuable or designed to win favor. Is this merely an observation that bribery works, or is it an ironic statement that bribery is everywhere? In verse 8b, **he turns** could be rendered: wherever the charm is used, it **succeeds.** Bribery is mentioned elsewhere, as in verse 23; 6:35 (condemned); 21:14 (bribery *does* work); 10:6 (ambiguous). It was a characteristic of society, but not recommended by the sage. The context and tone of such sayings are important. A gift that is well placed brings success; it's magic! Is this a pure (sarcastic) observation, a condemnation, or a recommendation? The Hebrew shows a strong alliterative pattern (cf. McCreesh, *Sound,* p. 54).

17:9 / Antithetic and juxtapositional. The effects of charitable silence or of tale-bearing are described: harmony or discord. With verse 9a see 10:12b and 19:11b; with verse 9b see 16:28b.

17:10 / Antithetic comparison. Docility and readiness to hear correction are a wisdom topos. In contrast to a docile person, even **a hundred lashes** (meant to be an exaggeration) cannot change a **fool.** See Additional Notes.

17:11 / Synthetic. The **evil** concentrate on obstinate resistance, but they will be brought into line by one who is **merciless.** The saying remains open: resistance to God, the king, or someone else? In any case, punishment is inevitable. The assonance between the two Hebrew terms, *ʾak-mᵉrî* and *ʾakzārî*, is striking.

17:12 / Synthetic comparison, but the style is unusual: literally, "meeting a bear . . . but not . . ." Danger to one's life (however extreme), is surpassed by an encounter with a real **fool.** The danger of bears was proverbial in ancient Israel (cf. 28:15).

17:13 / Synthetic; verse 13a is an absolute nominative or *casus pendens* (see introduction for explanation). Compare 20:22; 24:28–29; 25:21–22. Verse 13b emphasizes the social implication of such despicable conduct.

17:14 / The form is juxtapositional and unusual (there is no **like** in the MT). The sense of the NIV is correct, but it glosses over difficulties in the text; see Additional Notes. The point is: stop a **quarrel** at the very beginning.

17:15 / Subjects and predicates are in juxtaposition; 15a is a chiastic *casus pendens,* taken up in 15b. For the repetition of roots and sounds, see McCreesh, *Sound,* pp. 142–43. Toy *(Proverbs)* attempts to catch the assonance of the Hebrew text: "whoever rights the wrong and wrongs the right" (both an abomination). The point is the upholding of justice in judicial cases.

17:16 / Synthetic? The saying underscores the hopelessness of the **fool,** whose wealth cannot acquire **wisdom.** Besides, according to Job 28:14–19, wisdom is beyond any price. For the one who will listen, there is no charge for acquiring wisdom, according to Sirach 51:25.

17:17 / Antithetic? Commentators are divided on the meaning. Does true friendship rate higher than blood relationship (see 18:24; 27:10; cf. 18:19; 19:7)? Or, in a real crisis, is it a **brother** that one must depend upon? Probably the former. But it is also possible to take this saying as synonymous: brother merely intensifies **friend.** Friendship is a common wisdom topos; see chapter 27 and also Sirach 6:5–17 and passim.

17:18 / Synonymous? Juxtapositional. The action of 18a is specified in 18b. Going **pledge** for another is severely indicted by the sages; see 6:1–5 and the comment on 11:15. It is viewed differently in Sirach 8:12–13 and 27:1–20.

17:19 / Synonymous and juxtapositional (four participles). For further analysis, see McCreesh, *Sound,* pp. 103–4. The meaning is uncertain, because of verse 19b. There is no need to emend verse 19a (as Toy, *Proverbs;* Oesterley, *Proverbs).* But what is the meaning of building a **high gate** in this context? Some understand it as proud talk, but there is no biblical analogue to this metaphor. Moreover, **destruction** could also be translated "broken bones" (so NJPS, interpreting a high threshold as the occasion of a physical fall). See Additional Notes.

17:20 / Synonymous. One who is false in **heart** and in outward expression will suffer for it.

17:21 / Synonymous. This verse describes the grief caused by foolish offspring; compare 17:25, where the mother is explicitly mentioned (see also 10:1).

17:22 / Antithetic. It is a psychosomatic observation which describes the effect of the mind on the body. Verse 22a is similar to 15:13 (see Additional Notes).

17:23 / Synthetic; **in secret** is, literally, from the bosom (the fold of the garment, that served as a pocket). It is not necessarily "in secret," although the parallelism in 21:14 suggests it for that verse. But this verse can mean that the **wicked man** takes the **bribe** from his own bosom to give it to an unjust official. In 17:8 the effect of bribery was the point; here it is the evil intent.

17:24 / Antithetic. The saying contrasts the concentration of the sage with the lack of it in the fool, who is distracted and looking everywhere but to wisdom.

17:25 / Synonymous. See the comment on 17:21. On the style of this saying, see McCreesh, *Sound*, pp. 81–82.

17:26 / Synonymous parallelism; verse 26b heightens verse 26a. Flogging is far harsher punishment than a financial fine (NIV, **punish**). In addition, **officials** means properly nobles, a further intensification of the saying. Both actions are condemned.

17:27 / Synonymous and juxtapositional. This saying and the next illustrate the ambiguity of silence. It can be a sign of the wise who measure their words (cf. 10:19), or of fools who have nothing to say (v. 28). The **even-tempered** of the NIV is, literally, "cool of spirit" (reading the Kethib). This notion may be derived from the Egyptian (cf. L. H. Grollenberg, "A propos de Prov 8:6 et Prov 17:27," *RB* 59 [1952], pp. 40–43). Such a person coolly and calmly considers a situation and weighs what is to be said. The phrase is akin to "slow to anger" (cf. 15:18; 16:32). The opposite is the "short of anger/spirit" (cf. 14:17, 29).

17:28 / Synthetic; compare verse 17:27. Perhaps the best commentary on this verse is from Anchsheshonq 23.4, "Silence conceals foolishness" (*AEL*, vol. 3, p. 177).

Additional Notes §18

17:7 / The MT has, lit. "lip of excess (or surplus)." Efforts have been made to obtain a sharper contrast, reading Hb. *yōšer* "uprightness" (Gk. *pista* "trustworthy"). The contrast between a fool and a prince is not sharp, but see Isa. 32:6–8.

17:10 / The meaning of the Hb. *tēḥat* is not clear (penetrate?), and a conjectural emendation to *ʾaḥat* ("one, single") is tempting: "A single reprimand for an intelligent person . . ."

17:14 / The MT reads lit.: "One who opens water, the beginning of strife; and before the breaking out of dispute, leave off." The opening of water is interpreted as making an aperture, thus creating pressure for more water to rush out (as from a dam). The Gk. reads "justice" for "strife." It is also possible to think of water being wasted, and thus causing strife between people. Then the point is to prevent foolish causes of strife.

17:19 / It is not clear if the **high gate** is to be taken lit. (thus keeping people out?) or metaphorically (proud talk). This line seems to have given trouble in the Gk. tradition, where it is missing from this verse and is added to v. 16.

17:22 / Hb. *gēhâ* (healing?) is a *hapax legomenon*, but is usually rendered as **medicine**.

18:1 / The MT is ambiguous and the meaning uncertain. The NIV understands it as a description of the conduct of an **unfriendly** (lit. "separated") and foolish person.

18:2 / Antithetic. Without **understanding,** the **fool** lacks the sense to be silent or to learn, and instead reveals an (empty) mind.

18:3 / Synonymous. The saying describes the sad effects of wicked and shameful conduct.

18:4 / Antithetic? Juxtapositional. The NIV implies an antithesis between a and b. The disjunctive **but,** which is not in the MT, is inserted. In that case, **deep waters** stands for something unreachable (stagnant? obscure? and perhaps the waters of chaos, hence unruly and in need of discipline). In contrast is the availability and freshness of the source of **wisdom** in verse 4b (cf. NRSV). However, the relationship could be synonymous if deep waters is taken to mean "inexhaustible" and the **words** are presumed to be wise. In 20:5, "deep waters" seems to be used in a favorable sense. It is also possible to understand words as the subject, followed by three predicates (cf. NJPS), since there is no connective between a and b. See the Additional Notes.

18:5 / Antithetic. The verse recommends impartiality in judgment. See 17:15 for the thought and 17:26 for the form ("not good"). Partiality is expressed by "to lift up the head."

18:6 / Synonymous. Verses 6–8 are united by a common theme, foolish talk; this may be in a judicial process (cf. v. 5), or in ordinary conversation. The NIV points to the disastrous results of such talk. See the Additional Notes.

18:7 / Synonymous. Further harmful results of foolish talk: the **undoing** of the fool.

18:8 / Synthetic; the parallelism intensifies verse 8a. 26:22 repeats this proverb. **Choice morsels** is a common, if uncertain, translation of a rare word. The point of verse 8b is that such deep penetration makes gossip permanent (and pleasant to recall?).

18:9 / Synthetic. Even to be **slack in work** is said, with some exaggeration, to be simply destructive.

18:10 / Synthetic. The point is that *yhwh* is a refuge for **the righteous.** This is the only time that the phrase, **the name of the LORD,** occurs in the book. According to the Deuteronomic theology, the Lord's Name dwells in the Temple; the name is the person. **Safe** is literally "on high" (Hb. *niśgāb,* the word translated as **unscalable** in v. 11); see 29:25.

18:11 / Antithetic? There seems to be a deliberate contrast with verse 10. The safety for the **rich** is their **wealth** (this idea occurs in 10:15a without any moral judgment, but as a matter of observation). Is this true? Verse 11b seems to say: only in their imagination, not in reality. However, the meaning of the word for **imagine** is uncertain; see Additional Notes. In any case, there is sufficient contrast between religion and wealth to say that verses 10–11 modify the security provided by riches; the catchword is Hb. *niśgāb* (see v. 10 above). Verse 11 hearkens back to 10:15a and provides a new context for it.

18:12 / Antithetic. For the thought, see 16:18; verse 12b is the same as 15:33b. See also 29:23.

18:13 / The meaning is clear: one should listen before trying to answer; see also Sirach 11:8. See Additional Notes.

18:14 / Synthetic, in which there is a heightening in 14b. One can survive bodily **sickness** (and other evils), but not without a strong and lively **spirit.** Depression and other psychic difficulties are deadly (cf. 17:22).

18:15 / Synonymous. There are two sure ways **(heart** and **ears)** to wisdom: mental alertness and the ability to listen (to others). The need to listen is a frequent topos (cf. 4:20; 5:1); verse 15b strengthens verse 15a.

18:16 / Synonymous, with specification in the second line. **A gift** is not necessarily a bribe. If a bribe is meant, the verse is a statement of fact, not an exhortation. Therefore, a gift has its effect. For the "little" people to gain access to high places, a gift may have been in order. See Additional Notes, and the comment on 17:8, 23.

18:17 / Synthetic? The point is that both sides have to be heard. This applies to a judicial case (as the context afforded by v. 18 might suggest), or any evaluation (cf. Deut. 1:16–17).

18:18 / Synonymous, with specification in 18b. **Disputes** is the catchword with verse 19. The casting of lots (in whatever fashion) was considered to be under the aegis and agency of God. It was therefore decisive (cf. 16:33), even among the powerful.

18:19 / Apparently intended as synonymous, but the text is uncertain. See Additional Notes. The NIV seems to mean that when all mutual trust is lost (both metaphors in a and b point to **unyielding** resistance) there can be no reconciliation between the opposing parties.

18:20 / Synonymous. This verse seems to mean that utterances, whether good or bad, determine one's fate. Speech therefore carries consequences. For the metaphor of eating **fruit,** see 12:14a and 13:2a. McKane *(Proverbs)* understands the fruit in verse 20a as good fruit, and hence effective speech.

18:21 / Synthetic, with specification. The effects of speech upon the speaker are a matter of **life** or **death** (cf. 13:3 and 21:23). But the reference could also be to the effects on the person addressed (cf. 12:18; 15:4). See Sirach 37:17–24, who takes both aspects under consideration. See James 3:5 on the power of the tongue.

18:22 / Synonymous, with intensification in verse 22b. The repetition in verse 22a is striking. Therefore it is clear that "finding" is not casual. Rather it is **from the LORD** (19:14b), just as wisdom itself is a gift of God (2:6; 3:13; 8:35). Verse 22b finds a distant echo in 12:2a, 4a.

18:23 / Antithetic. Property or riches mean power. This is brought out by the contrast between the stereotypical description of the conduct of the **poor** (deference) and the **rich** (harshness).

18:24 / Any translation is uncertain; see the commentaries. The NIV means that one good solid **friend** is better than having **many companions.** See Additional Notes.

Additional Notes §19

18:1 / The Hb. preposition *lamed* before "desire" (NIV, **selfish ends**) is not easy to construe. "Desire" is "pretexts" in the Gk. Hence translations vary. Perhaps v. 1b can be translated lit. "he breaks out (in anger?) against all success." The LXX has "at every opportunity *(kairos)* he is disgraceful." Hence the uncertainty in the translations (see the footnotes to the NRSV and NJPS).

18:4 / The meaning of the words in the MT are easily translated, but their significance is not clear. Therefore the interpretations differ. It is important to observe that there is no connective between 4a and 4b.

18:6 / For NIV **bring,** the MT has lit. "comes with," or "enters into." The NIV seems to read the Hiphil *yābî'û,* with the LXX.

18:11 / Hb. *maśkît* seems to mean "image," and then imagination.

18:13 / The style is unusual; the subject is in v. 13a, a *casus pendens,* that is then taken up in v. 13b by the pronoun.

18:16 / Hb. *mattān,* or **gift,** is in effect a bribe in 15:27b. In 17:8, 23, another word for bribe is used, *šōḥad.* In 19:6 bribery is not the issue, but in 21:14 the two words are parallel.

18:19 / The uncertainties grow out of the only occurrence of Hb. *pš'* in the Niphal, which seems to modify **brother** and means "rebel, transgress" in the Qal stem. Also, the comparative Hb. *min* (which is the comparative *k* in several ancient versions) and the final comparison in v. 19b are simply not clear.

18:21 / The feminine suffix in v. 21b (rendered by **it** in the NIV) refers back to *lāšôn,* "tongue."

18:24 / Verses 23 and 24 are lacking in the LXX, which has a saying about a good wife and an adulteress after v. 22. The first line in v. 24 is obscure: lit. "man of friends for being broken(?)" There seems to be a contrast with a true friend in v. 24b and hence v. 24a must be speaking of friends who are less than that. "Man of friends" (the NIV inserts **many,** but it is not in the text) is a harsh construction and some explain Hb. *'yš,* which is usually translated "man," as related to *yēš,* "there is/are" (cf. v. 24b). The meaning of the final verb (in Hb. Hitpolel form) depends on the root it is to be derived from: *r''* (Aram.: to break); *r''* (to be bad); or *r'h* (to be friendly). Hence translations vary: "who mistreat each other," "who act friendly," etc.

19:1 / Antithetic comparison. Verses 1 and 2 are not in the LXX. The antithesis between **blameless** and **perverse** is clear, but not so for **poor** and **fool**. One would expect "rich" instead of fool. This is the reading of the apparent doublet in 28:6, adopted by many commentators and translations (NAB).

19:2 / Synonymous. In Proverbs, **hasty** action is generally suspect (e.g., 21:5; 28:20; 29:20). It suggests aimless (if not evil) and unplanned activity. The meaning of verse 2b enables one to translate the difficult verse 2a as the NIV does (contrast the NJPS): *npš* **(zeal)** that is aimless **(without knowledge)** will get nowhere.

19:3 / Synthetic with intensification. One cannot blame the Lord when, by the very nature of **folly**, the fool excludes God from consideration (Ps. 14:1—"there is no God!").

19:4 / Antithetic. Money makes a difference in the quality and quantity of one's **friends**. There are many similar sayings, for example, 14:20; 18:23–24. See also the testing of friends in Sirach 6:5–12 and the quality of a true friend in Proverbs 17:17.

19:5 / Synonymous. See the doublet in verse 9 and also similar ideas in 6:19 and 14:5, 25. These sayings refer to judicial process. Honest testimony was essential in the somewhat primitive procedures; it saved lives (14:25).

19:6 / Synonymous. Another saying concerning the difference that wealth and power create (cf. vv. 4, 7). There is no reason to understand **gifts** *(mattān)* as bribes. See Additional Notes for 18:16.

19:7 / Synonymous *a fortiori* conclusion. The first two lines in verse 7a are clear and develop the idea of verse 4b; see also 14:20a. **Relatives** have the greater obligation toward their own. The final line is corrupt; see Additional Notes.

19:8 / Synonymous. True love of self lies in the possession of "heart" (which the NIV renders as **wisdom**). **Cherishes** is weak; "keeps" is better.

19:9 / See the comment on verse 5.

19:10 / Synonymous *a fortiori* conclusion. According to sapiential (wisdom) thinking, the **fool** should not prosper so as to be in **luxury.** But as verse 10b exemplifies, there can be even greater social upheavals. On **slaves** as ruling, see 30:22 and Ecclesiastes 10:7. The saying does not envision a successful servant who rises to the occasion (cf. 17:2). For a lengthy treatment of servants, see Sirach 33:25–33.

19:11 / Synonymous with intensification. The ideal of the wise person is to be disciplined, calm, and resist anger (e.g., 14:29; 15:18; 16:32). The presumption is that the **offense** is not criminal. See 10:12.

19:12 / Antithetic. For verse 12a see 20:2. On the power of the **king,** see 16:14 and 28:15.

19:13 / Synonymous. These two examples of domestic problems could have been separate lines originally. For verse 13a see 10:1; 17:21, 25. The comparison in verse 13b is found in 27:15.

19:14 / Antithetic. On the whole, everything was under the control of **the LORD** (cf. 16:33). But some things were more dependent on human factors than others. Among these were inheritance laws that could ensure a more or less mechanical transfer. One need only be born in a family of some means. However, certain moves in life were beyond human control. Therefore a truly good **wife** had to be seen as a (mysterious) gift from God. See 18:22; 31:10–31; Sirach 26:1–4.

19:15 / Synonymous, with specification in verse 15b. The **deep sleep** is the word used of Adam in Genesis 2:21 and the participle appears in Proverbs 10:5. Here it is induced by **laziness** (cf. 6:9–11 for another association of laziness and sleep). The result is that one does not earn enough to feed a **hungry** appetite (Hb. *npš*).

19:16 / Antithetic with juxtaposition of participles. The **instructions** are those of the wisdom teacher (rather than of God), and it is to him that the **ways** refer. The death envisioned in verse 16b is a premature death, which is often invoked by the sages (e.g., 10:21; 15:10). Here the NIV rightly follows the Qere; the Kethib would imply a judicial sentencing to death. See the Additional Notes.

19:17 / Synthetic. Again, participles are juxtaposed in verse 17a. Kindness to the **poor** will be paid back by God, as it were, with interest (cf. 14:21, 31; 22:9; 29:7). **Reward** might be better rendered "payback." God is not the debtor; the poor are. They are to be considered as though in the place of God (Mein-hold, *Sprüche*).

19:18 / It is clear that corporal punishment is meant (cf. 23:13–14). One could also translate "while there is (still) hope"—a temporal rather than causal phrase. The second line is obscure. The MT has, literally, "Do not lift up your soul" to kill him. This is apparently a warning not to go to extremes (cf. 23:13).

19:19 / The text is doubtful and meaning uncertain. The NIV seems to suggest that if a person rescues **a hot-tempered man**, he will force that person to intervene for him over and over again instead of learning from his mistakes. See the Additional Notes.

19:20 / Synthetic. An admonition to abide by the wisdom of the sage. The **end** is not the end of life, but the end of whatever affair that calls for, and will profit from, advice.

19:21 / Antithetic. This saying resembles 16:1, 9. Hebrew ʿēṣâ in verses 20 and 21 **(advice, purpose)** is the catchword. As opposed to the many uncertainties or options a person might choose, the design of the Lord stands firm.

19:22 / Neither of the two readings suggested by the NIV for 22a is satisfactory. The text fails to translate the suffix ("his") attached to **love.** The margin gives a rare meaning **(shame)** to Hebrew ḥsdw (but cf. 14:34). The MT has, literally, "the desire of a man is his kindness." See Additional Notes. Verse 22b is rendered correctly, but the connection between the two lines is not clear. Translations vary considerably: "Greed is a reproach to a man" (the NJPS, marked as uncertain); McKane *(Proverbs)* follows the LXX, "A man's productivity is his loyalty."

19:23 / Synonymous. Verse 23b is harsh and the NJPS has marked it as of uncertain meaning. Literally, the MT has, "And satisfied he dwells, he will not be visited by evil." See the Additional Notes. Despite this, the meaning is clear: **fear of the LORD** brings security.

19:24 / Synonymous and chiastic. See also 26:15. The point of the exaggeration is to underscore the laziness of the **sluggard;** even hunger will not transform a lazy person.

19:25 / Antithetic. The saying deals with the effects of physical discipline and correction. The **mocker** will probably not learn from it, but the **simple** will. The **discerning** person does not need such a drastic example to learn a lesson. See 21:11.

19:26 / Synonymous. Verse 26a serves as a *casus pendens.* The characterization of such conduct is given in verse 26b. Parents are a frequent concern in such sayings (also 20:20; 23:22; 28:24).

19:27 / The NIV interprets verse 27a as a conditional clause, and so the verse is a general warning or recommendation to be attentive to the sage's teaching (cf. v. 20). So also many other translations convey this meaning, but the Hebrew text is unusual. See Additional Notes.

19:28 / Synonymous. Truth in cases of **justice** is a frequent theme in this book and lying is once more condemned (cf. e.g., 14:25; 25:18). **Gulps down** (see Additional Notes) is an unexpected verb here. Many change the text to read "pours forth" (cf. 15:28).

19:29 / Synonymous and chiastic. Those who reject wisdom will not be able to escape corporal punishment. Some translators exchange *b* for *p* in the Hebrew word *špṭym,* in order to specify the punishment, namely, "rods" instead of **penalties.**

Additional Notes §20

19:7 / This is a three-line saying, in contrast to the usual two lines. The final line does not make any sense: "the one who pursues words, not they" (or, if one follows the Qere: "his they are"). This has so far resisted all attempts at translation. The LXX has another line inserted ahead of it, and has added "will not be saved" at the end of the verse. The line is best left untranslated. The footnote to the NIV is an understatement.

19:16 / For the assonance and alliteration in this line (and also in v. 8), see McCreesh, *Sound,* pp. 100–103. The antithesis is helped in the NIV by its insertion of **but,** which is lacking in the Hb. In order to obtain stronger parallelism, many change Hb. *dᵉrākāyw* to *miṣwâ* ("command"; cf. 13:13), but the ancient versions agree with the MT.

19:19 / The Qere is to be preferred to the doubtful Kethib (thus, "great of anger"). There is no object (NIV, **him**) in v. 19b. **Do it again** of the NIV is, lit. "you will add still." Verse 19b opens up many possible options. Saving such a person once will not suffice; such an intervention will only increase the anger (of the person or the opponent). It is best to recognize a corrupt text here.

19:22 / Among other difficulties, the words are ambiguous. The Hb. *taᵃʾwat* can mean "greed" (see NJPS); *ḥesed* can (rarely) mean "shame." It is also possible, but doubtful, to read: "desirable in a person (is . . .)."

19:23 / One problem is that the subject (or antecedent) of the Hb. verb *yālîn* ("lodge") is nowhere expressed. The NIV supplies **then one** in order to get a smooth translation.

19:27 / The appearance of **my son** in this group of sayings (10:1–22:16) is unique. Lit., the MT has: "Stop listening to instruction, my son, to stray from the words of knowledge." This could be interpreted as ironical, and the transition from v. 27a to v. 27b is problematical. Perhaps the command is meant conditionally.

19:28 / Meinhold *(Sprüche)* argues for the MT on the basis of paranomasia: Hb. *blyᶜl* ("worthlessness"; NIV **corrupt**) in v. 28a and *yblᶜ* ("gulp") in v. 28b.

20:1 / Synthetic. Inebriation is condemned in 23:29–35 and 31:4–5. Here the drinks that produce it are personified: **wine** and strong drink (perhaps **beer**).

20:2 / Synthetic. For verse 2a see 19:12a. The point of the comparison is the **roar of a lion**, which like royal **wrath** produces panic. The meaning of verse 2b is uncertain.

20:3 / Antithetic. The idiomatic expression in verse 3a is literally, "sit (or dwell) from" (NIV, **avoid**). The precise meaning of Hebrew *ytgl^c* **(quick to quarrel)** is uncertain (cf. 17:24; 18:1).

20:4 / Synthetic. Winter, from October on, would be the **season** for plowing. The **sluggard**'s expectation for the **harvest** will be disappointed, and probably he can expect nothing from others.

20:5 / Synthetic. **Deep waters** is ambivalent (cf. 18:4). If it is understood merely as profound (rather than so deep as to be practically out of reach), the saying proclaims that (only) the person of **understanding** can make such **purposes** or plans come forth to clarity.

20:6 / Antithetic. The meaning of the NIV is clear enough. It brings out the contrast between a proclamation of love (that can be purely verbal) and true fidelity that is not easy to find. Verse 6a is ambiguous, subject to various translations. See the Additional Notes.

20:7 / Synthetic. The good effects of the integrity of the parent are to be seen in the virtue (and presumably prosperity) of the **children**. The association between parent and children is expressed also in 13:22; 14:26. Verse 7a can also be translated: "The one who walks in integrity is a just person."

20:8 / The saying characterizes the honest decision-making of an ideal **king**. Compare verse 26, which mentions winnowing (of wheat from chaff, good from bad) again.

20:9 / This question reflects the general biblical sense of human sinfulness. Only the Lord can judge (16:2); see also 15:3, 11 for God's sharp vision. Despite this **sin**, integrity and justice are also seen as within human reach (v. 7).

20:10 / Synthetic. See comment on 11:1 (cf. v. 23).

20:11 / Synthetic. The NIV seems to assert that righteous **actions** are the clue to the character of people, even as children. The behavior of children is significant for their future. But translations differ; see Additional Notes.

20:12 / Synthetic. The saying can be understood at various levels: (1) physical—the marvel of the senses created by God, enabling humans to fulfill these striking functions; (2) moral—the implication is that these organs should be used rightly; cf. Psalm 94:9. As to the form, see 22:2; 29:13.

20:13 / Antithetic: two imperatives stand in contrast. In Hebrew the imperative is often used for the conditional, "if you . . ." See verses 16, 19, 22 for other examples. Verses 12 and 13 are bonded by the word for eye (NIV, **awake**). The point is clear: avoid poverty by being diligent and alert (cf. 6:9–11).

20:14 / Synthetic. This is a somewhat humorous observation about purchasing. The charm lies in the contrast between the two scenes: undervaluing an object, and then boasting of a bargain. This observation is true of ancient bartering and modern sales.

20:15 / Synthetic with heightening. Precious metals are indeed valuable, but the (most) precious is wise speech (cf. 3:15; 8:11).

20:16 / Synonymous. The early sages were opposed to going surety for another (6:1–5; 11:15, etc.). This saying contains two imperatives (cf. v. 13 above). The first case deals with one who has gone surety **for a stranger.** In that case, get a guarantee by taking his **garment** (cf. Deut. 24:10–13). In the second case, if one has gone surety for a strange **woman** (reading the Qere, but not necessarily **wayward;** the Kethib has "strangers"), **hold** the garment (or possibly, him) **in pledge.** The verse seems to be a doublet of 27:13.

20:17 / Antithetic. This bread is described as "bread of deceit" (cf. 23:3). Instead of nourishing, it turns to sand in one's

mouth. It is a vivid comparison. The verse is associated with verse 16 by the Hebrew root ʿrb (**sweet** and "go surety").

20:18 / Synonymous. Compare 24:6; 11:4; 15:22. The sages insist on wise planning in all ventures, especially in the strategy of **war.**

20:19 / Synthetic. Verse 19a is practically identical with 11:13a, but here the conclusion is drawn that a garrulous person (lit. "one who opens the lips") should be avoided.

20:20 / Synthetic. The cursing of parents is strictly forbidden in the Law (Exod. 21:17; Lev. 20:9; Deut. 27:16); see also 30:11. On the **lamp,** see the comment on 13:9. **Pitch darkness** is literally, "the (eye) pupil of darkness"—the very center where light should be. See Additional Notes.

20:21 / Synthetic. The NIV adopts the Qere with the ancient versions ("hastily gotten") in place of the Kethib (doubtful meaning; "despised?"). In Proverbs "haste" is nearly always suggestive of something foolish or evil (13:11; 28:20, 22). It is not said exactly how the **inheritance** is obtained. The same word can also mean simply "possessions," but inheritance ties verse 21 more closely with verse 20.

20:22 / Synthetic. The "Lord" sayings occur in verses 22–25. For the spirit of this verse see also 24:17, 29 and 25:21–22. There is no expression of personal revenge, for everything is left **to the LORD.** This saying, according to Plöger (*Sprüche*), manifests a close relationship between wisdom and yahwistic devotion, a relationship that is even constitutive for wisdom. The formula, **do not say,** introduces several proverbs (e.g., 3:28; Eccl. 5:5; 7:10, etc.).

20:23 / Synonymous. Cheating is a frequent topic; see verse 10 and 11:1; 16:11. The MT has the abrupt phrase in verse 23b: "not good," parallel to "abomination" in verse 23a.

20:24 / Synthetic. This is another popular theme (cf. 3:6; 16:1, 9; 19:21; and Jer. 10:23). Since **the LORD** controls humans (cf. Ps. 37:23), two reactions (that do not necessarily exclude each other) are possible: hope (cf. v. 22), or a certain skepticism (as seen in the book of Job).

20:25 / Synthetic. The NIV warns against rash **vows** (cf. Eccl. 5:2–6). However, the text is difficult; see Additional Notes.

20:26 / Synonymous. For verse 26a, see verse 8. The idea is clear, but the mode of punishment is not clear. The NIV adds **threshing** to **wheel**, and thus continues the idea of **winnows**. See the Additional Notes.

20:27 / The Hebrew of verse 27a is ambiguous, as the margin of the NIV attests. The marginal reading is to be preferred. It seems to mean that the life-breath from God, by which a person lives (cf. Gen. 2:7; Job 32:8), penetrates to the very interior of a person. This could be taken as a warning, but better, as a consoling indication of how intimate God is to humans ("more intimate to me than I am to myself," as St. Augustine said). This is not merely the voice of conscience. See Additional Notes.

20:28 / Synonymous. The divine gifts of **love** and **faithfulness** (cf. 3:3) are practically personified here. They are the basis of a successful reign (cf. 16:12b).

20:29 / Antithetic. See comment on 16:31. The proverb should be taken as an even-handed compliment to both **young** and **old**. There is also a paradoxical contrast between **strength** and **gray hair**.

20:30 / Synonymous, but the translation is uncertain. The NIV understands the MT as pointing out the good results of corporal punishment. But see Additional Notes.

Additional Notes §21

20:2 / In v. 2b, the MT reads lit. "the one who is angered at him (i.e., the king) sins (as to) his life." One might expect the anger to be that of the king and many solutions have been proposed, as can be seen in McKane *(Proverbs)*.

20:6 / Some of the ancient versions (Syriac and Vulgate) vocalize Hb. *yqr* ("call") in the Niphal and render "many a person is called a man of *ḥesed*." The Hb. word *ḥesed* is a broad term for concepts like mercy, kindness, goodness, etc. See L. Alonso Schökel, J. Vilchez Lindez, with A. Pinto, *Proverbios* (Madrid: Cristiandad, 1984) for a discussion of five different translations of v. 6a.

20:11 / In the MT, Hb. *gam* (even) modifies actions, not child; it is conduct that reveals good character. There is no need to emend v. 11b (cf. 21:8b, which is almost identical). The Hb. verb *nkr* appears in Gen. 42:7 in the Hitpael in the sense of "dissemble" (cf. the NJPS, which indicates that the correct action of a child may be a case of dissembling).

20:20 / The NIV follows the Kethib reading **(pupil)** in v. 20b instead of the Qere ("in the hour"). Verse 20a is grammatically a *casus pendens* that is interpreted conditionally by the NIV.

20:25 / **Dedicate something rashly** is doubtful, although most versions have something similar; the phrase is lit. "say (rashly?) 'holy.' " Cf. the Hb. concept of *qorban* ("offering") in Matt. 15:5. Verse 25b is lit. "and after vows to search" (to search for what? excuses? means to fulfill what one should not have vowed?).

20:26 / Lit., v. 26b reads: "and he brought back (returned) a wheel upon them." This can hardly mean torture (cf. Amos 1:3), but it may continue the idea of **winnowing.** Some emend the MT on the basis of Ps. 94:23: "and brings upon them their iniquity"; but none of the versions support this.

20:27 / If one follows the NIV text rather than the marginal footnote, the **lamp of the LORD** is left undefined. Does this mean merely that the Lord **searches** (this word seems to be supplied from v. 27b) the "life-breath" (so the meaning of Hb. *nᵉšāmâ,* translated as **spirit** in the NIV)? Then there is only a rather flat parallelism in the verse.

20:30 / In v. 30a, the NIV follows the Kethib **(cleanse)** and the Qere seems to be a noun ("massage," on the basis of Esth. 2:3, 9, 12). In v. 30b, there is no verb; lit. "and blows, the dark places of the belly." The text is probably corrupt but the sense seems to be that corporal punishment plays an effective role.

21:1 / Synthetic. Not only ordinary humans, but even **kings** are thoroughly under the Lord's control. The **watercourse** is an irrigation channel, subject to the design of the gardener.

21:2 / Antithetic. The possibilities of self-deception are enormous; **the LORD** alone knows the truth of a person's **heart** (a catchword with v. 1). See 16:2 and comment, as well as 17:3.

21:3 / This is a frequent biblical theme (cf. v. 27; 15:8, and the so-called prophetic critique of sacrifice; also Sir. 34:21–35:8).

21:4 / The MT is ambiguous. Verse 4a is a kind of *casus pendens* that is taken up by **lamp** in verse 4b. Thus the hubris of the sinner is the guide to wrongdoing. This interpretation of the NIV rests on the reading of lamp for "tillage" of the MT; see Additional Notes. Perhaps the MT can be explained in the sense that pride is the tillage, the preparation for, or undertaking of, **sin.**

21:5 / Antithetic. The **diligent** are always praised (e.g., 10:24; 14:23), and their work leads to wealth (10:4). The sages usually look askance at hasty action, as in 19:2 and 29:20, and hastiness to become rich is explicitly condemned. Although the saying is antithetic, the Hebrew construction of the two lines is similar: an emphatic "only" (not clear in the NIV) occurs in both lines.

21:6 / Synthetic. As the margin indicates, the NIV corrects verse 6b. Ill-gotten goods will not only yield no profit (cf. 10:2; Sir. 40:13–14)—they are a **snare.** See Additional Notes.

21:7 / Synonymous. The **violence** perpetrated by the **wicked** is portrayed as a power that overcomes them because of their stubbornness in clinging to evil.

21:8 / Antithetic. This seems to be an obvious contrast between the actions of the **innocent** (v. 8b) and the wicked.

However, the Hebrew text of verse 8a is not clear; see the Additional Notes.

21:9 / A "better" saying. This is repeated in 25:24, and a similar idea is found in verse 19 (cf. also 19:13; 27:15). The contrast would be between an uncomfortable place as a dwelling and the unpleasantness of a **quarrelsome** woman. The male prejudice is obvious. The precise meaning of verse 9b is not clear; see Additional Notes..

21:10 / Synthetic. This is a strong condemnation of the **wicked,** who will not treat even a **neighbor** with kindness (cf. 4:16).

21:11 / Synonymous. The issue here is whether **the simple** (11a) and **he** are referring to the same person. In 19:25, a similar proverb, they are distinguished. The **mocker's** fate is a strong lesson for the simple; but one who is **wise** learns through wisdom.

21:12 / Many modern translations are in agreement with the NIV, but there are problems with the Hebrew text: (1) nowhere in the OT is the Lord called **The Righteous One** (not even in Job 34:17) and the NIV provides another choice in the margin; (2) the repetition of **wicked** is unusual; (3) he is distinguished from his **house** (i.e., family). The marginal reading of the NIV is less likely. It is the action of God, rather than **the righteous man,** who can bring about such destruction.

21:13 / 13a is a *casus pendens,* taken up in 13b in an emphatic way. By a kind of *lex talionis* (law of retaliation), such an insensitive person will **not be answered** in an hour of need (whether by man or by God).

21:14 / Synonymous. The note of secrecy (cf. 17:23) indicates that real bribes are meant (contrast 15:27; 17:8; 18:16). The fold of the **cloak** served as a pocket.

21:15 / Antithetic. The atmosphere is judicial. Verse 15a can mean that **the righteous** personally enjoys acting rightly, and is not merely reacting to the just actions of others.

21:16 / Synthetic. Folly leads to death. There may be some sarcasm in "resting" among the **dead** (Hb. *rᵉpāʾîm,* the "shades" in Sheol); see 5:5; 7:27; 9:18.

21:17 / Synonymous and chiastic. The reference is to high living; it will eventually lead to poverty (cf. Sir. 18:32–19:1). Moderation is the ideal.

21:18 / Synonymous. **Ransom** is the restitution (usually monetary) one makes for wrongdoing. It is used here metaphorically, as is also "in the place of" (rendered simply by **for** in the NIV). But this statement seems to be in conflict with the sages' notion of justice: the righteous should have no need of ransom; it is the wicked who need it. Perhaps this should be understood in the light of Proverbs 11:8 (see comment there). The medieval Jewish scholar Rashi cited Haman (Esth. 7:10) as an example.

21:19 / A "better" saying. See verse 9 and comment. The **desert** of the NIV is too drastic; although the land is withdrawn and desolate, it is still workable.

21:20 / Antithetic. The contrast is between **the wise** who grow rich (by being thrifty presumably) and the **foolish** who squander possessions. **Choice food and oil** of the NIV overloads verse 20a, but there is no convincing emendation. **All he has** of the NIV translates "it," meaning the possession of the foolish not of the wise.

21:21 / Synthetic. This proverb reflects the normal view about the rewards of the righteous (cf. 3:2, 16). Many modern versions eliminate **prosperity** (see also the marginal note in the NIV) as redundant. It is also lacking in the Greek.

21:22 / Synthetic. See also 20:18; Eccl. 9:14–15. The saying fits the ideal of the sages: wisdom is valued above strength.

21:23 / Synthetic, with juxtaposition of participles. Control of the tongue is essential for wisdom (cf. 13:3; 18:21). There is a neat play on **keeps/guards** (Hb. *šōmēr*) and the rhyme ending (-o), **his tongue** (Hb. *ûlᵉšônô*) and **himself** (Hb. *napšô*).

21:24 / Synthetic. Verse 24a provides a kind of definition of the scoffer. But hubris is not the only characteristic (cf. 1:3; 9:7–8; 13:1, etc.). The NIV renders Hebrew *lēṣ* consistently as **mocker.**

21:25 / Synthetic. The **sluggard** is torn by desires and by laziness (which prevent the achievement of any goal).

21:26 / The problem here is the subject in 26a; the NIV continues with the sluggard of the previous verse, but true parallelism is lacking. One can understand the construction as indefinite and thus it designates the opposite of the generous person (v. 26b). See Additional Notes. The contrast is then between the greedy and the generous.

21:27 / Synthetic. For verse 27a see 15:8. Obviously sacrifices coming from **the wicked** cannot be pleasing to God, but there is a heightening intended in verse 27b. However, it is not clear just what is meant by **evil intent** (to cover over a crime?); more than mere formalism is meant.

21:28 / For verse 28a see 19:5, 9. Verse 28b is probably corrupt, and neither of the two readings proposed in the NIV are successful. The MT reads literally, "and a hearing man speaks forever (or, for victory)." See Additional Notes.

21:29 / Antithetic. The MT has literally, "hardens his face," that is, is brazen-faced or impudent in action. This is in contrast to the **upright** who firms up (Kethib), or who ponders (Qere) the way (of life).

21:30 / Synthetic. This is a striking expression of the limitations of the wisdom enterprise. Despite the employment of **wisdom** and **insight,** the Lord's ways remain mysterious; there is no programming of God.

21:31 / Antithetic. Preparations for war **(horse)** can and should be made, but ultimately all depends on **the LORD** (1 Sam. 17:47), who alone is wise (Sir. 1:8). See also Psalms 20:7; 28:7; Jeremiah 9:23. This proverb specifies the more general saying in verse 30.

Additional Notes §22

21:4 / Many ancient and modern translations read the Hb. text as *ner* **(lamp)** instead of *nir* (tillage, as in the MT).

21:6 / The NIV reads Hb. *ûmôqᵉšê* ("snares of") instead of Hb. *mᵉbaqqᵉšê* ("seekers of"). The MT likens the pursuit of riches to the pursuit of death.

21:8 / The *wāzār* of the MT is translated by the NIV as **devious.** But the term is a *hapax legomenon* and various hypothetical meanings have been proposed. The NJPS takes it to mean "and strange," thus eliminating the *hapax.*

21:9 / **Share a house with** of the NIV is a questionable translation of the difficult Hb. *wbyt ḥbr* (lit. "and house of association") at the end of v. 9b (also appearing in 25:24). Although the phrase occurs also in the Ugaritic texts, the meaning is obscure (common house?).

21:26 / Verse 26a is lit. "the whole day he (or, one) desires a desire"—a cognate accusative construction. One should not be misled by the catchword in v. 25 **(crave).** Emendation of the text on the basis of the Gk., which introduces *asebēs,* "evil one," as the subject of v. 26a, is not helpful.

21:28 / The LXX reflects the MT except for Hb. *lāneṣaḥ,* "forever" (Gk. *phulassomenos,* "keeping guard"). This is not an improvement. The various hypothetical restorations are summarized in Toy *(Proverbs)* and McKane *(Proverbs).* The NIV understands Hb. *lāneṣaḥ* as a successful testimony which wins out in the end. The most recent study is by J. A. Emerton, "The Interpretation of Proverbs 21:28," *ZAW* (Supplement) 100 (1988), pp. 161–70.

22:1 / Synonymous. A **good name** or reputation was highly regarded in Israel. This is underlined by the comparisons made (see also Eccl. 7:1).

22:2 / Synthetic. The verb in verse 2a means either that they live near each other or better, as in the NIV, they have a **common** bond. The sense of verse 2b is descriptive, not prescriptive, as if **the LORD** created two classes. See 29:13 and also 14:31 and 17:5, which provide a certain context.

22:3 / Antithetic. This verse occurs again in 27:12. The point is that the immature will forge ahead into **danger,** unlike the wise person.

22:4 / The NIV inserts **and** with many other translations (e.g., NRSV) in verse 4a. But **fear of the LORD** might be construed as in apposition. In any case, the result is given in verse 4b (cf. 21:21).

22:5 / In verse 5a there is no **and** in the MT; this may be a case of apposition or hendiadys, "thorny traps" (cf. 15:19). Instead of **soul,** translate "life" (cf. 16:17).

22:6 / Synthetic. The imperative in verse 6a is equivalent to a conditional clause. The Hebrew has literally, "according to his way," which has been variously interpreted; most agree with the NIV. The point is that proper training early on will have lasting results. The verse is lacking in the Greek.

22:7 / Synonymous. This is an observation. Indebtedness, of whatever degree, is a form of servitude; money means power. Contrast verse 9.

22:8 / Synonymous. The farming images (cf. 11:18) tie together wrongdoing and punishment in verse 8a. If the MT is correct, **the rod of his fury** (an obscure phrase) may designate the excessive oppression exercised presumably by the wrongdoer. It is said of his rod that it "shall fail." All in all, verse 8b remains obscure. See Additional Notes.

22:9 / Synthetic. **Generous** is literally, "good of eye"; contrast "stingy," or evil of eye in 23:6 and 28:22. This generosity to the **poor** is a common topos (cf. 14:21b; 19:17; Sir. 7:32). The blessing comes both from God and from humans.

22:10 / Synthetic. The **mocker** (the consistent translation in the NIV of the somewhat difficult Hebrew *lēṣ*—a word that occurs almost exclusively in Proverbs and Psalms) appears in many contexts; here he is seen in particular as a troublemaker.

22:11 / The MT is hardly translatable. The NIV inserts **and whose,** but the entire saying is not convincing. The NJPS interprets this as a three-line saying. Modern and ancient versions alike differ widely. See Additional Notes.

22:12 / Verse 12a raises doubts. Why would **the LORD** guard **knowledge** (cf. 2:8)? Elsewhere in the Bible the Lord's **eyes** are *upon,* but are not said to **keep watch,** or guard. The two main verbs occur also in 13:6. See Additional Notes.

22:13 / Synthetic. The humor in this saying lies in the fact that lions did not roam the **streets** in Israel. The point is that the **sluggard** will go to any extreme to come up with an excuse to keep from working (cf. 26:13).

22:14 / Synthetic. In this section of the book the "strange woman" (NIV, **adulteress**) occurs only here and in 23:27, in contrast to the frequent references in chapters 1–9. Her seductive speech is singled out (see ch. 7 and also 2:16). There is an air of determinism present in verse 14b; this is not an episode of simple punishment.

22:15 / Synthetic. This affirms once more the necessity of corporal punishment (cf. 13:24; 23:13–14; 29:15).

22:16 / The MT has been interpreted (and also emended) in various ways. See Additional Notes. The NIV distinguishes two subjects and they both end up in disaster. Presumably **poverty** is the punishment for their immoral behavior (oppression and bribery). However, there is no **and** in the Hebrew. There is more of a paradox if the oppressor and the wealthy are one and the same (apposition or implicit comparison). Such conduct leads to . . . poverty!

Additional Notes §23

22:8 / Hb. *ʿbrtw* can also be translated "arrogance"; the suffix must refer to the subject in v. 8a. The Gk. appears to read *ergōn autou* for this Hb. *ʿbdtw* ("his labors"). The Gk. verb is *syntelesei* ("bring to an end, destroy"). This is followed by the NAB: "destroys his labors"; but the **rod** is left unexplained. McKane *(Proverbs)* adopts Gemser *(Sprüche):* "smites him," emending the Hb. verb to *ykhw*.

22:11 / The Gk. has three lines: "The Lord loves holy hearts; all the blameless are accepted by him"—but the third line does not fit: "a king feeds (his flock) with his lips." Some would consider Hb. *mlk* (king) at the end of the verse as the subject: the king loves the pure of heart; gracious speech (is) his friend. For various proposals, see Plöger *(Sprüche)*.

22:12 / Some commentators (Gemser, *Sprüche;* H. Ringgren, *Sprüche* [Göttingen: Vandenhoeck & Ruprecht, 1962]) take the abstract for the concrete: "the one who is knowledge," or the wise person. McKane *(Proverbs)* stoutly defends the MT "as a basis for belief in the operation of a theodicy in much the same way as 15:3."

22:16 / The Hb. *lô* (to bring increase—to him) of the MT seems to refer back to the oppressor—but this hardly squares with sapiential teaching. The ambiguous text leaves open the possibility that the poor person profits (v. 16a), but the relationship to v. 16b is not clear. One can take the verse as antithetic: the oppressor profits but loses his gain to the rich (so NAB; cf. NJPS).

The Sayings of the Wise (Prov. 22:17–24:34)

The title for these chapters is taken from the Greek, since the MT buries the phrase in verse 17. See the introduction for the international character of wisdom and the influence of Israel's neighbors, especially Egypt. There can be no doubt that this section has been influenced by the Egyptian text known as Teaching of Amenemope (about 1100 B.C.E.), but there is considerable difference of opinion on the extent and manner of the influence. There is a certain concensus on the following points. The Hebrew is dependent upon the Egyptian from 22:17 to 23:11. Although the number "thirty" seems assured as the correct reading in 22:20, there is no general agreement on the *numbering* of the thirty sayings in 22:17–24:22 (i.e., at which point a new title and small collection occurs). The manner of the transmission of the Egyptian work (either oral or written) cannot be determined, but it is likely that courts of both countries played some role in communication. The Hebrew work is remarkably free in its total relationship to the Egyptian. There are striking agreements in some details and a wide divergence in other instances. For example, thirty (chapters) occur in Amenemope at the end, but in Proverbs at the beginning, where the word itself is an emendation. The dependence is by no means slavish. Moreover, the influence of Amenemope is not restricted to these chapters; it also appears elsewhere in the book of Proverbs (e.g., 15:16; 17:1). Although the discrete sayings prevail in 10:1–22:16, the style now changes in 22:17 to admonitions, much like the genre of the teachings in Proverbs 1–9. The NIV printing of 22:17–24:22 is laid out in a manner to suggest thirty units. The commentaries of A. P. Ross ("Proverbs" in *EBC* [ed. F. E. Gaebelein; Grand Rapids: Zondervan, 1991], pp. 1065–76) and D. A. Garrett (*Proverbs, Ecclesiastes, Song of Songs* [Nashville: Broadman, 1993]), which are both based on the NIV, actually number thirty sayings. But, as already mentioned, there is no consensus on this. Plöger *(Sprüche)* divides this section into an introduction (22:17–21), a section influenced by extra-

Israelite literature (22:22–23:14), and an address to "my son" with various admonitions, ending with an unusual description of the inebriated (23:15–35).

For a detailed analysis, see G. Bryce, *A Legacy of Wisdom: The Egyptian Contribution to the Wisdom of Israel* (Lewisburg: Bucknell University Press, 1979). Since Bryce's study Egyptological research has concentrated mainly on the Egyptian composition. (Besides the translation in *ANET*, pp. 421–25, see also *AEL*, vol. 2, pp. 146–63.)

§24 Proverbs 22:17–24:22

22:17 / The NIV is correct in introducing this section as "Sayings of the Wise." However, the NIV should have followed the general consensus, which recognizes that the phrase comes from verse 17 (they are the first words of the LXX, v. 17) and thus translates verse 17a: "Incline your ear and listen." See Additional Notes.

22:18 / In verse 18a, **heart** is, literally, "belly."

22:19 / The explicit religious purpose **(trust in the LORD)** should be noted. The text of verse 19b, translated literally in the NIV, seems to be corrupt, but there is no satisfactory solution.

22:20 / The NIV wisely adopts the MT reading, **thirty**, and relegates the Qere and Kethib to the margins. This is a classic case of the Hebrew being understood out of the Egyptian work; see Additional Notes.

22:21 / The reliability of courtiers as messengers is a theme that appears also in the Instruction of Ptah-hotep (lines 140–60; *ANET,* p. 413) as well as in the introduction to Amenemope (lines 5–6; *ANET,* p. 421). See Additional Notes.

22:22–23 / This admonition is to be understood against the background of a legal **court** (lit. "gate," since it was at the gates of a city that legal judgments took place). **Because they are poor:** the poor lack the means to marshal a strong defense. Thus, they are vulnerable, but on their side is **the LORD,** who will turn the tables on their oppressors.

22:24–25 / The warning against the **hot-tempered** occurs several times in Amenemope (ch. 9; *ANET,* p. 423). The ideal "silent" person is counterpoint to the "heated" person (e.g., Amenemope ch. 4; *ANET,* p. 422). See also 15:18; 29:22.

22:26–27 / This admonition against going surety for another is frequent in Proverbs (6:1–5; 11:15; 17:18; 20:16), but it is not to be found in Amenemope.

22:28 / See 23:10. The customary motivation clause is absent. It was expected that the boundaries established by the ancestors were to be honored. There is a parallel in Amenemope, chapter 6 (*ANET*, p. 422).

22:29 / The question form is used again in 26:12 and 29:20. The last two lines of Amenemope (ch. 30; *ANET*, p. 424) are a distant parallel; they refer to the scribe, whereas the scope of this verse is broader.

23:1–3 / These verses contain admonitions regarding manners at table with a **ruler.** The NIV notes the ambiguity of the MT by providing a footnote, and prefers **what** for "who." The vivid language of verse 2a inculcates self-restraint and this is served by the prohibition in verse 3a. The **food** is termed **deceptive,** a vague and ambiguous term. Perhaps the one who eats will be the victim of too great an appetite, or perhaps the host is testing the dinner guest as to self-restraint. The topic reappears in verses 6–8, where verse 3a is repeated in verse 6b. The general topic of table manners appears also in Ptah-hotep, lines 119–144 (*ANET*, pp. 412–13) and Amenemope, chapter 23 (*ANET*, p. 424). See also Sirach 31:12–32:13.

23:4–5 / This is an admonition concerning riches. The self-restraint called for in verses 1–3 is now applied strongly to riches. One's own **wisdom** should dictate such **restraint** (v. 4). Verse 5 adds a particular reason: **riches** don't last, they are only momentary and escape **like an eagle** from their possessor. See the Additional Notes for the nuances of the Qere. The seventh chapter of Amenemope (*ANET*, pp. 422–23) likewise opposes greediness and warns that theft will bring no profit since riches take on wings like geese and fly to the sky. The Egyptian material relates closely to the Hebrew, even if the Hebrew author remained quite independent in using any source.

23:6–8 / An admonition not to dine with a miserly host. **Stingy** translates "evil of eye" (cf. 28:22 and the comment on 22:9). Verse 6b repeats verse 3a. The reason given in verse 7 refers to the host's hypocrisy; he really begrudges the food to his guest, but the first part of this verse is obscure (note the three readings proposed in the NIV) and probably corrupt. See the Additional Notes. Verse 8a expresses the nausea one feels on such an occasion and the meaninglessness of such social intercourse.

23:9 / An admonition with motivational rationale. See 26:4. As **fool** and unteachable, such a person is simply incorrigible. See Sirach 22:9–15.

23:10–11 / An admonition with motivational rationale. For verse 10 see 22:28 and comment. For the spirit of the saying, see 22:22–23. The Hb. *gōʾēl,* or **Defender,** is the close relative that comes to the aid of the needy; here it is applied to the Lord (cf. Job 19:25).

23:12 / An admonition and chiastic arrangement. **Heart** and **ears** occur as in the opening instruction in 22:17. Several appeals to listen and to cultivate wisdom, with direct address to "my son," occur in the rest of the chapter. It is not easy to determine whether this verse is an *inclusio* with 22:17, or joined with what follows. Hb. *mûsār* **(instruction, discipline)** binds verses 12 and 13 together.

23:13–14 / An admonition with motivational rationale. The topic of corporal punishment has been noted before (cf. 13:24; 19:18; 22:15). Commentators point to the similar words in Ahiqar (lines 81–82; *ANET,* p. 428), but this admonition is a commonplace in the ancient world. The NIV footnotes **death** with **Sheol** (which is the literal Hebrew) in verse 14. The point is that the **child** who responds to **discipline** should enjoy long life; if not corrected, the youth may die prematurely.

23:15–16 / Note the chiastic arrangement, expressing the joy that a **wise** student **(my son)** brings to the teacher. The catchword **heart** occurs twice in verse 15a, and it is repeated several times throughout the rest of the chapter.

23:17–18 / An admonition with motivational rationale. The prohibition in verse 17a is reflected in 3:31 and 24:1, 19 (cf. Ps. 37:1). The sinner is not to be envied. The NIV presupposes the same verb with a slightly different nuance **(zealous)** in verse 17b, where the **heart** is directed toward **fear of the Lord** (or perhaps "those who fear the Lord," understanding the abstract for the concrete). **Future hope** (cf. 24:14) is literally, "an after," or "a future." This does not refer to a life beyond death, but rather a full life in the here and now that will be blessed and not cut short. See the Additional Notes.

23:19–21 / An invitation, with warning and motivational rationale. **Son** and **heart** appear again (see comment above in 23:12); see also 4:14 and 9:6 for the **path** to travel. The warning against drunkenness and gluttony (cf. Deut. 21:20) is motivated by the threat of poverty (v. 21). The admonition prepares the way for the vivid ridicule of drunkenness in verses 29–35. See also Sirach 18:32–19:1.

23:22–25 / Advice about correct attitude toward parents. Only verse 23, reminiscent of 4:5, 7 and missing from the Greek, stands apart from the specific recommendations about parents (see also Sir. 3:1–16). The **joy** of the parents in such offspring is the point of emphasis. See the Additional Notes.

23:26–28 / An invitation and an admonition. The appeal to the **son** in verse 26 is reminiscent of verse 19. In verse 26b the NIV prefers the Qere (with many ancient versions): **keep to** (instead of "delight in"). The warning in verse 27 is against a **prostitute,** who is paralleled by the "strange woman" (NIV, **wayward wife**). It is not clear if two different types of women are indicated, but both involve the threat of sexual transgressions. The **pit** is used to trap animals (cf. Jer. 18:20, 22), and from a **narrow well** (cf. Jer. 38:6–8) it is not easy to free oneself. Death and Sheol are associated with such metaphors (cf. 2:18; 5:5; 9:18). The comparison in verse 28 to a **bandit** who lays an ambush reflects the description of the woman in chapter 7 (see especially 7:12). The ambush prepared by the wicked woman is depicted particularly by means of her seductive language (cf. 2:16; 5:3; 6:24; 22:14).

23:29–35 / This satire about an alcoholic is without parallel in the book. Its placement here may have been prompted by verses 20–21. The admonition itself (v. 31) is unusual: do not (even) *look* at **wine!** The introduction (v. 29) consists of six questions, almost like a riddle. The answer to this rhetorical description is given in verse 30: the drunkard (cf. Isa. 5:11). In verse 31, the reader can almost see the wine being poured out—and that is the occasion for the admonition: not to even look at it! **Sparkles** is literally, "gives its eye." There is a play on vision: the **gaze** is answered by the "eye" (sparkle) of the wine. The dangerous results of over-indulgence are vividly portrayed in verses 32–35. The NIV interprets the difficult verb in verse 32b with the Greek, **poisons,** in conformity with the dangerous **viper.** The concrete results of intoxication are described: blurry vision **(strange sights)** and confused talk (lit. v. 33b has: your heart shall speak upside down things). The drunkard is described in two comparisons in verse 34. He imagines himself lying down "in the heart of the sea"— perhaps experiencing something like sea-sickness, or even already drowned in the depths of the sea (cf. Jonah 2:4). The other comparison is **lying** atop **the rigging.** This loss of balance and the sense of uncontrollable motion lie behind his inability to really feel the wounds inflicted upon him (v. 35). But he acknowledges that all this does not quench his thirst; he will be looking for **another drink** as soon as he sobers up. See Additional Notes.

24:1–2 / An admonition with motivational rationale. **Envy** of the **wicked** presupposes that the wicked are somehow prospering. For this commonplace, see comment on 23:17 (cf. 24:19–20). Here the motivation is not punishment, but the very evil (v. 2) upon which such people are intent. It is the siren song with which they entice others to evil (cf. 1:11–15). **Plot** of the NIV translates the Hebrew *hāgâ*, which literally indicates an audible sound (coming from the heart!). This initial admonition is followed by couplets of sayings in verses 3–9.

24:3–4 / Probably **house** is not to be identified too strictly. It can refer to the physical building and also to the qualities necessary for an ideal home. In view of the references to wisdom and her house in 8:1 and to the qualities (**wisdom, understanding,** and **knowledge** in that order in 3:19 and 23:3) with which God created the world (3:19), the saying can have a wider application, such as to the harmony and peace of the hearth.

24:5–6 / The MT is difficult in verse 5: "a wise person is in strength, and a knowing person strengthens power." Many (NRSV, NAB) follow the ancient versions and read a comparison: a wise person is better (stronger) than a warrior, and a person with knowledge is better than a powerful one. See Additional Notes. This change fits better with the emphasis placed on **guidance** and **advisers** in verse 6, which itself repeats 20:18b and 11:14b.

24:7 / **High** is not a certain translation for a word that is usually translated (e.g., Ezek. 27:16; Job 28:18) as "corals"—something valuable. The **fool,** who is otherwise talkative when he should keep silent, will be of no help when decision is to be made **at the gate** of the city.

24:8–9 / These verses are linked by the word "scheme" (Hb. *zmm*), which is associated with **evil** and **folly.**

24:10–12 / These verses probably go together, urging one to a sense of responsibility for others. The translation of verse 10 in the NIV fits into this context. However, the NIV deliberately separates verse 10 from verse 11 and understands it in a general sense. Reaction to stress is an indication of one's **strength** (so also McKane, *Proverbs*). The problem is whether the **times of trouble** include the episode that follows. The NRSV, NJPS, NAB, and many commentators take verses 10–12 as a unit. The situation becomes clear in verse 11: there is danger of **death** (presumably for innocent people), and action is necessary. Verse 12 indicates clearly that an excuse for inaction is insufficient. Although not mentioned, God is the one who **weighs the heart, guards life,** and will punish whoever has tried to evade responsibility. It is difficult to be specific about the details of those who were **led away.**

24:13–14 / The admonition in verse 13 is continued by a comparison **(also)** in verse 14. Hence it is not a warning against overindulging, as in 25:16, 27. **Honey** is being compared to **wisdom** (cf. 16:24). However, verse 14a seems incomplete and the NIV fills in from the preceding line **(sweet).** A variant of 23:18 appears in verse 14b.

24:15–16 / An admonition with motivational rationale. The admonition warns against ruining the **dwelling place** of the **righteous.** It grants that the latter can suffer repeated adversity (the proverbial **seven times**), but in the long run he will prevail and the **wicked** will not. See the Additional Notes.

24:17–18 / The admonition not to **gloat** over the fall of an **enemy** is motivated by the displeasure of **the LORD** who will punish you instead of your enemy (v. 18; cf. 17:5). In other words, it is only for God to pass judgment. Others (e.g., McKane, *Proverbs*) claim that the motive is that God might stop punishing the enemy. *Schadenfreude,* or rejoicing over the downfall of the enemy, is common to ancients and modern alike. In Psalm 35:15–21, the enemies of the psalmist are guilty of it (but cf. Ps. 92:11). Job abjures such conduct (Job 31:29–31). Note the tie created by the repetition of the several words in verses 16–17.

24:19–20 / On this admonition, see especially 23:17–18, and in general Psalm 37. Here it is anger **(fret)** that is criticized. The motivation in verse 20 picks up metaphors in 24:14; 23:18; and 13:9.

24:21–22 / The NIV motivates the admonition by pointing out the punishment the LORD and **king** will inflict on the **rebellious.** But the MT is uncertain. It is difficult to determine if the **destruction** is sent by the Lord and king or if it is brought about by the machinations of the **rebellious.**

The LXX adds 5 verses to verse 22, numbered 22a–22e in Rahlf's edition of the Septuagint. These verses are followed by the insertion of 30:1–14, the "sayings of Agur." In the Hebrew text verse 22 is continued by a small collection of sayings (vv. 23b–34), for which verse 23a serves as a superscription.

Additional Notes §24

22:17 / Because the LXX has *akoue emon logon,* many would read "to my words" after **listen.** The comparison of 22:17–18 and Amenemope 3.9–16 (*ANET*, pp. 421–22) is particularly significant because important words occur in the same order: ear(s); hear; words; heart; profit/pleasant; casket of belly/belly; tongue/lips (adopted from Bryce, *Legacy*, p. 101). This cannot be a coincidence.

22:19 / The NIV translates the MT lit. Many others, with some help from the Gk. tradition, make v. 19b go in the direction of making known "his ways to you." The text is suspect.

22:20 / The NIV text is correct, and the marginal readings should be disregarded. The Hb. consonantal text reads *šlšwm,* **thirty.** The Kethib would mean "the day before yesterday" or "formerly." The Qere has "officers," which is interpreted to mean excellent (sayings). Most of the ancient versions understood the word as a number. The Teaching of Amenemope (27.7–8; *ANET*, p. 424) reads in its final and thirtieth chapter: "See thou these thirty chapters: they entertain; they instruct." This reference, along with the many similarities to the Egyptian teaching in 22.17–23.12, led to almost universal adoption of the conjectural "thirty." It is not essential that thirty sayings in 22.17–24.22 be identified, as (implicitly) in the NIV, although many commentators do so (e.g., Meinhold, *Sprüche;* McKane, *Proverbs*).

Gemser *(Sprüche)* interprets v. 20b as *beth essentiae* (that is, when the preposition *bet* is used in the sense of "serving as" or "in the capacity of") followed by a hendiadys, "knowledgeable advice."

22:21 / The verse is overloaded. It is better to eliminate Hb. *qšṭ* (truth) as a gloss on the first *ᵓemet*, than to omit the second occurrence of *ᵓemet*. These changes do not affect the general meaning.

23:4–5 / Verse 4b is lit. "from your wisdom (i.e., using the wisdom you have), desist." The Kethib of v. 5a is: "Will your eyes flee to it (presumably the riches), it is gone." The Qere has: "Will you cause your eyes to flee to it . . ." The interrogative particle is rendered by a conditional "if" in the Gk. and this understanding is implicit in the NIV. Read also the Qere with the NIV, **and fly off.**

23:6–8 / Verse 7 might be rendered lit. "for as he reckons in his soul, so is he." But "reckon" is a doubtful meaning for Hb. *šᶜr*, and various meanings have been attributed to it (see the commentaries). A line in Amenemope (ch. 11; *ANET*, p. 423) speaks of the possessions of a poor man blocking the throat of the greedy person. Although this is quite a different context, it has suggested various hypothetical emendations (cf. McKane, *Proverbs*, pp. 384–85).

23:18 / The translation of Hb. *kî ᵓim* as **surely** is not easy to justify. The Gk. reads, "For if you keep them . . ." The presence of a verb is also suggested by the repetition of these words about hope in 24:14.

23:22–25 / There are no serious textual problems here. The NIV correctly chose the Qere readings in v. 24. Many commentators question the double mention of the female parent in v. 25 and eliminate **mother** in v. 25a.

23:29–35 / There are some words of unknown or doubtful meaning, but the pericope (section) is clear enough. The NIV rightly reads the Qere **(cup)** instead of the Kethib (bag) in v. 31. **Sorrow** in v. 29 is an uncertain translation, but it fits the parallelism. Similarly, mast or **rigging** are common translations of the unknown Hb. *ḥibbēl* in v. 34a. The NIV adds **you will say** in v. 35a (with the Gk.) to indicate direct speech.

24:5 / The Gk., Syriac, and Targum suggest the comparison, hence reading Hb. *mēᶜāz* and *mēᵓammîṣ kōaḥ*.

24:16 / Hb. *rāšāᶜ* **(wicked)** of the MT is taken by the NIV as a kind of apposition; others understand it as a vocative.

24:21 / The translation of *šônîm* (lit. "those who change") is questionable, and the versions are not helpful. One would expect the suffix in v. 22 to refer back to God and the ruler.

§25 Proverbs 24:23–34

24:23a / Verse 23a is really a title to the collection of sayings in verses 23b–34. See 25:1 and the title at 22:17.

24:23b–25 / The impartiality urged by these verses is supported by Leviticus 19:15 and Deuteronomy 16:19. There is a contrast between those who judge unjustly and those who reprove (NIV, **convict**). The former will be accused and the latter will prosper.

24:26 / This seems to be an independent saying that says literally: "lips he kisses—the one who returns honest words." The NIV makes the comparison explicit. A true **answer** is ultimately a sign of love.

24:27 / "By wisdom a house is built" is stated in verse 31. Here the sequence is dictated: do the **outdoor work** first, then **build** the **house** (either a residence or the family). Commentators point out the broad possibilities in meaning: first things first; do the necessary things before making your move.

24:28–29 / A judicial setting (as in vv. 23b–24) is presupposed, but now the emphasis is not the judge but the witness. **Without cause** is not necessarily a false witness (so the LXX), but one who testifies gratuitously or out of revenge. Verse 28b is a question: "and do you mislead with your lips?" The LXX understood it as a prohibition (against giving deceitful witness).

By joining verses 28 and 29, the NIV implies that revenge would be an unworthy motive for the action in verse 28. But verse 29 can be understood independently. Even in a judicial process, revengeful motives can run amok and revenge in private life is clearly antisocial. See 20:22, where the Lord is invoked as the one who will punish.

24:30–34 / This is parallel to 6:6–11, with almost identical correspondence between 6:10–11 and verses 33–34. It is a kind of example story, or description of what has been observed. What is observed is the pitiable condition of the farm of a lazy person, overrun with **weeds** and its protective **stone wall** broken down. The sage meditates on this, and draws a moral in verses 33–34 that may have been a very popular one (cf. Eccl. 4:5). Verse 33 presents a vivid picture of sleeping instead of working. Laziness and folly go hand in hand (cf. 26:13–16). The comparisons in verse 34 are uncertain, as the footnote in the NIV indicates. The best comment on the text **(bandit, armed man)** is made by Toy *(Proverbs):* "Poverty . . . is personified as a powerful and ruthless enemy who destroys or carries off one's substance" (on 6:11, p. 125). The NIV footnote (see also McKane, *Proverbs*) has a reading that is difficult to understand. Perhaps it means that the possessions (even in the condition described in v. 31) can be taken over by any passerby **(vagrant, beggar).** See Additional Note.

Additional Note §25

24:34 / In contrast to 6:11, which has an explicit comparison and also the Piel participle of Hb. *hlk,* v. 34 reads the Hitpael participle. The meaning of "vagrant" or "tramp" is derived from the intensive forms of the verb. In v. 34b, "a man of (the) shield" seems to indicate one who is armed. The meaning "beggar" was suggested by W. F. Albright, "Some Canaanite-Phoenician Sources of Hebrew Wisdom," VTSup 3 (1955), pp. 9–10 on the basis of an alleged Hb. root, *mgn* (to give).

The Proverbs of Solomon (Prov. 25:1–29:27)

These chapters are introduced by a superscription indicating that they are from Solomon by way of the "men of Hezekiah." The sayings break from the admonitory style of 22:17–24:34 and resemble those of chapters 10–22:16. However, these sayings are much more vivid, and in chapters 25–27 they form larger units ("proverb poems," as they have been called). Explicit comparisons are frequent. We are unable to say much about the general setting of the collection, but the ambience of the court predominates in chapters 25–27. The characteristic sound patterns (assonance, alliteration, catchwords, etc.) mark this collection just as they did the previous chapters. For the sake of brevity these patterns will not be emphasized here, but the reader is referred to the studies of McCreesh, *Sound* (index), and for chapters 25–27 in particular, R. Van Leeuwen, *Context and Meaning in Proverbs 25–27* (Atlanta: Scholars Press, 1988).

25:1 / The superscription begins with the same words as 24:23; hence the **more** in the NIV is not advisable. **Copied** is a commonly accepted translation of a verb of uncertain meaning.

25:2–3 / Although separate in the NIV, these sayings belong together, due to the catchwords, **search** and **kings.** The first (antithetic) saying plays with the words **glory** and **matter.** It also contrasts **God** and **kings** as well as **conceal** and **search.** As Van Leeuwen points out (*Context*, p. 69), this contrastive saying amounts to: God hides, kings search (comparable to "man proposes, God disposes"; cf. 16:1, 9). The transcendence of God (see also Deut. 29:29) is affirmed even more by comparison with **kings.** Verse 3 exalts the **hearts of kings** which, however, are well known to God, according to 15:11 and 21:1. This exaltation is comparable to the **heavens** and the **earth,** which cannot be measured for height and depth. So the king has a certain "mystery" about him, too: **unsearchable.** Plöger *(Sprüche)* remarks of verse 2 that God can let a secret remain secret, and in what he reveals God shows who he is. See also Tobit 12:7, 11. See Additional Notes for 25:3.

25:4–5 / There is a comparison between the two verses: removal of **dross** refers to the removal of the **wicked;** both the **vessel** (marginal reading) and the **throne** are thereby bettered. The text of verse 4b is questionable; see Additional Notes. That justice should characterize a king's reign is a commonplace (cf. e.g., 16:12; Isa. 9:7).

25:6–7a / Admonitions to humility before **king** and **noblemen** are motivated by a "better" saying. The purpose is to warn against false claims to honor at the royal court. See Luke 14:7–11 for a similar thought.

25:7b–8 / The NIV incorporates verse 7b of the MT into verse 8, and the marginal note should be disregarded. Again the admonition is a caution: do not hasten into a legal dispute lest you be defeated and shamed. Mere visual evidence may not suffice (v. 7b). See Additional Notes.

25:9–10 / An admonition with motivation not to **betray** another's **confidence**. This could refer to a private settlement (cf. 17:14), or as the context of the preceding verse suggests, a legal trial. In any case, the sages emphasize the keeping of a secret (cf. 11:13).

25:11 / Juxtapositional. The NIV agrees with most translations in praising wise speech but the precise work of art **(apples of gold)** is obscure, and the translation, **aptly spoken,** is a paraphrase (see Additional Notes). It is usually taken to refer to a well-turned phrase or a word at the right moment (cf. 15:23).

25:12 / Juxtapositional. This verse is often joined with verse 11, with **gold** as a catchword. But the emphasis is upon obedience **(listening ear)** to the sage's **rebuke,** which is appropriately described as an **earring.**

25:13–14 / These comparisons contrast a **trustworthy messenger** with an unreliable boaster in terms of meteorological phenomena. Reliable messengers are a frequent topos (10:26; 13:17; 22:21; 26:6). It seems that **snow** and ice were gotten from the mountains, packed and transported—a luxury perhaps, but a vivid comparison. The emptiness of the words of one who merely promises **gifts** is neatly brought out by the comparison to **clouds** that fail to yield **rain** (v. 14 is juxtapositional).

25:15 / This saying underlines the success of **patience** in dealing with authorities by means of a paradoxical observation in verse 15b.

25:16–17 / Moderation in eating and socializing is counseled by warning to what excess will lead. Verse 27a also remarks upon the attractiveness of **honey. Too much** is the catchword for verses 16–17.

25:18–19 / Five vivid metaphors **(like** is absent in the Hb. of vv. 18–20) convey the pain of deception at the hands of a liar (in a legal case) or one who is untrustworthy.

25:20 / The implication is that it is foolish and tactless to try to console a sad person by means of joyful song. Such an action is compared to **vinegar** upon the natron (or **soda**) and to de-

priving a person of a needed **garment.** The text is uncertain. The
NIV seems to presuppose that vinegar would dissolve the soda
and render it ineffectual (e.g., for washing; cf. Jer. 2:22).

25:21–22 / Charity toward one's **enemy** is commanded,
but the motivation is unclear. **Heap burning coals upon his head**
has been interpreted to mean punishment, but also a pain that
presumably leads to remorse (thus one overcomes evil with good).
An Egyptian ritual in which coals were carried on the head as a
sign of shame has been adduced (S. Morenz, "Feurige Kohlen auf
dem Haupt," *TLZ* 78 [1953], pp. 187–92), but there is no evidence
that this was practiced in Israel. See also Romans 12:20.

25:23 / Juxtaposes two sayings that stress the inevita-
bility of certain results: **rain** brought in by the **north wind** in one
case, anger in the other; the comparison is implicit. Because it is
the west wind that brings rain, other translations have been proposed. See Additional Notes.

25:24 / An almost verbatim repetition of 21:9.

25:25 / Two sayings form an implicit comparison. Verse
25a is not unlike verse 13. For **good news** see also 15:30.

25:26 / Again, two juxtaposed sayings form an implicit
comparison and verse 26 is in partial contrast to verse 25. Here
the water is not potable and it is correlated with the spoiling of a
just person who gives in to the **wicked.**

25:27 / In agreement with the moderation urged in verse
16b, verse 27a says overindulgence **is not good.** Verse 27b is
probably corrupt, although the NIV gives a common interpretation. The MT has "seeking their glory is glory"; see Additional
Notes. The NIV is a simple condemnation of vainglory.

25:28 / Two juxtaposed sayings form an implicit comparison. An open, unprotected **city** is prey to attack from outsiders. Anyone **who lacks self-control** is likewise prey, but to
personal moods, passions, etc. See 16:32b.

Additional Notes §26

25:3 / The NIV almost always makes the comparisons in chs. 25–27 explicit by inserting "like," or "as," thus making similes out of the sayings that are only implicit comparisons.

25:4 / The MT reads lit. "and a vessel came forth for the silversmith." A change in vocalization is required. The NIV marginal reading is preferable, but read "for" instead of "from"; the line is elliptical.

25:8 / The NIV has a silent correction, reading Hb. *kî* (because) for Hb. *pen* (lest), with many other versions.

25:11 / **Aptly spoken** is lit. "on its two wheels," and the meaning is uncertain. Are the two wheels the two lines of a saying (cf. Sir. 50:27)? The **apples of gold** must refer to some kind of precious stones in a **silver** design (cf. v. 12a).

25:20 / The first four words of the Hb. text are uncertain, perhaps a dittography of v. 19b. Instead of **soda**, many prefer "wound" (Gk. *helkei*).

25:23 / **Sly** is an interpretation of Hb. *str*, "secret," and the word for **north wind** can also mean "hidden" (Hb. *ṣpn*), and thus form a parallel. A hidden (i.e., sudden) **rain** is compared to secret talk; both produce undesirable effects. The difficulty with the north wind is that it does not produce rain (the west wind does), but cold. See McKane *(Proverbs)* for other solutions.

25:27 / For the difficult v. 27b, see the discussion by R. C. Van Leeuwen, "Proverbs 25:27 Once Again," *VT* 36 (1986), pp. 105–14. His translation is: "and to seek difficult things is (no) glory."

§27 Proverbs 26:1–28

26:1 / There is a deliberate collocation of sayings in this chapter: verses 1–12 deal with the fool (Hb. *kᵉsîl*) and verses 13–16 with the sluggard (Hb. *ʿāṣēl*), and several phrases are repeated. Compare verse 5 with verse 12 (and also v. 16a), verses 4 and 5 (see also v. 11b), and verses 7b and 9b. The exceptional, even paradoxical, comparisons in verse 1a emphasize that **honor** is not to be given to a **fool**; see also verse 8.

26:2 / The comparison to the aimless, irregular flight of these birds underscores the failure of an **undeserved curse** to have its effect. Curses were taken seriously, but an unjust curse either boomerangs (Qere reading) or simply fails (Kethib).

26:3 / The implicit comparison of animals to **fools** depends upon their common failing: they won't obey and thus need to be disciplined (cf. 10:13b; 17:10b).

26:4–5 / Two famous proverbs that are apparently contradictory. The prohibition in verse 4 is motivated by ensuring that one's response is itself not foolish. This would reduce one to the level of a **fool** to whom no honor should be given, verse 1. The command in verse 5 is motivated by consideration for the **fool**. It would be worse for the fool to be **wise in his own eyes,** for according to verse 12 there is no hope for such a person. Plöger *(Sprüche)* thinks that the command in verse 5 is aimed at unmasking the fool for what he is. Thus circumstances can dictate when one should speak (just as silence itself is ambiguous; cf. 17:27–28). See K. G. Hoglund, "The Fool and the Wise in Dialogue" in *The Listening Heart* (Sheffield: JSOT Press, 1987), pp. 161–80, for a full discussion.

26:6 / The elements in this implicit comparison are all juxtaposed. Using a **fool** as a messenger is to fail in one's purpose and ultimately to bring harm to oneself (**drinking violence**—a strange metaphor here).

26:7 / An implicit comparison of the uselessness of a **proverb** uttered by a **fool;** he is unable to put it into practice—just as the **legs** of a crippled, **lame** person cannot provide forward progress.

26:8 / Despite the uncertain meaning of verse 8a (see Additional Notes), the explicit comparison points to the folly of honoring a **fool** (see also v. 1). The NIV understands verse 8a to be a self-defeating action; the **sling** will not be able to launch the missile.

26:9 / This implicit comparison simply juxtaposes two phrases; verse 9b repeats verse 7 and retains that meaning. But verse 9a is obscure: "a thorn (-stick?) comes into the hand of a drunkard." Does this indicate that the drunkard harms himself or others? Or is this merely a description of the unsteady gait of a drunkard who falls into thorns?

26:10 / Like the previous verse, this verse juxtaposes two phrases, but the verse cannot be translated with any certainty. The NIV compares to a careless **archer** anyone who will hire **a fool** or a mere transient. See the Additional Notes.

26:11 / See 2 Peter 2:22. This explicit comparison underscores the failure of fools to learn; they merely continue in their **folly.**

26:12 / Self-deception (to be **wise** in one's own estimation) is in a sense the greatest folly (and even the "wise" should be aware of it! cf. v. 16a; 28:11a). The blindness of such a person is simply incorrigible. The evaluation in verse 12b may have been a frequent one (cf. 29:20).

26:13 / The **sluggard** is the subject of verses 13–16 (cf. also 6:6–11; 24:30–34). The point of this verse is that he will use any excuse, however impossible, to avoid doing anything (cf. 22:13). For a detailed treatment of verses 13–16, see Van Leeuwen, *Context,* pp. 107–10.

26:14 / An implicit comparison between a **door** that **turns,** but goes nowhere, and the turning of a **sluggard**—while remaining in **bed!**

26:15 / Such a person is even too lazy to eat (cf. 19:24).

26:16 / The height of folly is indicated by this comparison of the **sluggard** to **seven** (i.e., an indefinite number) wise people. With the laziness goes self-deception (cf. v. 12a).

26:17 / The juxtaposition of two statements creates the comparison; in both cases the subject is simply asking for trouble.

26:18–19 / One who practices deceit and tries to cover it up as a joke is compared to the unstable person who wields deadly weapons in an indiscriminate manner.

26:20 / An implicit comparison by means of juxtaposition: **fire** is extinguished when no **wood** remains; a **quarrel** abates when there is no one to **gossip**.

26:21 / Another implicit comparison that by juxtaposition continues the thought of verse 20, expressing it positively: the **quarrelsome** one serves as **kindling** wood.

26:22 / This repeats 18:8; see comment there.

26:23 / An implicit comparison by means of juxtaposition: **fervent lips** hide the **evil heart,** just as **glaze** conceals mere **earthenware.** The NIV corrects the MT (see Additional Notes).

26:24 / The NIV prints verses 24–26 together, presumably because they deal with the **malicious** and their hypocrisy. Verse 24 is an antithetic saying that serves as an interpretation of verse 23, without metaphors.

26:25 / An admonition with motivational rationale, referring back to the malicious person of verse 24—**do not believe** his sweet talking.

26:26 / The NIV continues speaking of the malicious person of verse 24. He may succeed in hiding his hatred (NIV, **malice**) but it will eventually become public to all (it is not said just how this will take place).

26:27 / Two sayings in synonymous parallelism. Does this indicate something that happens regularly, or merely sometimes, and hence is unexpected? Much depends on the context. In Ecclesiastes 10:8–9, the events seem merely possible. But in Psalm 7:15–16, a sequence is indicated that has been called the "act/consequence" view. This is where a bad effect follows automatically from a bad action; a good effect from a good action. This view is advocated strongly by Klaus Koch, "Is There a Doctrine of

Retribution in the Old Testament?" in *Theodicy in the Old Testament* (ed. J. L. Crenshaw; Philadelphia: Fortress, 1983), pp. 57–87. However, the structure of verse 27 is merely to pair two participles (digger and roller), and their verbs **(fall, roll back)** can be translated with a modal nuance (may fall, or may return). There is no need to postulate an inflexible law of act/consequence, as if the direct agency of God has to be excluded. The NIV translates the verbs in the indicative. This can be justified by the context of verses 23–26, which is bent upon punishment for the malicious person. Even if one knows that the action in verse 27 is not inevitable, it expresses a kind of "poetic justice."

26:28 / Synonymous parallelism. **Those it hurts** is a doubtful translation of "its oppressed ones," but there is no successful emendation. The saying itself has some association with verses 24–26.

Additional Notes §27

26:8 / The MT in v. 8a seems to have "like tying of a stone in a sling" (the last word is a *hapax legomenon*, "stone-heap"?). With this proposed translation, an infinitive construct, "tying" (Hb. *ṣᵉrôr*), is parallel to a present participle, "giving" (Hb. *nôtēn*)—unless Hb. *ṣᵉrôr* is the noun meaning "purse" (cf. 7:20). Both the infinitive construct and the noun have the same vocalization.

26:10 / The difficulties in v. 10a come from the manifold meanings of each word: Hb. *rab* can mean "much," "master," "archer"? The verb can mean "bring forth" or "wound"; the object is "all." Literally, v. 10b reads: "and one who hires a fool and who hires passers-by." No emendations have achieved consensus.

26:23 / The MT is usually translated "silver dross" (NIV margin), presumably to indicate a covering that is not pure silver, but this is uncertain. The NIV adopts in the text the conjectural reading, Hb. *kspsgym*, which supposedly means "glaze" (but cf. M. Dietrich and O. Loretz, "Die angebliche Ug.-He. Parallele SPSG//SPS(J)G(JM)," *UF* 8 [1976], pp. 37–40).

Antithetic parallelism is frequent in this chapter, in contrast to chapters 25–26. The sayings seem to be generally related in couplets, thanks to content and also catchwords (e.g., Hb. *hll*, to boast or praise, in vv. 1–2). There are several admonitions and the final verses (23–27) form a special unit.

27:1 / One should concentrate on the present moment because of one's ignorance of the future. This is a commonplace. See Ecclesiastes 11:4, 6; James 4:13–15; and Amenemope 19.13 (*ANET*, p. 423).

27:2 / Synonymous parallelism. Self-praise can hardly be objective, but one can normally trust **praise** from others as being honest.

27:3–4 / Style (juxtaposition, comparison) unites these verses, although the thoughts are different. Difficulties are posed in verses 3a and 4a and the greater difficulty in verses 3b and 4b. Thus, physical burdens (**stone** and **sand**) are not as great as the **provocation** a **fool** can cause. Similarly in verse 4, but it is not clear if these emotions are subjective or are the reactions of others. In 14:30 **jealousy** (termed "envy" there) is subjective.

27:5–6 / A "better" saying and an antithetic statement are united by the Hebrew root *ʾhb* (**love, friend**) and the para-doxical qualities of these. In verse 5, love fails in that it is **hidden** instead of speaking out when needed, even for a **rebuke** (that would be a true sign of love). In verse 6, there is a contrast be-tween the frank though hurtful actions of a friend and the pro-fuse (but hypocritical) **kisses** of an **enemy**.

27:7 / Antithetic. This is partially matched in Ahiqar, line 188 (*ANET*, p. 430): "Hunger makes bitterness sweet . . ." The paradoxical observation is applicable to many situations in life.

27:8 / The point of the explicit comparison between the **bird** and the human is homelessness. Uprooting could be caused by various events, such as war or exile.

27:9 / Verse 9a is clear, but verse 9b is doubtful. The NIV glides over the fact that **one's** before **friend** has no antecedent. It seems to compare the pleasure of **perfume** to the **earnest counsel** (but literally this is "counsel of soul"). See Additional Notes.

27:10 / Two admonitions, followed by a "better" saying. These three lines deal with the topic of friendships, but in a rather disjointed manner. There is no apparent reason for the strange advice in verse 10b (but cf. 18:24b and 19:7). Verse 10c is intelligible in itself because of the distance factor. Three classes are treated: **friend, brother,** and **(nearby) neighbor.**

27:11 / An admonition of a father/teacher to a **son** to be **wise.** Thus the son will make him happy and enable him to reply to critics.

27:12 / This contrast between the **prudent** and the **simple** is virtually identical with 22:3.

27:13 / See 20:16. The sages advise against going surety for another (e.g., 6:1–5). One should deal even more strictly with those who make pledges on behalf of a **stranger.** See the Additional Notes.

27:14 / The NIV translates the participle by an "if" clause. It is assumed that such exaggeration in those circumstances harbors ill-feeling. The ambiguous "to him" in the Hebrew refers to the one who curses, as in the NIV.

27:15–16 / See 19:13b for the image of the **quarrelsome wife.** In verse 16 **restraining** is a mistranslation; Hebrew ṣpn means "hide," or "treasure up." Hence, translate with the NAB: whoever "keeps her stores up a whirlwind." The last line is also difficult; perhaps "oil meets his right hand." Then the two comparisons underscore what cannot be held: **wind** and **oil.** The situation is similar with the woman of verse 15. See Additional Notes.

27:17 / An implicit comparison between the sharpening of **iron** and the (mental) challenging of one's companion. **Another** is literally, "the face of his friend." See Additional Notes.

27:18 / An implicit comparison between a farmer who profits from his work, and a servant who profits from caring for the **master.**

27:19 / An explicit comparison between the image reflected by **water** and the image of a person that is mirrored in the human **heart.** The succinctness of the Hebrew is noteworthy: "like the water, face to face—so the heart of a person to a person." This leaves open the possibility of one person (v. 19b) seeing himself more truly, or of two persons (more probable?), one of whom sees him- or herself more truly in the reflection of another.

27:20 / Adopt the marginal reading of the NIV. Sheol/ **Death** is personified in the OT as a dynamic power that pursues human beings insatiably (cf. 30:15–16). There is an implicit comparison with human eyes that here represent the manifold human desires (cf. Eccl. 4:8).

27:21 / See 17:3, where the Lord does the testing. Here one's **praise** does the testing *(hapax legomenon)*, that is, the praise that one receives. Public reputation is a barometer of one's worthiness.

27:22 / The **fool** is simply incorrigible. This notion is exemplified by the metaphor of **grinding** to bits; **folly** remains as it was. It is remarkable that the possibility of the conversion of a fool is never really envisioned. Wisdom speaks to the simple or naive (1:22; 8:5; 9:4), for whom there seems to be some hope, but not to fools.

27:23–27 / A short poem in the style of an admonition to attending to farming and animal husbandry. **Lambs** and **goats** were vital to Israelite life and served many purposes. The motive given in verse 24 is that this will be more profitable than **riches,** even a (royal!) **crown,** since that will not last (cf. 23:5). To this negative motivation is added a positive description of the benefits of careful farming. Verse 25 introduces the provisions of fodder for the livestock (the second **growth**). Furthermore, there will be **clothing** from the lambs and expansion: a **field** obtained through selling of goats (v. 26). The homestead itself (including the servants) will have plenty to live on (v. 27). This passage is very detailed, when one considers the brief references to farming in 10:5; 12:10–11; 24:27; 28:19. It is less likely that we have here a parable (see Van Leeuven [*Context*]) about the king's care for his people.

Additional Notes §28

27:9 / V. 9b is also ambiguous in that the Hb. preposition *min* can be translated as indicating source (see NIV, **springs from**) or comparison ("better than one's own counsel" as in the NJPS). Many emendations have been suggested, but the line remains puzzling.

27:13 / The issue is whether the Kethib in 20:16, identical with this verse in other respects, should be adopted here—thus "strangers" instead of "strange woman," which the NIV interprets as **wayward.**

27:16 / Hb. *yāmîn* (right [hand]) is feminine and cannot be the subject of Hb. *yqrh*, and so the verb should be vocalized as derived from Hb. *qrh* (to meet), not Hb. *qr ᵓ* (to call).

27:17 / In order to obtain the (correct) NIV rendering, one must change the vocalization of the Hb. verb, *yḥd*, as the *BHS* suggests on the basis of the ancient versions. Therefore, Hb. *yḥd* in v. 17a, with the vocalization of the MT, reads, "be sharp" (Hb. *yāḥad*) rather than the proposed vocalization, "sharpen" (Hb. *yaḥad* or *yāḥēd*).

§29 Proverbs 28:1–28

Many consider chapters 28 and 29 to be a collection separate from chapters 25–27. In contrast to the latter, which has many groupings, the style here returns to the (apparently) discrete sayings of earlier chapters (e.g., chapters 10–15). Antithetic sayings are the most frequent. See comment on 29:27.

28:1 / Antithetic and chiastic. The **wicked man flees,** not merely because of a bad conscience but because of some kind of judgment to come. In contrast, the **righteous** have nothing to fear.

28:2 / Antithetic. The implication of verse 2a is that rebellion and instability is marked by **many** who vie for supremacy. The MT can also be translated: "because of the wrongdoing of the country its leaders will be many." The translation of verse 2b is very uncertain and many translations have been proposed (see Additional Notes). The parallelism suggests that an intelligent person can produce **order**—the general meaning proposed in the NIV.

28:3 / An implicit comparison through juxtaposition. The NIV relegates the MT reading **(poor)** to the margin, perhaps because it is deemed unusual for the poor to oppress one of their own. The comparison is vivid: the storm ruins the harvest. See Additional Notes.

28:4 / Antithetic. Hebrew *tôrâ* means instruction or teaching (of a parent or sage) in chapters 1–9. The NIV maintains this meaning also in those chapters, but here and in verses 7 and 9, it is rendered as **law,** which suggests that the translators mean the Mosaic Torah. Both meanings are possible.

28:5 / Antithetic. The understanding of the wicked and the devout differs radically. One does not comprehend **justice,** but the other comprehends *everything* (a more literal and better rendering than the NIV). In verse 5b, "everything" is quite general, referring to what is good/evil and to the meaning of life.

28:6 / Antithetic "better" saying, in chiastic form. See 19:1. The contrast between **rich** and **poor** appears also in verse 8. Possessions, or the lack thereof, can be ambiguous; virtue is what counts. **Ways** is literally "two ways" (the dual), but the NIV reads the plural here and in verse 18.

28:7 / Antithetic contrast by juxtaposition. See comment on verse 4, but here the content of verse 7b suggests the instruction of the **father** (cf. 10:1; 13:1).

28:8 / Synthetic. The underlying principle is that the evildoer cannot profit from evildoing; hence the illicit gain eventually returns to the **poor.** Charging **interest** to other Israelites was forbidden in the Law (e.g., Lev. 25:35–38) and kindness **to the poor** is urged in 19:17. The MT has a neat play on words: *hônô* and *hônēn* **(his wealth; will be kind).**

28:9 / Synthetic and juxtapositional. There is a neat opposition between the deafness of a person (to the **law**) and the deafness of God to that person's prayer (an "abomination"). See comment on verse 4; perhaps both Law and the instruction of the sage are included.

28:10 / The unusual length makes this suspect; perhaps a line is missing. The principle of deed/consequence is applied in the metaphor of the pit (see comment on 26:27). The seducer falls into **his own trap:** poetic justice.

28:11 / Antithetic and chiastic. The **rich** person **wise in his own eyes** is worse than a fool according to 26:12; no wonder the **poor** person **sees through** them. Wisdom cannot be identified with riches.

28:12 / Antithetic. The general meaning is clear; the administration of **the righteous** is a great benefit. In its absence, people are driven underground. The meaning of the verbs is somewhat uncertain: **triumph** is literally, "rejoice"; **go into hiding** (lit. "is searched for") seems to derive its meaning from 28:28a, where a different verb is used.

28:13 / Antithetic with juxtaposition of participles. It is assumed that **sins** are confessed (publicly) to God and forgiven (cf. Ps. 32:3–5). In contrast, whoever **conceals** equivalently denies wrongdoing.

28:14 / Antithetic with a blessing formula. Although the Hebrew is not the usual word for "fear" of God, it probably carries the same connotation. The verse is, as it were, a commentary on verse 14b, the hardened sinner.

28:15 / An implicit comparison by means of juxtaposition. A tyrant's affliction of poor subjects is compared to the instinctive roar and speed of wild beasts (cf. 29:2b).

28:16 / Antithetic. The text is uncertain; see Additional Notes. The NIV understands verse 16a as a kind of continuation of verse 15. On verse 16b see 10:2.

28:17 / Synthetic. The NIV supposes that a murderer will be driven on by a sense of **guilt** till the end of his life. A command is issued that no **support** be given him (lit. "do not lay hold of him"—thus one is not to prevent the Lord's vengeance from fulfilling its purpose?).

28:18 / Antithetic. The NIV silently reads the plural for the dual (v. 18b in the MT: "two ways"; cf. v. 6).

28:19 / Antithetic. This is identical with 12:11 except for the last two words; here there is a play on the word, "have one's fill," which occurs in both lines (cf. the REB). The saying calls for purposeful work.

28:20 / Antithetic. By **faithful** is meant one who is a person of integrity, in contrast to one who hastens (NIV, **eager**) **to get rich.** Haste is always suspect, often implying wrongdoing of some sort (19:2; 23:4–5; 28:22).

28:21 / Synthetic. A legal ideal is affirmed in the "not good" sayings (cf. 18:5; 24:23). The ideal, however, can be transgressed for even the slightest profit.

28:22 / Antithetic. Literally, "one evil of eye" (cf. 23:6 as opposed to 22:9) is **stingy,** but somewhere in the future there **awaits** an unexpected reversal, **poverty.** On haste, see comment on verse 20.

28:23 / A comparative contrast. The sages repeatedly emphasize the value of an honest rebuke as opposed to flattery; cf. 27:5–6. **In the end** of the NIV is literally, "after me"; see Additional Notes.

28:24 / Synthetic, participial juxtaposition. The NIV prints in three parts what the MT has in two. This is a condemnation of brazen stealing from parents (not specified in the Law); see also 19:26.

28:25 / Antithetic. The **greedy** (lit. "broad of desire") encounters strife, in contrast to the prosperous life of the one **who trusts in the LORD.**

28:26 / Antithetic. A contrast between ill-placed **trust** and true **wisdom.** The motif of trust continues verse 25b and the security given by wisdom is very similar to verse 18a. There is only a shade of difference between trusting in self and being wise in one's own eyes (26:12).

28:27 / Antithetic in juxtapositional style. Paradoxically, generosity to the **poor** does not deplete one's possessions, but the one who **closes** the **eyes** (cf. 21:13, whoever shuts the ears) will be cursed by the poor and perhaps by the Lord (cf. 3:33, where the same word is used).

28:28 / Antithetic. A contrast of the results of the presence or absence of **wicked** leaders. Verse 28a is almost identical with verse 12b, and verse 28b is similar to 29:2 **(the righteous thrive).**

Additional Notes §29

28:2 / The MT of v. 2b can be translated: in/by/with a man (or men?) intelligent, knowing, right lasts. The rendering of Hb. *kēn* as "right" (NIV, **order**) is doubtful and it is not clear what one **man** (the king?) can achieve. The Gk. has a quite different text.

28:3 / The MT has "a poor man"; the NIV proposes *rō'š* (head, chief) for Hb. *rāš*.

28:16 / The MT has lit. "A prince lacking in understanding and great in oppressions—those who hate ill-gotten gains will live long." A verb seems to be missing in v. 16a; perhaps Hb. *yārēb* (for *wᵉrab*), "increases" (oppression).

28:18 / **Suddenly** translates the MT "in one"; perhaps read "in the grave" (Hb. *bᵉsaḥat*) for "in one" (Hb. *bᵉ'eḥāt*).

28:23 / The NIV makes a silent correction, perhaps reading Hb. *'aḥᵃrît* (finally?).

§30 Proverbs 29:1–27

29:1 / Synthetic. On the downfall of the **stiff-necked**, see 28:14b; verse 1a repeats 6:15b. See comment on 28:23.

29:2 / Antithetic. See the comment on 28:12, 28b. The lot of the community is emphasized.

29:3 / Antithetic. Love of **wisdom** is a frequent theme in chapters 1–9 (e.g., 4:6; 8:17). Here it is contrasted with whoring (not a frequent topic in chs. 10–31). The emphasis seems to be on the financial ruin (cf. 6:31) the son incurs, rather than on shame.

29:4 / Antithetic. Compare verse 2. The effects of the just rule of a **king** is a commonplace. In contrast, "the man of gifts" (i.e., one who is obsessed with taxes and bribery—possibly also a king) ruins the country.

29:5 / Synthetic. Flattery is seen as seductive and harmful (cf. 26:28; 28:23). It is not clear if **his feet** refers to the flatterer or the **neighbor;** the ambiguity may be deliberate.

29:6 / Antithetic. The MT reads literally, "in the wrongdoing of an evil man is a trap"; see 12:13a. Here again one can ask: a trap for the evil person or for someone else? The NIV understands it to refer to the **evil man.** By contrast, then, the **righteous one** is joyful because there is no fear of a trap (not joyful because the **evil man is snared**).

29:7 / Antithetic. The contrast between the **righteous** (Hb. *ṣaddîq*) and the **wicked** (Hb. *rāšāʿ*) occurs over and over. This verse portrays their different attitudes toward the **poor.** The NIV, along with the NJPS, NRSV, and NAB, paraphrase verse 7b (lit. "does not understand knowledge").

29:8 / Antithetic. The NIV has **stir up;** better, "inflame." It takes the **wise** to bring about calm.

29:9 / Synthetic. Verse 9a is not a conditional, but a statement of fact, and is followed by "and anger and laughter and no rest." In verse 9b, the NIV inserts **the fool** in order to resolve the ambiguity of the emotional outburst, since the **wise** are calm by definition. However, the result is a lack of **peace;** hence the wise should avoid such a dispute.

29:10 / The NIV considers this as synonymous parallelism, but the rendering of verse 10b is doubtful. If there is a contrast between the two lines, verse 10b must mean something like the concern the **upright** have for a person of **integrity.**

29:11 / Antithetic. The sages are continually emphasizing self-control by using the **fool** as a foil (cf. 14:16, 29; 16:32). The MT of verse 11b reads literally, "the wise person stills it (anger) back," but there is no compelling reason to change the text.

29:12 / Synthetic. Any tolerance of **lies** by a **ruler** will surely have a corrosive effect on his **officials;** bad morale would result. See Sirach 10:2.

29:13 / Synthetic. The saying is reminiscent of 22:2 and it is at least an implicit warning to the **oppressor.** Verse 13b reads literally "makes bright the eyes of both"—in Psalm 13:3, the phrase means "to keep alive."

29:14 / Synthetic, with two lines juxtaposed. On the security of the **throne,** see 16:12b; 20:28b; and 25:5. This stability is achieved by equitable treatment of the **poor** (in 25:5, by removing the wicked). See also verse 7a.

29:15 / Antithetic. Physical punishment is mentioned also in 13:24; 23:13–14. See also verse 17.

29:16 / Antithetic. Similar ideas are found in 11:10–11; 28:12, 28; and 29:2. The implication is that the **righteous** look with pleasure, since by the **downfall** of the **wicked** justice is served.

29:17 / Synonymous. See verse 15; this verse emphasizes the positive results accruing to the parents.

29:18 / Antithetic (vision as opposed to **law; people** as opposed to an individual). **Revelation** translates the Hebrew *ḥāzôn* and it means (prophetic) vision. This suggests that the Mosaic Law is meant in verse 18b (see comment on 28:4, 7). Prophecy and Law are thus complementary.

29:19 / Synthetic. Physical discipline is to be used on the **servant** or slave as well as upon the child (cf. v. 15; 19:18). **Words** do not suffice.

29:20 / Synthetic. See 26:12, where the same verdict is rendered upon those who consider themselves wise. **Haste** is always condemned by the sages; here it means "without thought."

29:21 / Synthetic. The *hapax legomenon,* Hebrew *mānôn,* remains unknown (**grief?**). The MT refers **the end** to the master, not the slave. In spirit, this saying belongs with verse 19.

29:22 / Synonymous. The **angry** one is short-tempered and hot-headed. There is frequent warning about such (e.g., 22:24; 15:18). In verse 22b, the MT has literally "great in sin."

29:23 / Antithetic. The NIV brings out the paronomasia, **low, lowly.** This kind of advice is recurrent, for example, 11:2; 16:18–19.

29:24 / Synthetic. The NIV interprets this as a description of the plight of an **accomplice** in theft. Literally, "he hates his life" (v. 24a) because a curse (NIV, **oath**) can strike him as well as the actual **thief,** who is presumed to be absent or unknown. Commentators usually refer to Leviticus 5:1 as being a judicial case to which the proverb can be applied. The MT has "does not speak up" for **dare not testify** of the NIV. The power of a curse is assumed in the saying (cf. 26:2).

29:25 / Antithetic. **Fear of man** can mean anxiety about oneself or (more probably) worry about what others think. The antidote to this is trust in *yhwh* (cf. 18:10).

29:26 / Antithetic and chiastic. Recourse to a **ruler** can be honest or dishonest (cf. 19:6) and the end result is not certain. Only from *yhwh* can one expect true **justice.**

29:27 / Antithetic. Meinhold *(Sprüche)* observes that the final proverb contrasts the **righteous** (plural) with the **wicked** (singular, collective), just as in 28:1. This is apparently a kind of inclusion. Moreover, each half-line begins with *tāw,* the last letter of the Hebrew alphabet. The feeling between the two classes is mutual.

Additional Note §30

29:10 / Verse 10b would normally be translated as "and the just seek his life" (with the meaning, "to kill him"). The NIV translates the sense of the passage, making "the just" (Hb. *yᵉsārîm*) the object, but "his life" (Hb. *napšô*) is clearly the object. The line is difficult. Many translations render "seek" with the meaning "seek the good of," "care for," but this meaning is not attested for the Hb. verb *yᵉbaqqᵉsû*.

The Sayings of Agur (Prov. 30:1–14)

The title that is incorporated into verse 1 clearly indicates a new collection. But it is difficult to ascertain the extent of the sayings: does it extend to verse 4, 9, or 14? The fact that the 14 verses are found in the LXX after 24:22 would suggest that they were taken as a unit.

§31 Proverbs 30:1–14

30:1 / Agur is identified as son of Jakeh, but the next two words create some confusion (see Additional Notes) because both belong to prophetic speech: "burden," "oracle." It seems better to emend it slightly and read "of Massa" (mentioned in Gen. 25:14), and then take the second word and read literally with the MT, "The oracle of the man to. . . ." Because the proper names that follow are mysterious, many solutions have been proposed to replace them (as in the marginal reading of the NIV). See Additional Note.

30:2 / Synonymous with two juxtaposed nominal sentences. This admission of subhuman ignorance is either exaggerated or ironic (in view of the questions in v. 4). The avowal can be likened to Qoheleth's failure to acquire wisdom. It is a relative statement, relative to the knowledge of God (v. 3).

30:3 / Synonymous and chiastic. **The Holy One** is God, as in 9:10, where the plural form (normally indicating members of the heavenly court; cf. Job 5:1) appears. Is Agur comparing his ignorance to the **wisdom** of the wise that is a gift of God (2:6)?

30:4 / A series of questions, reminiscent of Job 38:5–11. Most agree that God, not humans, is the answer to the four "who" questions. In that case, Agur is stressing the mystery, inaccessibility, and power of God. He seems to be addressing an imaginary person, asking for a **name** and even the name of the child. Or perhaps this question refers to God and the "sons of God." There is no mistaking the irony in the very last line (as in Job 38:21). It has been proposed that the whole is a riddle, and the answer to it is: Israel, son of *yhwh* (an interpretation of Agur, son of Jakeh). See Skehan, *Studies*, pp. 42–43.

30:5–6 / These verses seem to be an instruction about God's **word,** with verse 5 being inspired by Psalm 18:30, and verse 6 following the admonition of Deuteronomy 4:2; 12:32. In context, this seems to be an assurance to any one upset by the words of Agur. God is indeed a mystery, but also a **shield,** and nothing is to be added **to his words.**

30:7–9 / A prayer, unique in the book, in the style of a numerical saying (cf. Job 13:20–21). The number is not to be taken strictly: **two** in verse 7 is followed by three in verse 8 and two more in verse 9. It is also possible to count two: removal of **lies** and granting of enough to live on (the middle way). **Before I die** means "as long as I live." Verse 9 describes the dangers that arise from having **too much** or too little—the motivation for the prayer.

30:10 / An admonition with motivational rationale. **Slander** of the NIV is too strong; that would be wrong in itself. The NJPS translates "inform," a neutral term, and the counsel is to mind one's own business. The fear of a **curse** is real (cf. 26:2). **Pay for it** (presumably a fine?) in the NIV is perhaps over specific. The Hebrew word means "be guilty." The only relation this verse has to the context is the catchword, curse.

30:11–14 / These verses are united by the fourfold repetition of Hebrew *dôr* ("generation," rendered in the NIV, **there are those** . . .) at the beginning of each verse. Four classes of wrongdoers are singled out for (implicit) condemnation: those who dishonor parents, hypocrites, the proud, and those who exploit the **poor.**

Additional Note §31

30:1 / Hb. grammar would call for the insertion of a gentilic *yod* to yield "the Massaite." Then "oracle" (Hb. *nᵉʾum*) is to be construed with "the man" (Hb. *haggeber*). The translations proposed for the rest of the verse are many, as can be seen from the survey by Whybray (*Composition*, p. 150, n. 3). These versions range from "There is no God . . ." to "I am not God . . ." There is simply no compelling translation. From the context (v. 2), it would seem that the beginning of the oracle must voice some desperation: weariness or weakness.

Numerical Sayings (Prov. 30:15–33)

This title is not found in the text, but it describes the form of the proverbs found here. The numerical proverb is a literary device found elsewhere in the Bible (e.g., Amos 1:3–2:6) and is usually expressed in the formula, X and X + 1, which dominates this section. But the numerical saying can also function with just a given number, as "four" in verses 24–28.

§32 Proverbs 30:15–33

30:15a / Verse 15a is a separate saying. Its place here is perhaps due to the number **two**, preceding **three** in verse 15b, and also because of the image of insatiability, which leads into verses 15b–16. The MT names the **daughters Give! Give! (they cry** is not in the MT). These are the suckers of this worm **(leech).**

30:15b–16 / A typical numerical saying in the X and X + 1 style describes **four** insatiable phenomena: **Sheol** (so NIV margin; cf. 27:20), which was viewed as Death that stalks human beings, the **womb** that has failed to deliver even one child (cf. Gen. 30:1), the **land** that never gets enough **water** in the ancient Near East, and finally the **fire** that depends upon fuel for existence. This seems to be merely a group of observations with no moral directly intended.

30:17 / Synthetic. See verse 11. The **eye** ("the lamp of the body," Matt. 6:22) seems to express the attitude of the total person. Perhaps it is chosen in view of the punishment inflicted by wild birds **(pecked out).** The NIV inexplicably puts the last two verbs in the passive voice.

30:18–19 / Another numerical proverb, on the 3/4 pattern, that singles out **four** marvels that surpass the sage's comprehension. All of them are united by the Hebrew word *derek* **(way),** and this must point to something in common to all. Following the lead of Wisdom 5:10–11, some argue that the common feature is the absence of any trace. This is inadequate for the last three examples. Others have seen the common element in the absence of any visible means of movement. But this pays no heed to the fourfold repetition of **way.** Rather, the point seems to lie in the mystery of the **way** that the **ship** traverses, the **snake** crawls, and the **eagle** flies. One cannot pinpoint these ways; there is something unknown, mysterious, about them. Similarly in the relationship between the sexes, there is the mysterious attraction behind the **way.** The point lies in the **way** to be traveled, not the way that leaves no trace. In all four instances, the **way** is not recoverable, but all four are marvels. One does not understand the **way** (perhaps the beginning and the end, but not the way). There is a mood of admiration and mystery about them all. What brought the **man** and the **maiden** together? The examples are not haphazardly chosen; they are from air, land, water, and a delicate human relationship. The mood is close to that of the Song of Songs.

30:20 / The NIV wisely separates this conclusion from the previous two verses because it is out of character with them. One may best understand this to be the reflection of a reader who interpreted the examples in verses 18–19 as indicating that no trace is left. Then the idea is applied to the conduct of an **adulteress** whose symbolic gesture removes traces (of an evil deed) and who claims to be innocent. This kind of observation obviously doesn't fit with the "marvels" of the previous saying, and it is also outside the 3/4 numbering, the pattern for the next three proverbs.

30:21–23 / Another numerical proverb in 3/4 style, with repetition of "under" and "when" (NIV, **who**) in the examples. The earth-shattering character of the **four** examples (two each of males and females), seems exaggerated. McKane *(Proverbs)* and others suspect a humorous intent. R. Van Leeuwen ("Proverbs 30:21–23 and the Biblical World Upside Down," *JBL* 105 [1986], pp. 599–610) understands this as a development of the topos, "the world upside down." The association of the physical with the social order is a given in OT thought (cf. Amos 1:2; 7:10, and Luke 1:52–53). The most serious example is the first in verse 22, as it suggests a revolution. The second example refers to a significant (and unwarranted, in the view of the sages) change in social status (cf. 28:19; 20:13). The final examples point to disorder in the household: the case of a **woman who is married** but is not loved (Gen. 29:31–35, Jacob and Leah). The case of a maid displacing her **mistress** is illustrated in Genesis 16:1–6 (Sarai and Hagar). These are all instances of things being topsy-turvy.

30:24–28 / The 3/4 pattern is broken, and a list of **four** creatures is given: **small,** but **extremely wise.** These are examples of various kinds of "wisdom" that can be learned from the conduct of insignificant animals. The **ant** proves that to be wise does not depend upon size; it is diligent and provides for its future (cf. 6:6–8). The **coney,** or badger, is small but it uses the crevices in rocky precipices for a safe home (cf. Ps. 104:18). Hordes of **locusts** wipe out crops, like an army, but with **no king** or leader. The **lizard** (or spider) is easily **caught,** but it can end up in unexpected places, such as **palaces.** The Hebrew style for these "parables" is quite expressive.

30:29–31 / Another numerical proverb in 3/4 style. The only certain items are the **lion,** whose **stately** stride is augmented by his irresistible power, and also the **king.** The translation of verse 31 is uncertain (see Additional Notes). Moreover, **three** items are mentioned without the usual description (as provided for the lion and, apparently, the king). The NIV is in general agreement with most other versions despite the uncertainty.

30:32–33 / An instruction presumably followed by a motivation **(for),** but the connection between the two verses is not clear. The advice given is to keep silent in the wake of unwise and scheming (NIV, **planned evil**) actions. Silence would seem called for *before* such actions, not after them. They are conditional **(if)** and perhaps they can be translated as "if you intend to play . . ." (so Meinhold, *Sprüche*). Verse 33 is characterized by a threefold repetition of "pressure" (on **milk, nose, anger**). If the final line is taken as the point of the comparisons (which are only implicit in the MT, which lacks the **as** of the NIV), the verse can be interpreted as reinforcing the command to be silent. See Additional Notes.

Additional Notes §32

30:29–31 / The translation of the first two words in v. 31 would be "girt of loins." But Hb. *zarzîr* is a *hapax legomenon* and is rendered as "rooster" in the LXX. Other guesses are: greyhound and warhorse. The MT has an inexplicable "or" before he-goat. Perhaps there is a corruption behind it. In v. 31b, Hb. *ʾalqûm* cannot mean "not rising up," but the various hypothetical readings that have been proposed have not achieved any consensus. The NIV appears to read the Hb. text as *lāqûm ʿal ʿammô*. The margin of the NIV follows the Vulgate understanding. See the discussion in McKane *(Proverbs)* and Plöger *(Sprüche)*. It would appear that three animals are compared to the **king**, the fourth item.

30:32–33 / The NIV translates the *hapax legomenon mîṣ* (probably "pressure") in three ways in order to bring out a viable meaning. Pressure upon **anger** (Hb. *ʾappayim*, a play on the word nose, *ʾap*, in the preceding phrase) only increases it and thus leads to **strife**.

The Sayings of Lemuel (Prov. 31:1–9)

The opening words indicate that a new collection appears. These sayings are clearly limited to verses 1–9, since an acrostic poem begins at verse 10. Moreover, they are a rare example of advice given by the queen mother to her son.

§33 Proverbs 31:1–9

31:1 / As in 30:1 (see the comment), "Massaite" should be read instead of **oracle** (see the NIV margin). The prestige and role of the queen mother in the ancient Near East was great. The role of women in society (and education) is not as prominent elsewhere in the OT as it is in Proverbs, although much can be inferred from other books.

31:2 / The MT has "what" (*mah*, see Additional Notes), rendered as **O** in the NIV. **Son of my vows** is not found elsewhere, and the paraphrase in the NIV margin seems to be inspired by Hannah in 1 Samuel 1:9–11. There may be an allusion to the meaning of Lemuel ("to God," that is, dedicated to God).

31:3 / A prohibition to Lemuel against frequenting (and over-indulging?) the harem. This is also an action that may have involved plots and intrigue. The NIV interprets the problematical text of verse 3b in parallelism with verse 3a, but several changes have been proposed (see Additional Notes).

31:4–7 / The subject is the use of alcohol. **Kings** and **rulers** are warned not to abuse it, lest they neglect the law and thus deny the **rights** of the **oppressed** (cf. Hos. 4:11). See the Additional Notes. The words of the queen mother continue with a different suggestion (vv. 6–7) for the use of alcohol. It should be provided for **those who are perishing** and **in anguish,** to help them **forget** their pitiable condition. The intention seems to proceed from pity, since justice has been insisted upon.

31:8–9 / The commands in verses 8–9 return to the ideals of justice expressed in verse 5, especially for those with special needs: (e.g., **those who cannot speak for themselves**). See Additional Notes.

Additional Notes §33

31:2 / Hb. *mah* ("what") of the MT has been interpreted as a negative, "No!" and as an imperative ("listen," Arabic). Others have followed the LXX, "what am I to say to you?" **Lemuel** (or v. 4, **Lemoel**) can be interpreted as the long form of Lael (Num. 3:24), "to God."

31:3 / **Vigor** of the NIV is an uncertain translation of the MT, which is normally "ways" (so NRSV), but it fits the parallelism. Hb. *lamᵉḥôt* seems to be revocalized in the NIV to yield "(female) destroyers of kings" (Hb. *lᵉmīḥôt*).

31:4 / **To crave** of the NIV interprets *ʾw* (Kethib; the Qere is *ʾy,* "where") as derived from Hb. *ʾwh,* "to desire."

31:8 / **Destitute** is an uncertain translation of "vanishing?"—the form is the infinitive construct of Hb. *ḥlp* ("change," "disappear"). Many other solutions have been proposed but uncertainty reigns (cf. McKane, *Proverbs,* pp. 411–12).

The Ideal Wife (Prov. 31:10–31)

An acrostic poem (vv. 10–31) is a rather surprising ending to a book that consists mainly of collections of sayings and it adds to the intriguing nature of this work. The Hebrew phrase, ʾēšet-ḥayil (cf. Ruth 3:11), "wife of noble character," has been rendered in many ways: *mulier fortis* (Vulgate), etc. Her qualities are described from a male point of view. But the description of the woman is such that no human being could possibly possess all these qualities. Hence many look to another level of meaning in the poem; cf. T. P. McCreesh, "Wisdom as Wife: Proverbs 31:10–31," *RB* 92 (1985), pp. 25–46; C. V. Camp, *Wisdom and the Feminine in the Book of Proverbs* (Sheffield; Almond, 1985), pp. 90–97.

§34 Proverbs 31:10–31

31:10–12 / **Who can find?** is a rhetorical question that suggests the answer—no one. Compare Job 28:20, where the question is used of personified Wisdom that is known only to God. Yet this woman is clearly "found." In 18:22 and 19:14, a wife is considered a gift from God. The comparison of personified Wisdom to precious jewels is often made: **rubies** in 3:15 (Qere) and 8:11 (cf. 18:19; 16:16). The fortunate **husband** (vv. 11–12) is noted again in verse 23 (prestige) and in verse 28 (his praise of her). His trust in her is magnified because of the gain **(lacks nothing of value)** she continually brings him.

31:13–22 / The portrayal of her energy and talents is really incredible. Verse 13 opens up as a description of her varied and expert activity for her **household** and others (the **poor**, v. 20). She spins **wool** to provide clothes (v. 13; cf. vv. 21–22). The comparison to **merchant ships** (v. 14) indicates that she is active in acquiring things beyond her immediate home circle. She is untiring and up early to provide for the **family** and **servants** (v. 15; cf. 27:27). Verse 16 indicates unusual responsibility, buying a **field** and planting a **vineyard** from the profits she makes. Verse 17 gives a picturesque description: "she girds her loins with strength"; vigor is her girdle (cf. Ps. 93:1). She "tastes" (v. 18; NIV, **sees**) **that her trading** yields profit (cf. the successful trading qualities of Wisdom in 3:14), and she works far into the **night.** Her active **hands** and **arms** are at work spinning wool (cf. v. 13) and also providing for the **needy** (vv. 19–20). Her **household** (v. 21) has no reason to fear the cold due to their **scarlet** (or double?) clothing. Verse 22 has her making covers for herself (not necessarily for the **bed,** but cf. 7:16) and also elegant clothing for her own person.

31:23–28 / Her husband's presence **at the city gate** indicates that he is among the **elders** who manage the affairs of the community (v. 23). Verse 24 picks up her industry and business acumen again (cf. vv. 15–16). Her true clothing is **strength and dignity** (v. 25); it is not surprising that she looks confidently to the future. **Wisdom** in verse 26 is parallel to *"tôrâ of ḥesed"* (perhaps "loving advice"), and the verse is expressed in chiasm. It has been pointed out by A. Wolters ("*Ṣôpiyyâ* [Prov 31:27] as Hymnic Participle and Play on *Sophia*," *JBL* 104 [1985], pp. 577–87) that in verse 27 the Hebrew word ("she watches over") sounds very much like the Greek word for wisdom (Hb. *ṣôpiyyâ* and Gk. *sophia*). This seems to be a deliberate play on words since it is the only time a participle is used to describe the woman's activity. This may be an indication of the date of the poem. The Greek language is taken for granted. If **bread of idleness** in verse 27b means merely that she is not lazy, that is flat and anticlimactic. Meinhold *(Sprüche)* interprets it to mean that laziness will not merit any food in her household (no work, no food). The praise of her entire family in verses 28–29 is well deserved.

31:29 / The words of praise are quoted, and there is an inclusion with verse 10 where she was described as a woman of *ḥayil* (hardly recognizable in the NIV, **noble things**).

31:30–31 / These verses are not part of the praise; they belong to the writer of the poem who ends with a generalization about the relative **beauty** and virtue and fear of **the LORD** (see Additional Notes). Meinhold *(Sprüche)* points out that verse 31 is a summary in which six of the seven words repeat terms used in the body of the poem. The acrostic poem has been called a coda (see McCreesh in Additional Notes) to the book of Proverbs. See the introduction for the relationship of this poem to personified Wisdom.

Additional Notes §34

31:15 / The NIV translates Hb. *ṭerep* as food (in light of the LXX, *brōmata*), although the word properly means "prey."

31:21 / The **scarlet** (so the MT) in the context of clothes in cold weather has raised some problems. The Vulgate apparently read *šᵉnayim* (double) for *šānîm* (scarlet), and the Gk. has "double coverings" in v. 22.

31:22 / The MT reads lit. "she makes covers for herself," and parallelism would indicate that this refers to her dress. Because of the only other occurrence of this rare word in 7:16, coverlet is also possible.

31:30 / Verse 30b is generally rendered as in the NIV (cf. NAB, NRSV). But the Masoretic vocalization of Hb. *yrʾt* suggests the feminine construct of Hb. *yirʾâ* (= the fear of). The customary adjectival translation seems to presuppose the feminine form of the adjective *yārēʾ*, which one would expect to be vocalized as *yᵉrēʾat* or *yᵉrēʾt*. "Fear of the Lord" was read by the Gk. ("an intelligent woman will be praised, but let her praise the fear of the Lord"). It is possible that the original reading was: woman, the fear of the Lord, she *(hyʾ)* is to be praised. The apposition of woman and fear of the Lord (the beginning of wisdom) would confirm the symbolism of the woman in vv. 10–31. Both Woman Wisdom (in 9:1–6) and Wisdom in 31:10–31 (where "house" occurs four times) are the mistress of a house! See the discussion by McCreesh, "Wife."

Ecclesiastes

Elizabeth Huwiler

Introduction: Ecclesiastes

Ecclesiastes and Other Biblical Texts

The book of Ecclesiastes[1] has a distinct voice among the texts of the Bible. No other text treats God so impersonally while at the same time giving significant attention to God and God's work. There are other texts in which, as in Ecclesiastes, God's behavior is enigmatic, approaching God is dangerous, God's will is difficult to discern, God is remote, or divine sovereignty is affirmed over human ability to effect outcomes. There are no other texts, however, in which all these concerns are combined, and in Ecclesiastes they are explored relentlessly.

The book addresses two principal questions. The first issue is whether human experience is meaningful, controllable, and predictable. The author judges that it is not. People are unable to put meaning into life, to discern a coherent pattern in their existence, or to control or even know what will happen to them. The only certainty in life is death. This judgment, however, need not lead to despair. The second question is whether human well-being is possible. To this, the author of Ecclesiastes, to whom we shall refer as Qohelet, offers an affirmative answer. It is possible to enjoy the pleasures of eating, drinking, working, and family. Thus, the two conclusions to these questions are in tension: life has no meaning, but it can still be enjoyed. There is a possibility of joy, but it exists only within the context of human limitations and the ultimate limitation, death.

Ecclesiastes is neither to be dismissed nor to be treated as though it contained the entire message of Scripture. The book has been particularly embraced by skeptics and dissenters within and outside the Jewish and Christian traditions, and it functions appropriately to challenge all easy certainties and attempts to manipulate God.

Ecclesiastes stands in contrast to most of the canon. There are no great stories of God's presence in the people's midst. Its assumptions about the fate of the just and the unjust, the wise and the fool, are certainly different from those expressed elsewhere in the OT. It is precisely that distinctiveness, however, that exemplifies the value of having a biblical canon: a collection of sacred texts rather than a single book. Qohelet affirms the concept of a time for everything. If one accepts that claim, surely there is a time for not only the ancestral stories of Genesis, the holy songs of the Psalms, and the bold proclamation of the prophets, but also the relentless questioning of Qohelet.

Ecclesiastes and the Biblical Wisdom Tradition

Ecclesiastes fits within the wisdom corpus of the OT, along with Proverbs and Job; if one includes apocryphal/deuterocanonical books, then Sirach (Ecclesiasticus) and the Wisdom of Solomon may be added. The wisdom books contain observations and interpretations of human life and behavior, along with advice on how to live. They are characterized by a tendency to contrast positive and negative persons and qualities, using a distinctive vocabulary (e.g., wise/fool; diligent/lazy; righteous/wicked; intelligent/simple). Proverbs, Job, and Ecclesiastes do this without making direct reference to the great events of Israel's history (such as Exodus, covenant with Moses, settlement in the land, establishment of davidic dynasty). Nor do they express an expectation that God will intervene in a decisive way in the future. In the later books (Sirach and Wisdom of Solomon) wisdom begins to make connections with the persons and events of Israelite history.

Wisdom is also characterized by distinctive forms, such as saying, instruction, parable (or brief exemplary story), and alphabetic acrostic. These forms are most clearly evident in the book of Proverbs; Qohelet uses similar sayings and stories, but incorporates them into extended treatments that are not exactly instruction but more reflective essay.

The wisdom tradition is frequently described as having two branches, variously described as practical and speculative, secular and theological, or optimistic and skeptical. In the Bible, practical/optimistic wisdom is most clearly identified with the book of Proverbs, and speculative/skeptical wisdom with Job and Ecclesiastes.

The goal of traditional wisdom is to pass on what one has learned, both from instruction and from observation and experience; it is thus an educational enterprise. Like the other wisdom books, Ecclesiastes contains observations and interpretations of human life and behavior along with advice on proper behavior. It combines overall concerns with God, the created world, and discovering what is good in human existence with practical advice about enjoying life and avoiding unnecessary trouble, especially from superiors.

It is clear that Qohelet was familiar with the wisdom tradition and spoke in its language. The author works with polar opposites such as righteous and wicked, good and bad, wisdom and folly, and uses wisdom forms such as the "better" saying (for examples see "Genre and Forms," below). Wisdom methodology is evident as well. Qohelet quotes traditional claims, observes the world and human experience, and reflects on those claims on the basis of observation and evaluation. Yet Ecclesiastes differs from traditional wisdom, as exemplified in Proverbs, in important ways. Traditional wisdom seeks evidence that supports its claims and tends toward harmonizing diverse observations. Qohelet takes a more confrontive approach, placing claims and observations over against each other, looking for the exception rather than the general rule. If Proverbs provides guidance for coping with typical or ideal experience, Ecclesiastes explores the atypical and even disastrous.

The issue of retribution (or the relationship between behavior and outcome) is important throughout wisdom. Proverbs consistently assumes that positive behavior results in positive outcomes, while negative behavior produces negative outcomes. Specific results may vary: positive behavior may correlate with material wealth, physical longevity, or spiritual or emotional well-being. Nonetheless, in Proverbs some positive relationship is always affirmed. In Ecclesiastes, this relationship is called into question and sometimes even denied: the wise and the foolish share the same fate (2:14–16); the righteous may get what the wicked deserve and vice versa (8:14). Qohelet occasionally affirms traditional claims, but when doing so he qualifies them; see, for example, 7:11–12 on the benefits of wisdom, and 8:12 on fearing God.

Wisdom itself is a thematic concern in Ecclesiastes; not surprisingly, it is dealt with paradoxically. The speaker claims to have more wisdom than any predecessor (1:16), but admits "wisdom was beyond me" (7:23); calls wisdom a good thing (7:11), yet admits that it is possible to be too wise (7:16); and says that wisdom is better than strength and weapons, while observing that wisdom can be ineffective (9:16–18). Throughout all of this, wisdom as a concept is brought to the foreground and explored relentlessly. On the one hand, wisdom is good and profitable; on the other, wisdom is not always effective in the short term, and makes no difference in one's ultimate fate. Like the sages of Proverbs, then, Qohelet seeks to affirm a preference for wisdom and other virtues; unlike them, Qohelet acknowledges that there is no lasting benefit and then continues to pursue the exploration.

Ecclesiastes and Non-Israelite Wisdom Texts

Both practical and reflective wisdom are found not only in the Bible but also in the surrounding world. Biblical wisdom has affinities with that of other ancient Near Eastern societies; Ecclesiastes most strongly resembles texts from Egypt and Mesopotamia, although there is no text that matches it precisely in either genre or content. The Egyptian and Mesopotamian wisdom traditions go back thousands of years before the book of Ecclesiastes was written. One cannot claim with any certainty that Qohelet had access to any of the specific texts, although the possibility exists. What these parallels do demonstrate is that Qohelet addressed issues that were part of the intellectual heritage of the region.

A few texts resemble Ecclesiastes closely enough to be mentioned specifically.[2] The speaker in an Egyptian tale, "A Dispute over Suicide," from the end of the third millennium B.C.E., debates the relative value of life and death in internal dialogue; Ecclesiastes too questions life and death, and the Hebrew is marked by repeated addresses to the speaker's heart. "The Protests of the Eloquent Peasant," another Egyptian tale from around the twenty-first century B.C.E., incorporates traditional sayings into a narrative critique of social injustice. A Mesopotamian poem, "I Will Praise the Lord of Wisdom," from around 1100 B.C.E., laments the impossibility of knowing how to please one's god. In another Mesopotamian poem, "The Babylonian Theodicy," one speaker claims that although it is possible to find out how to satisfy the deities, no one knows how to do it. In addition, the Mesopotamian corpus contains a poem, "The Dialogue of Pessimism," in which a servant demonstrates the ability to argue both sides of any issue the master raises. Perhaps the most striking parallel comes in the Old Babylonian version of "The Epic of Gilgamesh." It is in the context of Gilgamesh's grief over the death of his friend Enkidu and his first fear that he may be mortal, that the ale-wife Siduri advises him,

> Thou, Gilgamesh, let full be thy belly,
> Make thou merry by day and by night.
> Of each day make thou a feast of rejoicing,
> Day and night dance thou and play!
> Let thy garments be sparkling fresh,
> Thy head be washed; bathe thou in water.
> Pay heed to the little one that holds on to thy hand,
> Let thy spouse delight in thy bosom!
> For this is the task of [mankind]![3]

In this striking parallel to Ecclesiastes 9:7–10, Siduri approaches Qohelet's insistence on facing the reality of death as well as living the pleasures of life in this world. The above call to joy happens when Gilgamesh first encounters death and before his failed search for immortality. This placement limits its power for the reader. One longs for a resumption of the call after Gilgamesh has realized that he, too, is inescapably mortal. In context, the call to joy in Gilgamesh pushes the reader to experience joy as a stage in the hero's experience. Qohelet, by contrast, returns to the call to joy after each successive disillusionment, thus maintaining the paradox as central to human experience.

Most interpreters agree that Ecclesiastes belongs within a Greek-influenced worldview and a few even argue that it represents an early attempt to do Greek-style philosophy in the Hebrew language. Parallels with various Greek philosophical traditions such as stoicism, epicureanism, and cynicism have been suggested. The parallels, however, are not so close as to make acquaintance with specific Greek texts likely. It is more likely that Ecclesiastes simply reflects a Hellenistic milieu; at least, its concerns with happiness, meaning, and the good in human life are also popular in Greek philosophical movements.

Repetitions and Their Function

"Hebel" *Pronouncements.* The book of Ecclesiastes begins and ends with the judgment that everything is *hebel* (1:2; 12:8). Between these two general statements, Qohelet examines various human behaviors and elements of the human condition, concluding after each that it is to be judged *hebel.* The precise meaning of the word in Ecclesiastes is difficult. Although the NIV usually translates it as "meaningless," the most frequent translation remains the traditional "vanity"; other possibilities include "futility"; "breath"; "absurd."[4] The concrete meaning of the word is "vapor, mist"; it is also the proper name of Abel (Gen. 4). In Ecclesiastes, *hebel* is sometimes used with a specific referent: "everything" (1:2; 3:19; 12:8); "all the things done under the sun" (1:14) or "the work that is done under the sun" (2:17); "much dreaming and many words" (5:7); the few and shadowy days of human life (6:12); Qohelet's life (7:15); the life of the reader (9:9); "everything to come" (11:8); "youth and vigor" (11:10). More often, though, it is used in the summary "this too is meaningless" (2:1, 15, 19, 21, 23, 26; 4:4, 8, 16; 5:10; 6:9; 7:6; 8:10, 14), describing a situation or the conclusion Qohelet draws from it. "Chasing after wind" sometimes joins and sometimes replaces "this too is meaningless."

The repeated "this too" functions to build up evidence that enables the reader, skeptical of the motto at the beginning, to accept it at the conclusion. Thus in 2:19, "this too is meaningless" refers to the fact that another person, who may be wise or a fool, will inherit the proceeds of the speaker's toil, and in 2:21 it pronounces the verdict over the general situation of inequity in reward; in 2:23 the motto seems to refer to the distress associated with work.

In many cases, it is difficult to be sure of the scope of the reference. The use of *hebel* in 2:1 could refer either to pleasure itself or to the experiment with pleasure; it could refer in 2:15 to wisdom, the gain of being wise, or the fact that the fool and the wise share the same fate.

The word thus has varying nuances in different contexts within Ecclesiastes. With that understood, "meaningless" is an appropriate translation, although the careful reader will observe specific instances in which meaning is not entirely the issue.

Several sub-themes contribute to the overall conclusion of *hebel.* All people, regardless of virtue or vice, share a common fate of death and oblivion (2:14–16; in 3:19 this is extended to animals as well). Labor can be drudgery (2:17, 23). People work for profits that they cannot count on keeping or passing on to heirs (2:19–21, 26). Achievement springs from envy (4:4). Even people whose work results in wealth may be unsatisfied (4:8; 5:10). Rewards and punishments in this life do not correspond with merit (8:9–14). Humans ultimately lack the certainty for which they long (3:11; 6:11–12).

Affirmations of pleasure. In counterpoint to the relentless insistence on *hebel* is a series of affirmations of joy or pleasure (Hb. *śimḥâ*) in human existence—in eating, drinking, working, loving (2:24–26; 3:22; 5:18–20; 8:15; 9:7–10; 11:7–8). Qohelet repeatedly announces what is good in human life; these announcements regularly include the enjoyment of food and drink, and sometimes other elements (e.g., work, life with a beloved woman). The commendations of pleasure vary; some state that enjoyment simply is good, while others use the less restrained "there is nothing better," and a few actively call the reader to enjoy life.

Such positive expressions most often occur in complicated contexts that also include some negatives. These commendations of pleasure serve multiple functions. They provide some balance for the frequent "meaningless" judgments and underscore Qohelet's conviction that there is some good in life. At the same time, they qualify and restrict that goodness, putting it into the context of human limitations.

A particular challenge for interpreters is the fact that Qohelet clings tenaciously to both claims: all life is *hebel,* and yet joy is both possible and good. It is important not to make one of these claims the only message of the book and dismiss the other as either a distraction or a grudging qualification. Qohelet insists on both, and often in the same passage. Thus any interpretation that attempts to separate them or exclude one is a distortion.

Wisdom. Qohelet uses the vocabulary common to wisdom literature. References to wisdom, knowledge, understanding, seeking, and finding occur frequently, and are often used with negatives (not know, not find). Like other wisdom texts, Qohelet deals in polar opposites, such as the fool and the wise person. Another favored pair of opposites is good and bad. "Good" appears repeatedly in the affirmations of pleasure and the "better" sayings. "Bad" (the Hebrew root r^{cc}) also occurs frequently and is sometimes translated "evil" or "unpleasant." Because this Hebrew word is used both with and without moral connotations, the reader should question the adequacy of "evil" as a translation.

Money, Profit, Inheritance. Qohelet expresses a striking portion of the book's argument in language that has to do with wealth or commerce. Although the wording of the NIV conveys much of the vocabulary of finance and ownership (money, wealth, possessions, inheritance), the translation sometimes obscures this milieu. The opening question, "What does man gain from all his labor at which he toils under the sun?" (1:3), uses a financial term for "gain" (Hb. *yitrôn*; also in 2:11, 15; 3:9; 5:9, 16; 7:12; 10:10, 11). In the enigmatic investigation of 7:23–29, Qohelet may be seeking to find the "balance" rather than the "scheme" (7:25, 27). Seow notes seven general terms having to do with wealth and possessions, and eleven words that belong specifically to a business milieu.[5] Readers should be alert for words such as "advantage," "lack," and "lot," all of which have specialized financial meanings that are at least in the background in their use in Ecclesiastes.

This is not to say that Qohelet's only concern is financial. Clearly the investigation involves all of human life. It is, however, significant that Qohelet describes both tangible and intangible outcomes in the language of finance and commerce more frequently than, for example, in the parlance of agriculture or the royal court. The book makes the most sense in a milieu in which this financial language would resonate.

Contrasts and Contradictions

Ecclesiastes contains expressions that are contradictory from one section to another, and even within a single section. For example, in 4:2 Qohelet claims, "I declared that the dead, who had already died, are happier than the living, who are still alive." But in 9:4, "Anyone who is among the living has hope—even a live dog is better off than a dead lion!" "Wisdom is better than folly . . . the same fate overtakes them both [wise and fool]" (2:13–14).

Interpreters have dealt with these tensions in the following three principal ways:

(1) Some claim that Qohelet wrote a thoroughly skeptical document to which one or more pious redactors added some traditional views. If this is the case, the redactor(s) did a rather poor

job: the book is still quite challenging. In addition, the book without the more orthodox expressions does not hold together well.

(2) Others suggest that Qohelet quotes traditional wisdom only in order to refute it. If this is true, one might wish that Qohelet had taken care to mark the quotations in some consistent way. In addition, even some of the "traditional" expressions use Qohelet's favorite vocabulary. Thus it is more likely that the text reflects authentic struggling with complex issues.

(3) A third understanding is that Qohelet's views encompass, and even grow out of, the contradictions. This is probably closest to the truth. Indeed, the recognition of contradictions in life (as well as between values and experiences) is part of what leads to the overall judgment of meaninglessness.[6]

The anguish of Qohelet's investigation of life is knowing that the following two observations about life are true at the same time: On the one hand, the advantage of wisdom in life is real, but wisdom must exist in the limited context of a human lifetime. On the other hand, the common fate of life is also real and is enhanced only by how well one spends the time one has.

With no other biblical book is the danger of citing individual verses out of context so clear. Qohelet deals with tensions and contradictions and repeatedly offers competing views. Quoting one side of a tension without acknowledging the other leads to serious distortion. The reader is challenged to allow the competing claims to be heard, and to find truth in their clash.

Unity and Structure

There is no consensus about either the unity or the structure of the book of Ecclesiastes. Most recent treatments agree that with the exception of the superscription (1:1) and the epilogue (12:9–14), it is difficult to make confident claims of more than one author. In this commentary, it is assumed that the pre-existing materials, whatever they may have been, now function as part of the final work and that Qohelet is the speaker of 1:2–12:8.

A recent, influential attempt to define strict structural elements of the book is that of Addison Wright.[7] Wright argues that the book falls into two major sections of 111 verses each (1:1–6:9 and 6:10–12:14), for a total of 222 verses, or six times the numerical value of the key word *hebel*. Units in the first half of the book are marked by a *hebel*-formula, and those in the second half by either "find/not find" (chs. 7–8) or "not know" (chs. 9–12). Without the epilogue the book contains 216 verses, which happens to be the numerical equivalent of the motto in 1:2 and 12:8 (NIV "Meaningless! Meaningless! Utterly meaningless!").

Although Wright's proposal has been influential enough to determine the organization of the New American Bible, it has not convinced most commentators. Aside from technical problems,[8] it is a bit too neat to express the thought of the book. The suspicious reader may conclude that if there are number games in the book, Qohelet may have skewed them so that the book (like human existence, in Qohelet's view) does not finally "add up," thus reinforcing the insistence that human beings do not know and cannot find out.

It is likely, as Wright asserts, that the repeated phrases function at times to mark structural units of the book. They do not, however, always occur at major thematic breaks. A cluster of several such repeated phrases is especially likely to indicate a transition, particularly when followed by a phrase that indicates a new beginning. But even this is difficult; Qohelet often doubles back to pick up a theme that has already been treated. Although the style is basically exposition, the text is not organized in strict paragraphs. Transitional segments may be equally plausibly connected with either what precedes or what follows.

There is an additional complication in Qohelet's use of repetitions or refrain lines that might be considered structural markers. The majority of repeated expressions make negative evaluations of specific experiences or of the human experience in general: "this too is meaningless (and pursuit of wind) (and a grievous evil)"; "no one knows" (or "one does not know," or "cannot find"). Yet one of the repetitions, usually the most elaborate, is the affirmation of joy or pleasure. Interpreters who use refrain lines to indicate the structure of the book have difficulty giving equal emphasis to the negative evaluations and to the positive call. The choice of divisions, then, is not only debatable but also gives weight to a particular interpretive option.

Section breaks in this commentary do not necessarily follow those of the NIV. Rather, breaks are indicated only after verses that express the ambivalence of the book as a whole, and before verses that indicate a new beginning, through a change formula (e.g., "I turned and I saw") or a formal change. This division into sections is somewhat provisional and does itself imply an interpretive direction: it foregrounds the speaker's ambivalence. By breaking sections at these points, this commentary does not allow either side of Qohelet's ambivalence to be lost. Neither the admission that all is meaningless nor the insistence that joy is possible maintains dominance.

The difficulty one experiences in attempting to follow the speaker's thought is related to the theme of the book itself. Because Qohelet experiences life as finally incoherent, it is appropriate that the reader too should struggle with the question of form and meaning. If indeed Qohelet's failed quest in 7:23–29 (especially 7:27–28) is taken seriously, it suggests that in Qohelet's attempts to make sense of the universe, things don't add up. It is appropriate that Qohelet's expression of human experience is communicated in a book in which the overall structure is at least enigmatic and perhaps incomprehensible.

Genre and Forms

The book as a whole does not fit easily into a single category. One might call it a reflective essay, but such a label is not much help; the book presents a unique genre within the Bible.

Ecclesiastes does, however, use forms that are known from biblical and extrabiblical sources. The experiment beginning in 1:12 in which Qohelet adopts the persona of Solomon (see "Speaker and Audience," below) has affinities with the extrabiblical royal testament.[9]

The type of wisdom saying that occurs most frequently in Ecclesiastes is the "better" saying (of the form "X is better than Y," as in Prov. 8:19, or "X with A is better than Y with B," as in Prov. 15:16–17), which frequently functions as a kind of values clarification. Qohelet uses and modifies the form, most extensively in 7:1–11 and 9:16–10:1, to make both traditional and surprising, and even contrasting, claims.

Qohelet's speech is also characterized by the use of rhetorical questions. Typically, a positive rhetorical question anticipates a negative answer and a negative one anticipates a positive answer. Thus the obvious answer to the question, "Who knows?" is "No one." Understanding this aspect of the text is essential to perceiving the strength of Qohelet's claims.

Translators do not agree on which parts of the book are poetry and which are prose. The NIV uses poetry more extensively than do most translations (that is, the NIV prints in lines material that most versions print in paragraphs). Distinguishing biblical poetry from prose is a matter of judgment, and the reader who compares translations need not be disturbed by the discrepancy. Like other Hebrew poetry found in the OT, most verses in Ecclesiastes can be divided into two or three lines of similar length that are often in a parallel relationship. However, unlike most Hebrew poetry, the text of Ecclesiastes lacks features such as the loss of particles and a general compression of speech.

It is also important to keep in mind that while the book is not a narrative overall, it does have a narrative aspect. A process of investigation and reflection is followed throughout the book: sometimes Qohelet comes to tentative conclusions which are questioned in the next stage of the investigation. One must therefore be careful with judgments introduced with "I said" or "I thought" or the use of evaluative or emotional judgments in narrative context. For example, "I hated life" (2:17) is not a permanent conclusion that life is hateful but a description of the speaker's state of mind at one particular stage of exploration; it in turn is called into question by the following affirmation of joy.

Date, Author, and Setting

Because of a lack of references to identifiable events, the date of Ecclesiastes is determined by internal linguistic and formal evidence combined with external references to it. The language overall is decidedly unusual in the Bible, which leads to a variety of conclusions: the book may reflect a dialect otherwise unattested, foreign influence, or even translation from a non-Hebrew original. The occurrence of Persian loanwords in the text suggests a date during the postexilic period; there is no evidence of such loanwords earlier.[10] Many readers note similarities in vocabulary and syntax to the Mishnah. This perhaps suggests that it is one of the latest books in the Hebrew Bible.[11] The book of Sirach (about 200 B.C.E.) includes apparent references to Ecclesiastes interspersed with those to other books of the Hebrew Scriptures. Thus the book must have been known and used by the time Sirach was written.

With these considerations in mind, most interpreters conclude that the book fits most naturally into the postexilic period. Interpreters who emphasize the similarity of Qohelet's concerns with those of Greek philosophy and the lateness of known references to Ecclesiastes date it in the Hellenistic period, while those who emphasize the existence of Persian but not Greek loanwords consider the Persian period more likely. Either of these is possible.

If a postexilic date is correct, the author cannot be Solomon, as is hinted in 1:1 and 1:12. The author was, however, familiar with the wisdom tradition which is associated with Solomon and works within that tradition. Most interpreters make little attempt to distinguish author from speaker, except in the superscription and epilogue. For further discussion of the speaker, see below.

The place of composition is difficult to determine. Such passages as 5:1 [MT 4:17], 8:10, and perhaps 3:16 imply access to the temple. Familiarity with wisdom traditions not reflected elsewhere in the Bible have led some to suggest authorship outside Palestine. The peculiarities of the language in Ecclesiastes have led to numerous conflicting suggestions, none of them substantiated.[12] I will suppose that Ecclesiastes was written in the vicinity of Jerusalem but recognize that this is not certain.

Speaker and Audience

Qohelet is the speaker of the book, except for the superscription (1:1) and epilogue (12:9–14). The latter identifies Qohelet as a sage and teacher of the people as well as a compiler and refiner of proverbs.

In 1:12–2:26 Qohelet adopts the persona of a king over Jerusalem, no doubt Solomon (although the reference to "all who reigned before me in Jerusalem" is a bit odd for Solomon). Aside from the superscription, Solomon is not implied elsewhere in the book. There are no references to experiences and events known about Solomon's life. There is no "inside track" on the monarchy; in fact, kings are described from a distance and as considerably more powerful than either the speaker or the addressees. For these reasons, most interpreters consider the royal claim part of a fictive persona that was useful for only one section of the book.

The speaker responds compassionately to the oppression of the poor, yet describes it as something seen, not as something experienced. In fact, aside from 1:12–2:26 and 7:23–29, Qohelet's first-person references describe observations rather than activities or experiences. The subjects involved in action are God, the addressees, unidentified third-person individuals, types (wise, fool) or humans generally, but never the speaker.

The personal complaint described in the text is not about a lack of material goods but is about the fear that those goods will go to another. Thus the reader imagines someone in socially and financially comfortable circumstances. Implicit is the leisure to study and reflect in the wisdom tradition.

The speaker is certainly male. This is suggested primarily by the family references (son, brother, wife/woman whom you love) and by the fact that the speaker displays a keen sense of systemic oppression but nowhere mentions the situation of women in that system. References to financial insecurity, for example, do not mention widows or divorcees, even though in Israelite culture the financial situation of these women would have been insecure.

The audience whom the speaker is addressing is directly indicated by second-person speech in the body of the book only in 5:1–8; 7:9–22; 8:2–3; 9:7–10; 10:4; 10:20–11:1; and 11:9–12:1. The second-person speech in 12:12–13 is in the epilogue and thus not part of the speaker's audience. Second-person speech is also used in internal dialogue and in apostrophes to unnamed countries. These references suggest a variety of audiences. These include those who might enter the presence of the king, see official oppression in the provinces, enter the temple, take vows, have servants, choose righteous or wicked behavior, and be engaged in agriculture or commerce. The addressee of 9:9 is implicitly male ("your wife") and of 11:9 explicitly young. From the content of the book, readers might also infer that the addressees are concerned with gaining and preserving wealth, with the disposition of their assets after their lifetimes, and with the meaning of life.

The implied readers, then, are young Israelite men who are living at better than subsistence level, probably in or near Jerusalem. They might include government officials, businessmen, and farm owners. If, as many suggest, the royal (and later provincial) court was the milieu for the development and transmission of wisdom texts, junior members of the bureaucracy may be the principal audience.

Canonization and History of Interpretation

Although the canonical or inspired status of Ecclesiastes was discussed by the rabbis (who recognized and were bothered by the book's internal contradictions), there is no record of a serious challenge to its place in the Jewish or Christian Bibles. Within Jewish tradition, it is one of the five festal scrolls and is read at the feast of Tabernacles. Tabernacles, also called Sukkot, Booths, or Ingathering, is one of the three major pilgrim festivals and celebrates the autumn harvest. Reading Ecclesiastes at Tabernacles, a particularly joyful festival, both highlights the affirmations of pleasure in the book and ensures that even a joyful festival maintains awareness of the brevity and limitations of human existence.

Both Christian and Jewish interpreters assumed Solomonic authorship until modern times. Traditional Jewish exegesis tended toward harmonizing Ecclesiastes with the Torah; traditional Christian interpretation used the "meaningless" theme either to urge asceticism or to focus attention away from this world and toward the next.

A curious fact of English publishing history attests to the continuing fascination with the book: Ecclesiastes and Proverbs were the first two books of the Bible to be published in English.[13]

The Theology of Ecclesiastes

The book of Ecclesiastes never uses the distinctive Hebrew name of God, Yahweh, but always the generic term Elohim (used both with and without the definite article). Neither do we find other Israelite or pre-Israelite epithets such as El Elyon or El Shaddai. There are no clear metaphors for the deity, such as rock or shepherd (except perhaps in the epilogue, 12:11). Nor is there any use of pronoun suffixes with the word for God: Qohelet does not refer to "my God," "your God," or "our God." There is, however, a likely reference to "your Creator" in 12:1.

Qohelet presents God as creator, provider, and judge. God makes everything (11:5), and made everything beautiful in its time (3:11). But God made some things crooked (7:13), good and bad times (7:14), and people upright (7:29). God gives humans burdens (1:13; 3:10), the ability to eat and find enjoyment (2:24–26; 5:19), the days of one's life (5:18; 8:15), wealth and possessions (5:19; 6:2), occupation (5:20), and spirit or breath (12:7). God judges both positively and negatively. God will call the past to account (3:15), tests people (3:18), takes no pleasure in fools (5:4), becomes angry (5:6), favors taking appropriate enjoyment in life (9:7), and will bring the reader to judgment (11:9). God considers some people good and others sinners (7:26).

God is also incomprehensible, distant, and awesome. People cannot fathom what God has done (3:11). God is in heaven and the reader on earth (5:2). The appropriate attitude before God is reverence (3:14; 7:18, 26; 8:12).

What can readers then conclude about God as described by Qohelet? First, Qohelet clearly believes in God. The speaker is not a modern with the option of atheism or agnosticism; that God exists, and has control, is assumed throughout the book. Qohelet is also a thorough monotheist: bad or unfortunate events and experiences are not explained away by blaming them on a malevolent deity in conflict with a benevolent one. Beyond that, God is a mystery, unknowable, and certainly uncontrollable. In fact, the central claim of the book, that human experience is meaningless, is directly related to the impossibility of understanding what God is doing.

Qohelet goes beyond merely expressing a state of confusion by noting that God's behavior is problematic. The problem is that God is not carrying out justice, at least not in a timely fashion. The idea that divine justice can be challenged is not unique to Qohelet. There are the words of Abraham, "Far be it from you to do such a thing—to kill the righteous with the wicked, treating the righteous and the wicked alike. Far be it from you! Will not the Judge of all the earth do right?" (Gen. 18:25). There are also the laments that call God to live up to the covenant (e.g., Ps. 89). What is different (and disturbing) in Ecclesiastes is that this is not a complaint to God but a complaint about God. The relationship assumed by Abraham and the psalmist is not operative for Qohelet.

Qohelet's theology has other points of continuity with the biblical tradition. Qohelet assumes without question that God is in control, affirms that life is better for those with whom God is pleased than for those God considers sinners, and acknowledges that all aspects of life are gifts of God. Qohelet, however, includes in the discussion problematic aspects of all these affirmations. He acknowledges a transcendent and incomprehensible God. Although other strains of the biblical tradition also emphasize transcendence, nowhere else is the human inability to understand God and to know what will be pleasing to God emphasized so starkly.

The Relevance of Ecclesiastes

People of faith in every age have found the book of Ecclesiastes relevant. It maintains its traditional value, but in addition is particularly appropriate for our current cultural situation. Ours is a pluralistic age. Western culture generally and American culture in particular continue to grapple with materialism. Postmodernism offers the awareness that our knowledge is at best provisional and that access to the fullness of truth is simply not available to humans. For all of these, Qohelet is a resource in at least seven ways:

(1) In every age, Christians and Jews have had to come to terms with their relation to the tradition. Ecclesiastes stands within the tradition while daring to challenge its easy answers. It affirms divine sovereignty and theoretical retribution. It insists with tradition that an afterlife cannot be counted on. Further, it accepts some common motifs of Israelite wisdom. Finally, it expresses reverence toward God. It challenges the tradition by questioning practical retribution and the ability of humans to know the will of God.

(2) The current cultural situation, especially in North America and Europe, calls for re-examination of the relationship between the individual and the community. In Ecclesiastes, issues of the individual predominate although they are issues regarding the individual's struggle to live within, and moreover to have an effect on, the life of the community. Individual well-being is not subsumed under the good of the group, and yet individual well-being is not enough if the community is awry.

(3) Although other books in the Scriptures may help us to live as God's people in the world, Ecclesiastes is a guide to living faithfully in a world in which God is problematic. No doubt everyone who has a living relationship with a living God goes through times when God is incomprehensible. Certainly anyone in the work of ministry will encounter people in anguish whose pain is partly directed toward God. In this context, it is a great blessing to have Ecclesiastes. Here is a message—canonically sanctioned, no less—that there is a possibility of trying to live faithfully, of working out one's role in creation, even when God is experienced as distant.

(4) The book reflects a pluralistic milieu: Israelite traditions (mostly wisdom but also monarchy and cult) are both utilized and called into question. Egyptian and Mesopotamian skeptical wisdom traditions provide some context. Ideas of Greek philosophy may hover in the background. In our own increasingly pluralistic world, it is helpful to see an ancient Israelite attempt to deal with a similarly pluralistic context by incorporating and critiquing internal traditions along with those of the surrounding cultures.

(5) Ecclesiastes says more in a direct fashion about greed and the interference of greed with happiness than any other biblical book. The book appears to belong to a setting in which work is too often toil rather than calling and is engaged in for the sake of its rewards. Qohelet repeatedly reminds his audience that working and striving can forestall the happiness they are meant to enable.

(6) Ecclesiastes states more emphatically and more consistently than any other biblical book that human access to truth and knowledge is limited. The provisional nature of human knowledge, a commonplace of postmodernism, is pushed to an extreme in Ecclesiastes.

(7) Like many postmodern texts, Ecclesiastes seems in ways to be a puzzle. There may be some numerological games, particularly with the number thirty-seven (the numerical value of *hebel*), and yet the numbers don't quite add up.[14] The end of chapter 7 hints toward wisdom personified but never quite makes her explicit. It is as though Qohelet wants the reader to struggle to figure out a complicated puzzle to which there is, after all, no solution.

In all of these areas, Ecclesiastes is a resource for people of our own time that turn to the Bible as source or resource. When facing an issue that appears to be "something new under the sun," we see in Qohelet a person who faced the same dilemma long ago, in the ages before us.

Notes

---

1. Ecclesiastes is the traditional rendition of the Hb. *qōhelet*. This is derived from the Gk. translation of *qōhelet*, which is *ekklēsiastēs*, "preacher" or "speaker" to assemblies. In this commentary, Ecclesiastes is used to refer to the book and Qohelet to refer to its speaker and author.

2. For a collection of non-Israelite wisdom texts, see *ANET*. Texts mentioned here are found on pp. 72–99, 405–10, 503–7, and 596–604.

3. *ANET*, p. 90.

4. "Vanity" remains the most common translation, and is the usual choice for NRSV; NAB; J. L. Crenshaw, *Ecclesiastes: A Commentary* (OTL; Philadelphia: Westminster, 1987); R. Gordis, *Koheleth: The Man and His World, A Study of Ecclesiastes* (3d ed.; New York: Schocken, 1968);

R. E. Murphy, *Ecclesiastes* (WBC 23; Waco: Word, 1992); and C.-L. Seow, *Ecclesiastes: A New Translation with Introduction and Commentary* (AB 18C; Garden City, N.Y.: Doubleday, 1997). "Futility" is in NJPS, REB, NJB. "Breath" is used by R. B. Y. Scott, *Proverbs, Ecclesiastes: A New Translation with Introduction and Commentary,* (AB 18; Garden City, N.Y.: Doubleday, 1965). "Absurdity" is preferred by M. V. Fox, who argues that the use of *hebel* by Qohelet is a near equivalent to "absurd" as used by A. Camus (*Qohelet and His Contradictions* [JSOTSup 71; Sheffield: Almond, 1989]).

    5. Seow, *Ecclesiastes,* pp. 21–23.

    6. For an expanded treatment, see Fox, *Qohelet,* pp. 18–28.

    7. A. G. Wright's analysis forms the basis for his own commentary, "Ecclesiastes (Qoheleth)," in *NJBC,* pp. 489–95. The technical basis is explained more thoroughly in his articles, "The Riddle of the Sphinx: The Structure of the Book of Qoheleth," *CBQ* 30 (1968), pp. 313–34; "The Riddle of the Sphinx Revisited: Numerical Patterns in the Book of Qoheleth," *CBQ* 42 (1980), pp. 38–51; "Additional Numerical Patterns in Qoheleth," *CBQ* 45 (1983), pp. 32–43.

    8. The pattern depends on the verse numbering system, which dates only to the middle ages. Many of the verse divisions are sensible ones, but not all are at the end of sentences or other obvious breaking places. Wright makes a great deal of the fact that the numerical value of *hebel* is 37, and forms of the word *hebel* occur 38 times in the body of the book. His assumption is that one of these crept into the text as an error of transmission.

    9. Several Egyptian instructions with kings as speakers have been labeled "royal testaments." They differ most clearly from Ecclesiastes in their subject matter, which always relates to governance (Seow, pp. 98–99).

    10. Seow's treatment of the language of Qohelet is very thorough, with detailed discussion of previous proposals and extrabiblical usage (*Ecclesiastes,* pp. 11–21). He is one of few recent interpreters who insist on a date in the Persian period.

    11. See especially R. N. Whybray, *Ecclesiastes: Based on the Revised Standard Version* (NCBC; Grand Rapids: Eerdmans, 1989), pp. 3–16.

    12. See n. 11.

    13. I am grateful to Robert Johnston for telling me of a volume he saw in the Lambeth library, printed in 1534: *Proverbs and Ecclesiastes,* translated by George Joye; printed by Thomas Godfray.

    14. See discussion of A. Wright and sources cited above.

§1 Opening Matters (Eccl. 1:1–11)

This opening section of the book of Ecclesiastes consists of three distinct segments. First, a superscription identifies the work but is not part of the book proper (1:1). The following verse provides a motto for the book (1:2). Closing the introductory section is a poem that incorporates many of the themes and much of the vocabulary to be developed in the remainder of the work (1:3–11).

Because this section functions as an introduction to the book as a whole, it is not surprising to find that it anticipates many of the major issues of the book. The motto in verse 2 raises the central problem by stating it as a conclusion rather than a question: all is meaningless. The poem that follows then specifies aspects of that lack of meaning that will be developed in the following chapters. The question of gain from human labor (v. 3) is developed in the context of repetition throughout creation without goals (human generations, v. 4; natural phenomena, vv. 5–7; the perceptions of the individual, v. 8). There is nothing new, no remembrance of what has been, and no hope for remembrance of what is yet in the future.

The reader who is not new to this book will notice not only the themes that are raised in these opening verses, but also those that figure prominently in the book but are not present here. First and perhaps most significant, the opening verses do not mention God, the social order, or human relationships. Second, and perhaps related to this, there is no mention here of retribution or the relation between behavior and outcome. Finally, this section includes no call to joy nor acknowledgment of the good that is possible in human life. The themes are raised in the abstract; as yet there is no appeal to specific experiences.

1:1 / The superscription identifies the speaker of the main portion of the book. This speaker is identified by a title (NIV **the Teacher,** and further specified as **son of David, king in Jerusalem,** leading to the traditional ascription of the work to

Solomon. The hint of Solomon as speaker anticipates the persona adopted in 1:12–2:26. This persona is not carried through the remainder of the book, where the narrative voice speaks about kings but not as a king (see, e.g., 8:2–4).

1:2 / This verse, which provides a motto for the entire book, forms an *inclusio* with 12:8. The section from 1:2 to 12:8 is thus the main body of the work. Of the eight words in the Hebrew of this verse, five are forms of the root *hebel,* translated **meaningless** in the NIV. The vocabulary underscores the sense: Qohelet claims that **everything is meaningless,** and in this verse, nearly everything is.

1:3–11 / The opening poem (which some identify rather as stately prose), has stylistic continuities and discontinuities with the rest of the book. Although it is framed with statements about the human situation (vv. 3–4, 10–11), the heart of the poem (vv. 4–7) refers to natural phenomena: **earth, sun, wind,** water. As these represent the traditional four elements, these references support the claim in v. 8 about **all things** (so Murphy, *Ecclesiastes,* p. 9). The sense of completeness is heightened in vv. 5–6, with references to the rising and setting places of the sun (implicitly east and west) and the southerly and northerly direction of the wind; thus the four directions as well as the four elements are included.

Some interpreters suppose that this passage comes from a hand other than that of the author of the rest of the book. If so, it is well chosen: the poem introduces key terms and concepts to be developed later in the book. Among these key terms and concepts (see introduction for further discussion) are such things as **gain** (v. 3), **labor/toil** (v. 3), **under the sun** (vv. 3, 9), **wind** (v. 6), **what has been** (v. 9), **nothing new** (v. 9), and **remembrance** (v. 11).

Unlike much of the book, this passage contains no use of the first person singular: the speaking voice is impersonally authoritative. The poem is, however, situated in historical time (**our time,** v. 10).

There is a concentric pattern to the poem. At its center is the core statement, **all things are wearisome** (v. 8a). The Hebrew term for **things** (Hb. *dᵉbārîm*) is broad enough to include both things (natural phenomena) and words (human expression). Bracketing this claim are the goalless repetitions of the sun, wind, and **sea** (vv. 5–7), along with the similarly unfilled **eye** and **ear** (v. 8b). The next bracket is the picture of one generation replacing another against the backdrop of a permanent earth (v. 4), and the proclamation that there is nothing new (vv. 9–10). The outer bracket of the poem contains the question about the **gain** of human **labor** (v. 3) and the conclusion: **there is no remembrance** (v. 11). Thus the rhetorical question of v. 3 has the implied answer: "there is no gain."

Two elements of verse 11 are somewhat problematic. First, Qohelet claims that there is no remembrance of those who were before while at the same time insisting that what exists has been already. Thus, Qohelet claims to know both that everything has been before and that what existed before is forgotten. Secondly, Qohelet claims that those still to come will not remember; the rest of the book expresses a lack of knowledge about what is to come. The speaker is thus situated outside the lack of memory and advanced knowledge which characterize the human experience.

The occurrence of **under the sun** in verses 3 and 9 suggests an opening and closing formula. Thus it is possible that the existing poem is an expansion of an earlier version that did not include verses 10 and 11.

Additional Notes §1

1:1 / **The Teacher:** The word used here (Hb. *qōhelet*) occurs only in this book of the Bible, although its root is familiar from *qāhāl* ("gathering" or "assembly"). The form is a feminine participle, which may refer to a particular office. The precise nature of that office is not clear. The traditional title Ecclesiastes derives from *ekklēsia,* the Gk. equivalent of *qāhāl.* Both "preacher" and the NIV's **teacher** are possible specifications of an office within the assembly. It is also possible that "assemble" refers to the gathering of sayings rather than people, in which case one might call Qohelet "the collector." The epilogue to the book supports either possibility. It claims that Qohelet both **imparted knowledge to the people** and **set in order many proverbs** (12:9).

1:2 / **Meaningless:** The Hb. word *hebel* is variously translated meaningless(ness), vanity, futility, emptiness, absurdity. The word is related to wind and mist, and in Ecclesiastes it is used for things that do not last, cannot be grasped, or are not worthwhile. There is no corresponding English word with the same range of meaning. The NIV translation is as good as any but does not allow the various nuances of the word in different parts of the books. Some uses of *hebel* in Ecclesiastes may well indicate a lack of meaning while others suggest a lack of endurance. For more discussion, see the introduction and specific uses.

1:3 / **Under the sun:** This expression occurs frequently in Ecclesiastes (29 times), but is never used elsewhere in the Bible.

1:6 / The non-productive movement of **the wind (south, north, round and round, ever returning)** sets the framework for understanding **chasing after the wind,** a frequent refrain through the first half of the book (1:14, 17; 2:11, 17, 26; 4:4, 6, 16; 6:9). In addition, if **the sun rises, the sun sets** in v. 5 refers indirectly to east and west, the mention of north and south in this verse completes the reference to the four directions.

Wind: Throughout Ecclesiastes, the word for wind (Hb. *rûaḥ;* also "breath" or "spirit") is used without positive connotations and frequently with negative ones. This is not unique but neither is it characteristic of biblical usage.

1:8 / **All things are wearisome:** Another possible translation for Hb. *dᵉbārîm* (NIV **things**) is "words." Both senses are operative here: the sense of "things" includes the natural phenomena in vv. 5–7; "words" anticipates the inability to speak. The word translated **wearisome** (Hb. *yᵉgēᶜîm*) may also be translated "weary": there is a sense in which things not only are tiring to people but are themselves worn out.

1:10 / **Is there anything of which one can say . . . ?** There is no interrogative particle in the Hb. One might translate "There may be something of which it is said"; or "If there is anything of which is it said." In any case, the end of the verse announces that even what one hears proclaimed as new has long existed.

1:11 / **Men of old:** The Hb. expression does not specify whether the reference is to people of previous ages or to the previous ages themselves. The same is true of the reference to **those who are yet to come.**

§2 *Qohelet's Experiment (Eccl. 1:12–2:26)*

Qohelet, using the implied persona of Solomon, under-takes to explore "all that is done" (1:13). "All" includes gaining wisdom, amassing possessions, building monuments, and en-gaging in celebrations. Solomon is an effective choice as speaker: he is the one character in Israelite tradition who can take wisdom, wealth, and extravagance to their extremes.

This section records an experiment: a project that involves engaging in particular behaviors, recording the results, and ana-lyzing them. Results include both the physical outcomes (for ex-ample, ownership of possessions) and emotional responses (such as joy and hatred). The analysis consists of reflection on the meaning, value, and permanence of those results. The project, then, has a philosophical purpose, although it involves physical as well as mental endeavor.

Qohelet's evaluative comments take the reader through a complex series of responses. The section begins and ends with negative evaluations: "What a heavy burden God has laid on men! I have seen all the things that are done under the sun; all of them are meaningless, a chasing after the wind" (1:13–14) and "This too is meaningless, a chasing after wind" (2:26).

The intervening verses contain a mixture of positive and negative comments. Qohelet offers repeated affirmations of the good. "My heart took delight in all my work, and this was the re-ward for all my labor" (2:10). "Wisdom is better than folly, just as light is better than darkness. The wise man has eyes in his head, while the fool walks in the darkness" (2:13–14). "A man can do nothing better than to eat and drink and find satisfaction in his work. This too, I see, is from the hand of God, for without him, who can eat or find enjoyment? To the man who pleases him, God gives wisdom, knowledge and happiness" (2:24–25). Nonethe-less, Qohelet's efforts are repeatedly judged "meaningless" (1:14; 2:1, 11, 15, 17, 19, 21, 23) and "chasing after the wind" (1:14, 17; 2:11, 17). At one point Qohelet even acknowledges, "I hated life"

(2:17). The good in life, then, is contained within an overall framework of meaninglessness.

1:12–18 / The exploration of wisdom is announced but its process (unlike that of the following examination of pleasure) is not described. Instead, Qohelet immediately announces a general verdict: human activity is a **heavy burden** (or worse), divinely imposed and **meaningless.** The segment concludes with the negative side of **wisdom** and **knowledge:** they bring **sorrow** and **grief.**

2:1–11 / This segment explores **pleasure** and announces in advance the verdict: **that also proved to be meaningless** (2:1). Pleasure is examined through **laughter, wine, folly,** building and landscaping projects, and the amassing of **slaves,** livestock, and possessions. All this was done without loss of **wisdom** (2:9). Qohelet both acknowledges taking **delight** in the **work** (2:10) and proclaims it **meaningless, chasing after wind,** and without gain (2:11). Thus the initial reaction of receiving pleasure is overshadowed, but not eliminated, by the verdict **meaningless** bracketing the description of the experiment (2:1, 11). The addition of the final phrase **(nothing was gained under the sun)** has the effect of making this project seem even more meaningless than was the pursuit of wisdom.

2:12–16 / Here the speaker reflects on **wisdom** and **folly** in the context of death. Wisdom is better than folly (2:13–14a), but in the end does not exempt its owner from the universal **fate:** death and oblivion (2:14b–16). The lack of remembrance is reminiscent of 1:11. As in the preceding section, it is important neither to deny the affirmation of wisdom nor to skip over the denial of an ultimate difference between wise and foolish persons.

2:17–26 / The section closes with a pair of contrasting evaluations. The first is negative: Qohelet hated life (2:17). This admission is to be neither glossed over nor given exaggerated weight. It is expressed as a first-person narration rather than as a general statement: **I hated life,** and not "life is hateful." Thus the reader encounters it as a narrative stage rather than as an absolute conclusion. Therefore, at that particular moment, Qohelet did indeed hate life. That is not the last word, however. Qohelet goes on to commend eating and drinking and enjoying one's work as at least a relative good; they come from God

(2:24–25). Similar positive claims will appear in 3:12–13, 5:18–19, 8:15, 9:7, and 11:8.

The last verse of the section (2:26) is an affirmation of retribution. Thus **God gives** intangible rewards **(wisdom, knowledge and happiness)** to those who are God-pleasing. However, to sinners God gives the thankless task of working for the benefit of the God-pleasing. **This too is meaningless, a chasing after the wind** concludes the chapter. The reader may wonder how broadly to understand the referent for "this." Does the verdict "meaningless" apply only to the sinner's task of gathering and storing up wealth to hand it over to someone else? Or does it refer to the entire situation in which God gives blessings to some people and takes them from others? At this point in the book, when retribution has been affirmed but not yet made problematic, the reader is more likely to take the former view. Later, when it becomes clear that people have little control over (or even knowledge of) whether they are pleasing to God, this provisional decision may need to be revised.

Additional Notes §2

1:13 / Heavy burden: The NIV translation, while possible, softens the blow of Qohelet's statement. This is the same expression used in 4:8 and 5:13, where NIV translates **miserable business** and **grievous evil** respectively.

1:17 / Madness and folly: Both words are rare and uncertain; the NIV translation is as likely as any.

2:1 / To find out what is good: The form of the Hb. (lit. "to see into good") suggests not only expression of purpose, but a call to the speaker's self to experience what is good: "So enjoy!"

2:12 / What more can the king's successor do than what has already been done? The second half of 2:12 is difficult. First, the syntax is cryptic, lit. "For what the man who comes after the king? What they have already done/made it/him." The NIV, with many translations, assumes an unstated form of "do" in the first clause; this is possible but not certain. In the second clause, there is no expressed referent for the plural verb (omitted in NIV), and the object suffix could be understood personally as easily as impersonally. That is, the expression could be referring to what the king's successor will *do* or what that successor will *be*. Equally unclear is whether (and if so, how) Qohelet identifies with the expression. If the persona of Solomon is still understood, the speaker could be either the king (reflecting on the one who will succeed him) or the successor (reflecting on his relationship with his predecessor). If, on the other hand, this is a more general statement that does not assume the Solomon persona, it need not reflect on the relationship between the speaker and either predecessor or successor. A final difficulty is that the entire second half of 2:12 disrupts a natural flow from 2:12a to 2:13.

2:24 / **Nothing better than:** The comparative understanding depends on supplying one additional Hb. letter, a *mêm*. This addition is reasonable, given the similar expressions later in the book, and because the preceding word ends with a *mêm* it is plausible that one was lost in transmission. The Hb. text without emendation says, "It is not good for a man that he . . ."

2:25 / **Without him:** The Hb. reads "without me," although the sense is clearly "without God," as NIV implies. If the Hb. is correct, it suggests that Qohelet is quoting a saying in which God is the speaker that the readers would have recognized.

§3 Time (Eccl. 3:1–22)

Qohelet turns here to a consideration of "time." The poem on time (3:1–8) is the most familiar passage in the book of Ecclesiastes, and is used in settings from funerals to folk-rock concerts. In the poem, pairs of opposites illustrate that there is a proper time for all human activity. When it is read in isolation from its context, the poem provides the reader with a sense of comfort and reassurance. There is a time for everything. In the unpleasant seasons of life, one can recognize that there will be balancing good times. Thus one is enabled to accept grief as part of a larger picture (when using this as a funeral reading), or to strive to work toward the time for peace (as in the Pete Seeger song "Turn, Turn, Turn").

Following the poem is a prose reflection on the same subject (3:9–15). It is more characteristic of Qohelet's voice, both in the ruthlessness with which it insists on human limitations and in its affirmation of finding pleasure in one's food, drink, and work.

The reassurance that the reader may have found in the poem on time is strictly circumscribed when one reads it in connection with the prose reflection. One can still "be happy and do good" (3:12), and even understand the ability to "eat and drink, and find satisfaction" in one's work as a "gift of God" (3:13). Yet the lack of understanding remains heavy "burden" (3:10).

It is not coincidental that the letdown occurs when the role of God is made explicit. It is God who has "set eternity in the hearts of men" but withheld the ability to "fathom what God has done from beginning to end" (3:11). The passage develops and explains the exclamation of 1:13, "What a heavy burden God has laid on men!"

The next verses (3:16–17) introduce the issue of injustice, here in the context of "a time for everything." The chapter closes with an interlude (3:18–22) in which Qohelet claims that humans are like beasts, or even that they are in fact beasts. The preceding segment on injustice may allow the reader to infer that this conclusion is based on the way people treat one another, but Qohelet does not make this connection explicit. Rather, it is the likeness of their fates (death and return to the ground) that links humankind with animals.

3:1–8 / The poem on **time** is carefully balanced. Time exists for opposite activities, although with some of the word pairs the precision of the opposition is questionable. God is not mentioned in this section, but is implicit as the One who appoints the proper times.

The elements the poem describes are all normal human activities and emotions. There is little emphasis on the specific vocabulary and concerns of wisdom or on the particular concerns of the book of Qohelet. Although the opposites have positive and negative connotations (beginnings and endings, pleasures and sorrows), they should not be assigned moral significance: all of them are activities proper in their time, which cannot be claimed for immoral behavior. Notably, the poem does not include "a time to be wise and a time to be foolish"; or "a time to be righteous and a time to be wicked"; or "a time to fear God and a time to sin"; or "a time to be lazy and a time to be diligent." Perhaps more significantly in light of what follows, Qohelet does not acknowledge "a time to oppress and a time to do justice." Although there are times for both pleasant and unpleasant activities, Qohelet never suggests that there is a proper time for injustice or wickedness.

3:9–15 / Following the poem, Qohelet offers reflections on the concept of proper time, seriously qualifying its usefulness for human behavior. In this segment, **God** is explicitly and ominously present. God has established an appropriate point in time for everything, and God has also put time in the sense of duration (NIV **eternity**) into the human heart. The human predicament is being caught between these two aspects of time. God has determined the proper specific times for different behaviors and has put the larger sense of time into our hearts, but we are unable to determine **what God has done.** Thus we are unable to discern proper times and are simply confounded by time in its broader aspect.

The serene tone of the preceding poem, then, comes to an abrupt end. There is a time for everything, but we humans are unable to comprehend this. In the final analysis, we simply cannot understand God's work. And yet, there is nothing better than happiness, eating and drinking, and finding satisfaction in one's work. This is not only from God (as in 2:24), but should be understood as **the gift of God.** God's work endures and is designed to inspire reverence on the part of humans.

3:16–17 / A brief transitional segment provides the first reference in the book to human injustice. The problem is a grievous one, but it is described from the perspective of one who sees oppression, not one who experiences it. At first reading, it may appear as though the issue of space has supplanted that of time. There is a **place** for **judgment** and a **place** for **justice,** but in both of these places there is **wickedness.** However, the temporal concern is implicit in the claim that **God** will impose **judgment** on the **righteous** and the **wicked:** because there is a **time** for everything, there must be a time for judgment. This claim has potential for comfort, coming as it does after both the poem asserting the existence of proper times and the prose reflection acknowledging human inaccessibility to the divine time scheme. The reader might expect Qohelet to relinquish control and accept God's wisdom about when the time for patience is over and it is time to execute justice. The potential consolation, however, is not realized and Qohelet never observes the longed-for justice. The tone of the segment remains poised between confidence and despair; as usual, there is no retreat from either side of this difficult, even paradoxical, combination. Qohelet knows both that judgment will happen and that it has not yet happened. There is no suggestion here of judgment at the hour of death, a concept which might mitigate the tension.

3:18–22 / The relation of the final verses of chapter 3 to the preceding reflection on injustice is not explicit, yet the placement of this segment pushes the reader to find a connection. Most likely, the deferral of judgment provides the opportunity for testing, and the prevalence of oppression is what occasions the likening of humans to beasts. In any case, Qohelet claims that humans have the **same fate** as do **animals:** death and return to the **dust.** In this context, Qohelet concludes again that **everything is meaningless** (3:19). This is the only use of the key word in this chapter and it does not include its frequent expansion, "chasing after wind."

Who knows in 3:21, like other rhetorical questions in Ecclesiastes, assumes a negative response. No one knows whether the human **spirit** has a different destination after death than does that of an animal. The previous verses hint toward an absolute denial of an afterlife, but this phrase is less ambitious. It simply implies that certainty is impossible. Reference to the possibility of an afterlife suggests a milieu in which the idea was available but debated. Qohelet is clearly inclined to deny the existence of a life after death (3:19–20), but finally unable to draw a definite conclusion.

This uncertainty leads to the third commendation of enjoyment of life (3:22). Because people do not know what happens after their lifetimes, the best they can do is **enjoy** life while it lasts. The closing rhetorical question (**who can bring him to see,** 3:22) anticipates a negative response. This is the first specific reference to lack of knowledge of the future, which will become an important theme later in the book.

Additional Notes §3

3:2 / **A time to be born:** The translation **to be born** makes excellent sense given the pairing with "to die." However, since the Hb. verb form is active, "to give birth" would be a more fitting translation.

3:11 / **Eternity:** Although "eternity" is the usual translation for the Hb. *ʿôlām* (long duration, whether in time or space), its sense here is not immediately apparent. Possible translations include: "a sense of past and future" (NRSV, REB), "the timeless" (NAB); "an awareness of the passage of time" (NJB); "a sense of duration" (Murphy, *Ecclesiastes*); "the unknown" (Crenshaw, *Ecclesiastes*), and "the world" (Gordis, *Koheleth*).

3:15 / **God will call the past to account:** The sense is difficult; a more literal translation is "God seeks what is pursued." Is the sense that God seeks out (and finds) that which humans pursue (vainly)? Or is it (as the NIV footnote suggests) that God seeks out (and re-calls into being) the existence of that of which humans have no remembrance (i.e., the past)? The first part of v. 15 recalls 1:9; if the second half of 1:9 is to direct the reader's interpretation here, the latter option is to be preferred.

3:17 / **A time for every activity:** The use of the phrase, which in Hb. is an exact repetition of **a season for every activity** (3:1), indicates a close connection between this segment and the reflection on time that opened the chapter.

§4 The Human Dilemma (Eccl. 4:1–5:20)

The segments in this section are connected by the theme of the human individual, both in isolation and in relationships within social, familial, and religious systems. A concern with labor and material prosperity connects this section with the rest of the book. The development of thought is difficult to follow, though, and interpreters disagree not only about the logic of the argument but even about the claims that Qohelet is making.

Acknowledging these difficulties, the reader can find in the section an overall movement from despair ("the dead" are to be praised more than "the living," and the unborn above either, 4:2–3) to acceptance (it is good "to eat and drink" and "find satisfaction" in one's work, 5:18). Within this overall movement, the segments fall into two groups. The segments of the first group (4:1–5:7) are held together by "better" sayings (4:2–3, 6, 9, 13; 5:5). Those of the second group (5:8–20) resume concerns of segments in the first group. In 5:8–9, Qohelet returns to the problem of oppression (4:1–3). The challenge of 5:10–12 maintains that "more is better" (see 4:10–12). The plight of the solitary individual is lamented in 5:13–15 (see 4:7–12). Finally, in 5:16–17, there is the assertion that all gain will be lost (as may be implied by 4:13–16). The only two segments that mention God fall at the end of these two halves (5:1–7, 18–20): the former insisting on reticence and awe in the divine presence and the latter urging the enjoyment of God's gifts.

4:1–3 / Qohelet returns to the problem of oppression that was introduced in 3:16–17. The lack of a **comforter** for **the oppressed** is a grievous problem. From this, Qohelet concludes that **the dead** are more praiseworthy than **the living** and the unborn more fortunate than either. Some distance from oppression is assumed even here. The problem with being alive is not that one risks suffering oppression but that one will have to observe both oppression and the lack of a comforter for the oppressed. Because redress for the oppressed is an expectation of both God and the king in biblical religion (see, e.g., Jer. 22:11–19; Ezek. 22:6–16), criticism of either or both may be implicit here. Nevertheless, Qohelet is too keenly aware of the dangers of offending the powerful to express such criticism directly. It is clear that the persona of Solomon, used earlier for the experiment in wisdom and pleasure, is no longer used. A king this outraged about oppression could take action against it rather than merely lamenting its presence.

4:4–6 / These verses deal with striving. Verse 4 ascribes all human **achievement** to **envy**; verse 5 appears to note the self-destructiveness of the lazy **fool**; and verse 6 rejects working for more than one needs. If indeed all of these express aspects of Qohelet's point of view, it would seem that there is no course of action (or inaction) that is worthwhile, a specific reinforcement of Qohelet's general claim that all is meaningless.

Not all interpreters agree with this reading. The problem is the sense of 4:5 and its relation to context. It is possible to read this verse, "The fool folds his hands but eats his meat" (i.e., still has food). In this case, the fool would be affirmed, something that Qohelet never does elsewhere.

Commentators disagree, too, about whether 4:5 expresses Qohelet's point of view or whether it is a popular proverb, quoted to be rejected. In the latter case, the logic of 4:5–6 would be: [Some say,] "The fool folds his hands and ruins himself"; [but I say,] "Better one handful . . ." There is even a third possibility, that both 4:5 and 4:6 are popular sayings that Qohelet rejects.

The lack of consensus among commentators need not make the reader despair of finding meaning in this passage. It is clear that Qohelet rejects striving as a product of envy. Although it is less clear that this specific passage rejects inaction as well, the fact that the calls to joy usually include affirmation of pleasure in one's work suggests that overall Qohelet would reject the fool who **folds his hands**, whether or not his behavior is self-destructive.

4:7–12 / Loneliness, community, and family come together in these verses. It makes no sense for a loner to work so hard as to deprive oneself of **enjoyment**. The reader may wonder whether the change in 4:8 from third to first person indicates that Qohelet is quoting the person without **son** or **brother** or whether instead it suggests that Qohelet identifies with the worker.

Contrasted with the lonely worker is the person who has a companion. The treatment of companionship is uncharacteristically non-ironic. Qohelet does not discuss the possibility that the companion might be a fool or that the two envy each other. Qohelet finds a practical advantage in companionship. There is no claim of ultimate meaning, but neither do we find "this too is meaningless."

4:13–16 / **A poor but wise youth** contrasts with **an old but foolish king.** The vignette offers a combination of dissimilar elements: wisdom ought to go with wealth and age, folly with poverty and youth. In this example, wisdom begins as an advantage greater than age, social standing, or wealth. As readers have come to expect by now, the following verses undercut the claim of value. Like other concepts that Qohelet has examined, wisdom is of only relative worth.

Interpreters debate whether these verses reflect a situation in Israel's history (such as the Joseph story) or one contemporaneous with Qohelet. Some assert that the story is strictly fictional. Even the events narrated are unclear. Does the poor but wise youth supplant or become the old but foolish king, or do the two exemplify two extreme possibilities? Is the successor of 4:15 to be identified with the youth (as the NIV translation suggests) or is this the successor of the youth who has since become king? It is possible that a situation known to the ancient audience is behind this narrative, but to today's readers the gaps in the description make it difficult to discern. In fact, the ambiguity is so embedded in the narration (e.g., the use of pronouns that could refer to either the king or the youth) that it may be preferable to leave the story unclear.

The force of the segment as a whole, however, does not depend on knowing the details of the story. The passage offers a multifaceted rejection of the value of royal status. A king may be an old fool, come from nothing, or lose power. The world at large, viewed in historical terms, does not care about a king.

5:1–7 / This is the most clearly cult-related passage in the entire book, involving **the house of God,** presumably the temple. It is assumed that the reader will go to the house of God and Qohelet recommends that the motivation for going should be **to listen** rather than to **sacrifice** foolishly. The section warns against the danger of approaching God and possibly offending, whether through **the sacrifice of fools, hasty** speech, or unfulfilled vows.

The language and details of the segment contrast with those in the rest of this section. The use of imperatives, reference to the house of God, and lack of reference to material wealth all distinguish the passage from its context. The principal connection of the segment with the rest of this section is the emphasis on relationship, although here it is the relationship between humans and God rather than relationships among humans.

5:8–9 / The segment is a reprise on oppression (see 3:16–17; 4:1–3). Here the existence of a hierarchy makes oppression predictable. Rather than being a safeguard or a system of checks and balances, a complex bureaucracy enables oppression and the denial of **rights**. The NIV translation of 5:9 suggests that the injustice goes all the way to the top.

5:10–17 / The segment treats the problems of one who prospers materially. The difficulty with loving **money** is that one **never** gets **enough** to satisfy. This is true even when one cannot use everything oneself. The **laborer** sleeping soundly contrasts with the rich insomniac.

Hoarded wealth that harms **its owner** (how is not specified) and loss of wealth are the next problems. Qohelet includes more illustrations of the claim that it is not profitable to make one's goal the acquisition of material goods.

This segment exemplifies the worst-case scenario for Qohelet. The situation is twice labeled **grievous evil** (5:13, 16). The use of multiple words with negative connotations in 5:17 **(darkness, frustration, affliction,** and **anger)** makes it clear that this is something the speaker cares about intensely.

5:18–20 / At last, Qohelet returns to the positive. As in the previous affirmations of joy, what is good and proper is eating and drinking and finding satisfaction in one's work. This commendation is less positive than the previous ones, though, with **labor** labeled **toilsome** and the **days of life** labeled **few.** Although love of wealth is a problem, having **wealth and possessions** is **a gift of God.** The most serious limitation of this gift (at least for folks as reflective as Qohelet) is that this blessing from God keeps one too busy to contemplate one's situation in life.

Additional Notes §4

4:2 / **I declared that the dead ... are happier:** Lit. "I praise the dead." The object of the verb (Hb. *šabbēaḥ,* to praise) is unusual. Normally only God occurs as its object.

4:5 / **Ruins himself:** Lit. "eats his flesh." Later usage would allow the reading "eats his meat," acknowledging that even the inactive fool survives.

4:8 / **There is:** The Hb. expression *yēš* suggests a hypothetical situation: "imagine someone." The usage is almost like the "certain man" of Jesus' parables.

4:12 / **Cord of three strands:** The reference to "three" seems odd in the context of "one" and "two." Qohelet may be quoting a popular proverb.

4:14 / **The youth:** Hb. is unclear, simply using "he" rather than an explicit subject. It is also possible that this verse refers to the king.

May have ... or may have: NIV here understands Hb. *kî ... kî* as offering alternatives. This is a possibility and makes sense of a verse which is otherwise difficult.

May have been born in poverty within his kingdom: NIV's reading reflects a common motif used by outsiders when they rise to power in the ancient Near East. A literal translation, "even in his poverty he was born poor," implies that even a king brings nothing with him when he enters the world, anticipating 5:15 [Hb. 5:14].

4:16 / The verse is reminiscent of the poem in 1:3–11, specifically regarding the generations going and coming (1:4) and the lack of remembrance (1:11).

5:1 / In the Hb. text this verse is 4:17, hence the Hb. is numbered one verse behind the English translation throughout ch. 5.

5:6 / **My vow was a mistake:** NIV adds **my vow,** for which Hb. has only a pronoun.

5:9 / **The king himself profits from the fields:** The verse is ambiguous. The NIV provides a possible reading but it is also possible that the king is profitable for the land.

§5 What Is Good? (Eccl. 6:1–12)

This section spans the center of the book: the formal midpoint is 6:9. Its opening segment challenges God's disposition of human possessions, and the closing segment implies human inability to contend with the deity. These explicit and implicit divine references bracket a segment in which Qohelet questions the value of wisdom in the context of human appetites (6:7–9).

The question, "For who knows what is good for a man in life, during the few and meaningless days he passes through like a shadow?" (6:12), is reminiscent of the affirmations of pleasure (see discussion in introduction; cf. 2:24–26; 3:22; 5:18–20; 8:15; 9:7–10; 11:7–8). Yet Qohelet does not presume to know what is good, and the implication is that no one but God knows.

Readers may find themselves struggling against Qohelet's claims at the beginning of this section. It is not surprising to see "meaningless" or even "grievous evil" as a judgment on human experience, but Qohelet has not previously been so clear about assigning God the responsibility for this situation. It is even easier to reject the judgment that "a stillborn child is better off" than people who do not enjoy the fruit of their labor: Qohelet's "I say" (6:3) almost invites disagreement. Even resisting readers, however, are likely to be drawn into the closing section by its use of passive forms, and they may find themselves making inferences that they would not affirm as explicit statements. Thus it is entirely appropriate for readers to be unsettled at this point.

6:1–6 / Qohelet claims to describe **another evil,** but the situation described is not significantly different from those in 2:18–26 and 5:13–14 (and implicit in 4:7–8). God grants a person **wealth, possessions and honor** that are enjoyed by a **stranger.** Qohelet described the situation as evil, weighty, **meaningless,** and **a grievous evil.**

The discussion is carried to an extreme in the second part of this segment (6:3–6). The protagonist (still presumably the one who has prospered in 6:1–2) also has **a hundred children** and a long life. Qohelet judges **a stillborn child** to be **better off.** Because offspring, long life, and **prosperity** are central elements of the Israelite conception of well-being, Qohelet is suggesting that nothing makes life worth living for one who cannot **enjoy prosperity.**

6:7–9 / In the context of the insatiable human **appetite,** Qohelet calls into question basic values of wisdom and right **conduct.** As usual, the rhetorical questions imply negative answers. There is no advantage for the **wise** over the **fool;** the **poor** gain nothing by knowing proper conduct.

6:10–12 / God is the unnamed presence in this segment. The passive expressions **has been known** and **has already been named** allow the reader to infer "by God," as human knowledge is nonexistent for Qohelet. This implication sets up the understanding that the **one who is stronger** must also be God. The lack of explicit mention of God may be an expression of human (even Qohelet's) inability to **contend** with this **stronger** one, or it may be a rhetorical ploy by which the readers are pushed to take responsibility for their own inferences.

Readers may find some irony in the rejection of wordiness at this point. Qohelet has already warned against **many words** (5:3, 7). Even if the book were to end here, Qohelet could be accused of repetitiveness and, in fact, the second half of the book is only beginning.

The chapter closes by asking **who knows what is good** in human existence (6:12). The language is reminiscent of the calls to joy but this time Qohelet refuses to make any positive claim and does not mention enjoyment of the physical pleasures of life. As we have seen, rhetorical questions ordinarily imply negative answers. Here, because God has been implicit in the preceding verses, the implied answer is instead, "God knows." This, of course, is of no practical advantage to those **under the sun,** because God is not sharing the answer.

Additional Notes §5

6:1 / **I have seen another evil:** The Hb., lit. "there is another evil I have seen," may set up a hypothetical situation. It is possible that

Qohelet is describing the sort of thing that happens in our world rather than a specific event he has personally witnessed.

6:2 / Grievous evil: The language used here is very strong. The expression lit. translates "evil illness," and is not an expression that Qohelet uses elsewhere. At the same time, it is important to recognize that the Hb. word for evil *(ra*ᶜ*)* is used of any negative and need not have moral connotations.

6:3 / Does not receive a proper burial: The clause may be understood with either the man or the stillborn as subject. Most interpreters judge the stillborn more likely; thus, "Although it does not receive a proper burial, I say that a stillborn child is better off than he." The image of the stillborn child links with the one **who has not yet been** of 4:3.

6:6 / Do not all go to the same place? See 3:20. The place implied is the grave; Qohelet again argues against those who would claim an afterlife.

6:7 / Appetite: Here and in 6:9, the Hb. uses the multivalent *nepeš*, which can also mean "life, being." Although the constant desire for "more" is at issue and the reference to **mouth** suggests physical appetite, the reader may here understand a general reference to human insatiability.

§6 What Is Better? (Eccl. 7:1–14)

In this section Qohelet qualifies the negative conclusion of 6:12, which was that knowledge about what is good in life is unavailable to humans. Here Qohelet makes claims about what is good.

The section begins with a segment organized around "better" sayings. Although Qohelet has been unable to claim absolute good, there is relative good: some things are better than others. In the central segment, wisdom is judged to be good—at least when accompanied by an inheritance. The final segment discusses God explicitly; here, both good and bad times are attributed to the deity.

Initially, the reader may be relieved at the simplicity of form in the sayings that begin this chapter. The movement of the section, however, is as disturbing as that of the previous one. The positive valuation of death and sorrow invites the reader to question, if not to reject, the earlier affirmations of pleasure—and they are the only positives that Qohelet has offered the reader. It is the final segment, however, that provides the greatest challenge. Even a reader who wants to deny that God has made anything crooked (7:13) may admit that God has made both good and bad times, and that people do not have knowledge of the future (7:14).

7:1–6 / This segment consists of a series of "better" sayings with commentary. The first line of 7:1 sounds fairly conventional. It affirms the value of reputation over that of wealth. As it is standard even in Proverbs to prefer intangible positives over tangibles, this sounds unremarkable.

The second line of 7:1, however, expressing preference for **the day of death** over **the day of birth,** is distinctly unconventional. It pushes the reader to reinterpret the first line in the context of that "better" day: when one is dead, it is better to leave behind a good reputation than to be anointed lavishly.

Preoccupation with the day of death colors the segment as a whole, with its preference for **mourning** and **sorrow** over **feasting, laughter,** and **pleasure.** Although Qohelet has already expressed a preference for death over life (4:2–3) and for being unborn over death (6:1–6), no earlier passage rejects pleasure for those who are unfortunate enough to be alive. If the rhetorical questions of 6:12 called the affirmations of pleasure into question, this segment intensifies the effect of those questions. Here there is, in fact, something better than eating and drinking and enjoying life. It is mourning, sorrow, and the **rebuke** of the **wise.** Once again, however, Qohelet's conclusions are provisional and must be understood within their narrative context. The reader who suspects that Qohelet will offer no more commendations of pleasure will be proved wrong.

7:7–12 / The segment, in which third-person sayings (7:7–8, 11–12) surround second-person admonitions (7:9–10), is connected with the preceding segment by the "better" sayings in 7:8. Here both the sage (7:7) and **wisdom** itself (7:11–12) are called into question. Human wisdom is temporary (7:7–10), can be undone by **extortion,** bribery, or **anger,** and may lead to unwise longing for the good old days (7:10) rather than living in the present. Although wisdom has some practical usefulness, particularly when it is accompanied by inherited wealth (7:11), and can even **preserve** the **life** of those who have it (7:12), lengthened life is not a particular value for Qohelet.

7:13–14 / The closing segment returns to an explicit consideration of **God,** whose work is described as **crooked.** The allegation is Qohelet's most explicit challenge of the deity to this point. It is, however, in keeping with a strain of Israelite monotheism that insists on God's responsibility for everything, the **bad** as well as the **good.** See, for example, Job 2:10, 2 Samuel 24, and Isaiah 45:6–7. The closing verse, with its brief affirmation of happiness, emphasizes God's responsibility for both good and bad times and returns to the theme of human ignorance about the **future.**

Additional Notes §6

7:1 / **A good name is better than fine perfume:** There is nice balance in the Hb. of this line: *ṭôb šēm miššemen ṭôb*. It depends on the similarity in sound between *šēm* (name) and *šemen* (perfume), and on "name" carrying the implication of "reputation, good name."

7:5-6 / **Song . . . thorns:** There is more wordplay here, between *šîr* (song) and *sîr* (thorn).

7:10 / **Why:** The Hb. word used here *(mê)* has the sense of "what" more often than "why." Although "what" does not work here, a translation "how is it that" is preferable (so Murphy, *Ecclesiastes;* Seow, *Ecclesiastes*).

7:11 / **Like an inheritance:** The NIV does not quite follow the Hb. here, which reads "with *(ʿim)* an inheritance." That is, wisdom is fine as long as it is accompanied by wealth—but, implicitly, wisdom without an inheritance is worth little. Perhaps Qohelet has modified an existing saying that claimed wisdom to be *better* than an inheritance: the only difference would be the addition of a single Hb. letter, *ʿayin* (Hb. *mnḥlh* to *ʿm-nḥlh*). Fox (*Qohelet*, p. 231) notes that *ʿim* may be used comparatively, but Scott's (*Proverbs, Ecclesiastes*, p. 235) argument that a poor wise man is ignored (9:13) would favor the basic meaning, "with."

7:14 / **About his future:** The Hb. reads "after him," which suggests the time after a person's life is over, whereas the NIV indicates a later time during the person's life.

§7 *Where Is Wisdom? (Eccl. 7:15–8:17)*

Qohelet continues the exploration of wisdom in one of the most enigmatic sections of the entire book. The initial segment (7:15–22) considers the potential benefits and dangers of righteousness and wisdom over against wickedness and folly. As usual, Qohelet affirms contrasting points.

At the center of the section is a segment reflecting on wisdom and folly. The elusiveness of wisdom (7:23–29) is emphasized through images of women and accounting. Wisdom is simply not available and Qohelet's investigation of it does not add up.

A complex segment closes the section (8:1–17). Here the value of wisdom is considered in the context of people's power over one another and the apparent lack of retribution. As usual, Qohelet concludes with a combination of positive and negative refrains. The commendation of pleasure (8:15) is muted by the preceding "this too is meaningless" (8:14) and the following "no one can comprehend" (8:17).

The reader's response to this section is likely to be complex and perhaps even contradictory. On the one hand, it contains Qohelet's most thoroughgoing rejection of human wisdom: no one, not even the wisest, understands. On the other hand, Qohelet addresses readers directly in negative and positive imperatives (7:16–17, 21; 8:2–3). With a confident tone Qohelet commands the reader toward unusual behavior, namely, not to be too righteous or too wise and not to listen too carefully. This confidence combines oddly with the admission that even Qohelet has not been able to figure out what goes on in the world: it doesn't all add up. Given the speaker's lack of understanding, it is not surprising if readers question this advice. Why trust the judgment of a speaker who admits to a lack of understanding? And yet, since Qohelet describes an incomprehensible and even dangerous world, the reader's skepticism needs to be tempered by caution. With this caution, the reader may begin to approximate Qohelet's own stance.

7:15–22 / This segment is a powerful rejection of traditional wisdom. Qohelet claims to have seen everything (rather than only **both of these,** 7:15). **Righteousness** does not ensure survival, nor does **wickedness** prevent it. In fact, extreme righteousness and wisdom can be self-destructive, as extreme wickedness and folly can cause premature death. Qohelet does not explain the reasoning behind these questions.

The claim that a single sage is **more powerful than ten rulers** (7:19) sounds almost like traditional wisdom until one considers that careful behavior before rulers is a commonplace of wisdom—including the book of Ecclesiastes. This apparent denial of the social order that wisdom ordinarily works to maintain will itself be challenged in 8:2–6.

Qohelet goes on to insist that no one is entirely **righteous** (7:20). The tension between this verse and the observation of righteous people in 7:15 is real, and yet the absolute righteousness denied here need not preclude relative righteousness in the earlier verse. The closing verse (7:22), with its admonition not to **pay attention** to all that **people say** and its assertion that the reader has **cursed others many times,** contrasts with wisdom's usual emphasis on careful listening and circumspect speech. This accusation may subtly bolster Qohelet's claim that no one is truly wise.

7:23–29 / Describing a test made by means of **wisdom** reminiscent of 1:12–2:26, Qohelet acknowledges his inability to obtain wisdom or to find "that which is." The speaker then turns to investigate wisdom, and to determine whether life adds up. What Qohelet finds is not wisdom and understanding, but **the woman who is a snare, whose heart is a trap and whose hands are chains** (7:26). Although many interpreters have taken it as a rejection of women generally, or of a specific woman (e.g., Qohelet's mother or wife), the rest of the book does not indicate any rejection of women as a whole. Further, there are no references to women in Qohelet's life. In fact, the language used is reminiscent of the seductress of Proverbs 7, in whose company the simple youth is "like an ox going to the slaughter, like a deer stepping into a noose . . . like a bird darting into a snare, little knowing it will cost him his life" (Prov. 7:22–23). Moreover, the segment as a whole describes a search for wisdom (7:23, 25). In this context, the **woman among them all** whom Qohelet has not found (7:28) is at least symbolically associated with wisdom personified.

Qohelet on the one hand claims to have used wisdom to test **all this** and on the other hand admits failure in the search for wisdom. There is a tension here, much like that involving a righteous person in 7:15 and 7:20. No positive absolute is available to humankind, including absolute wisdom.

The use of economic and accounting images in this passage is striking. Qohelet sought **the scheme of things** (7:25); one might more readily translate "accounting" or "sum." Should the reader fail to notice the character of the language, Qohelet makes it even more explicit in 7:27 where he speaks of **adding one thing to another to discover the scheme** (or sum). Finally, Qohelet concludes that while God made people straightforward, they **have gone in search of many schemes** (or calculations; 7:29). Perhaps this is an admission that the reason Qohelet did not find wisdom (the **woman among them all**?) is that the search itself was wrongheaded and could lead only to folly (**the woman who is a snare**?). The search for a scheme in 7:25, 27–28 is acknowledged in 7:29 to be out of harmony with the work of God: human experience finally does not "add up."

8:1–17 / This final segment is bracketed by a question and answer, the former implying that the sage is incomparable, the latter that even the wise lack knowledge.

Qohelet asks who is like the sage and who knows the explanation of things. As with his other rhetorical questions, the implied answers are negative. No one is like the sage; no one **knows the explanation of things.** The two questions fit together uneasily. If no one (not even a sage) knows the explanation of things, what makes the sage incomparable? The last half of the verse suggests an answer. **Wisdom brightens** one's **face** and alters its **hard appearance.** The value of this change in the sage's face is not specified and the reader might well suppose that Qohelet is ambivalent about it (contrast 9:7–10 with 7:1–6).

Verses 2–11 deal with power, first the specific instance of royal power (8:2–6), and then the more generalized situation of humans having power over one another (8:7–11). The royal image is of an absolute ruler who cannot be questioned. The subject's wisest course of action is to live in such a way that the king will not do one harm. In spite of the visible lack of retribution, Qohelet acknowledges that it will be well with those who fear God and not with the **wicked** (8:12–13). The correlation of fearing God with good outcomes is familiar from traditional wisdom

(Prov. 10:27; 14:26, 27; 16:6; 19:23; 22:4). Yet Qohelet is not willing to ignore the situation **on earth** (8:14). It is meaningless that people do not get what they **deserve**. In this context, one might expect to find in the commendation of pleasure (8:15) the hollow ring of a resigned conclusion: since meaningless experience cannot be escaped, one might as well enjoy life. But the usual qualifiers ("meaningless"; references to brevity) are not found in the commendation itself. The final two verses (8:16–17) repeat Qohelet's conclusion that the ways of God are incomprehensible, even to the wisest of humans.

Verses 7–11 are related to the preceding ones in a movement from particular to general—from the specific case of the **king** and a subject to the general situation of one person having power over another. In 8:11, Qohelet praises deterrence like a law and order politician. In the related 8:12, however, Qohelet sees the survival of the **wicked**, which undermines the traditional wisdom claim that it will be **better** for God-fearers. As usual, it is difficult to be sure whether **I know** means that Qohelet knows *about* the traditional teaching (without necessarily accepting it) or, at least in the long run, *affirms it as true* (even without having seen it carried out so far). This and the following verse represent not facile rejections of traditional theory, but a struggle with the discrepancy between observation (what is) and values (what ought to be). It is in the context of this discordant state of affairs that the reader can identify with the conclusion: **this too is meaningless** (8:14).

In 8:15–17, Qohelet repeats the commendation of joy, following it with a verse reminiscent of 1:13. It is interesting but probably insignificant that this time Qohelet refers to the **labor** (better: "business") done **on earth** rather than "under the sun." The combination of frequently-used expressions (**meaningless, enjoyment of life, nothing is better, under the sun, God has given, God has done, no one can comprehend, cannot discover**) suggests that these verses provide a major conclusion.

Additional Notes §7

7:15 / **Both of these:** Lit. "everything," the same word used in the motto "everything is meaningless" (1:2, 12:8). Qohelet's claim may well imply more than the NIV allows, esp. as the admonitions of 7:16–17 refer not only to righteousness and wickedness but also to wisdom and folly.

7:16–17 / **Do not be a fool:** Of the four possibilities (righteousness, wisdom, wickedness, and folly), folly is the only one that is rejected outright, without an intensifier (**overrighteous, overwise, overwicked**).

7:18 / **It is good to grasp the one and not let go of the other:** The antecedents of **the one** and **the other** are not clear; most likely they refer to self-destruction (7:16) and premature death (7:17).

Avoid all extremes: This is one possible meaning of literal "go forth [from] all of them." The NIV puts Qohelet into the Greek thought world of the golden mean, which is consonant with the rejection of being overrighteous, overwise, overwicked, or a fool (7:17). On the other hand, Qohelet does not elsewhere plead for moderation in all things. It is more likely that the God-fearer will survive any situation.

7:24 / **Whatever wisdom may be:** NIV inserts "wisdom"; Hb. has simply "That which is." "Wisdom" is unlikely even as an implied subject: "that which is" is grammatically masculine (taking a masculine verb and adjectives), while wisdom in 7:23 is grammatically feminine (taking a feminine pronoun and adjective). Qohelet is unable to achieve wisdom because all of existence (including but not limited to wisdom) is beyond human grasp.

7:25 / **The scheme of things:** "Sum" is another sense of Hb. *ḥešbôn*.

7:28 / **While I was still searching but not finding:** The Hb. begins with the multipurpose particle *ʾašer*, which may relate the phrase to either what precedes or what follows. It is possible to read this verse as a whole: "What I was still searching but not finding is [the proverbial saying] I found one upright man among a thousand" (so Murphy, *Ecclesiastes*, p. 77).

One upright man . . . one upright: The Hb. contains no word corresponding to **upright**, which the NIV imports from 7:29.

7:29 / **God made mankind upright:** Note the contrast between this claim and 7:13 ("Consider what God has done: Who can straighten what he has made crooked?"). Perhaps this is an admission that the "crookedness" of human behavior is not God's doing after all.

8:2 / **Because you took an oath before God:** The NIV has the probable sense, although the Hb. "because of [in regard to] the oath of God" is more ambiguous, allowing for either an oath made to/before God or God's self-oath.

8:6 / **There is a proper time and procedure for every matter:** The Hb. is reminiscent of 3:1, 16–17; all the major words in this clause occur there.

8:8 / **Over the wind to contain it:** As the NIV footnote indicates, the Hb. *rûaḥ* can mean either "wind" or "breath." If the latter is the correct sense, it indicates lack of control over life and death.

8:10 / **Buried:** A slight emendation yields "approach," which better fits the context.

8:11 / **Sentence:** The word used, *pitgām,* is a Persian loan-word. Here it may refer either to the judicial sentence for a crime or to a divine judgment.

§8 Destiny (Eccl. 9:1–10)

This short section considers divine omnipotence and human limitations: everything is in God's power, and humans have nothing but consciousness. Qohelet observes that there is a single fate for all people, a further specification of the theme developed concerning humans and animals in 3:18–22. Verses 7–10 comprise the longest version of Qohelet's call to joy, typically tempered by context. The benefit of living is that one knows that one will die. The references to meaninglessness (or transience) and Sheol within the call itself put it in further perspective.

The reader experiences the entire section as tempered by the preceding insistence that "no one can comprehend" and "even if a wise man claims he knows, he cannot really comprehend it" (8:17). The "common destiny" that Qohelet claims for all people (9:2) may itself be beyond the speaker's ability to comprehend.

9:1–6 / Qohelet returns to the theme of one fate for everyone. The language hints at the cult, especially in the reference to sacrifice. The reference to **oaths** in this section contrasts with 5:3–4. In chapter 5 Qohelet suggested that taking oaths unnecessarily was particularly dangerous; here it seems insignificant. The building up of parallels in 9:2, first strict then loose, has a cumulative effect of emphasizing **everything**. Verse 3 recalls 1:13 (who but God can be responsible for this evil?). Yet Qohelet clings here to the idea that life is better than death. The reader notes a contrast with 4:2. Qohelet repeatedly observes the limits of life. Sometimes he concludes that it is better than the alternative and at other times that it is worse. This tension between the goodness and the pain of life is never finally resolved and, in fact, lies at the heart of the book.

9:7–10 / In the face of the preceding anguish, there comes an extended call to joy: "enjoy life, not simply because life is to be enjoyed, but because you are in the shadow of death." The details of the section contrast with the somber mood of 7:2–4. Yet they fit with those verses because these too come after facing the reality of death and oblivion. Indeed, these details contain repeated reminders of the emptiness and transience of human life: **meaningless; under the sun; toilsome labor;** and **the grave, where you are going.**

There is little new content in these verses. What is different is the tone. The call to pleasure itself is in imperative language. Qohelet does not merely announce that pleasure is a good thing, but calls the reader specifically into that pleasure. What is more, Qohelet, who rarely knows that God approves of anything, here uncharacteristically labels this enjoyment of life as favored by God (9:7). The details, too, are developed more than in the parallel sections, complete with festive clothing, anointing oil, and a beloved woman (the implied reader is clearly male).

Nonetheless, the call to joy is bracketed by insistence on the common fate shared by all and the randomness of misfortune. Within the call itself, we find the qualifying language that was notably lacking in the commendation at the end of the preceding section (8:15): **this meaningless life; all your meaningless days;** and **toilsome labor** (9:9). The effect is that good times, while vividly evoked, feel like an oasis in the midst of the emptiness that surrounds and threatens. This is an invitation to be accepted while it is available.

Throughout this section, the Hebrew *hebel* (NIV **meaningless**) may have the primary sense of "brief" or "transient." While a secondary sense of "meaningless" is no doubt present for the reader by means of association with other uses in the book, the emphasis is nonetheless on the brevity of life. The recognition of this enables the reader to take the affirmation seriously.

Additional Notes §8

9:1 / **Whether it is love or hate:** The syntactic relation of this phrase to its context is not specified. The NIV reading is possible, as is the idea that even love and hate (whether God's, other people's, or one's own) are in the hand of God.

9:2 / **And the bad:** The NIV adds this phrase, with ancient versions, to complete the balanced pairs of opposites.

9:4 / Even a live dog is better off than a dead lion! Cf. 4:2–3 and 6:3–6. Qohelet continues to wrestle with the value of life. Although a living, thinking person will experience limitation, here that limitation is better than no knowledge at all.

9:5 / For the living know that they will die, but the dead know nothing: The value that Qohelet places on knowledge is nowhere clearer than in this verse, in which even the knowledge that one will die is better than lack of knowledge.

9:9 / Your wife, whom you love: This is the only reference to a wife in the book.

§9 Wisdom and Folly (Eccl. 9:11–11:10)

The section is a loosely woven collection of vignettes and sayings, punctuated by phrases characteristic of Qohelet's own voice. It is difficult to break it into segments because the themes of randomness, social order, wisdom and folly, and language overlap and sometimes clash. The reader may find it difficult to follow a coherent line of reasoning. The overarching theme is that of living in an unpredictable world, and the section moves from random disaster (9:11–12) to random success (11:6).

Qohelet's attitude toward the social order contains tensions. On the one hand, it is unfortunate that a poor wise man may not be heeded (9:13–16) and it is possible for those with social power to use it badly (9:17; 10:5). On the other hand, 10:6 implies that fools and the rich are a contrasting pair. Thus, folly is properly associated with poverty and wisdom with wealth. Further, 10:16–17 correlate social standing with decorous behavior. In any case, a king or ruler's power is such that the prudent one will be circumspect not only in behavior (10:4) but even in thought and solitary speech (10:20). Throughout this section, there is an advantage to wisdom, skill, and social standing. However, this advantage can be undone by circumstances and there is a greater danger in folly, impropriety, and laziness.

9:11–12 / Again, Qohelet acknowledges the randomness of human existence. Therefore, one does not get what one deserves and outcomes happen unexpectedly and suddenly. The imagery of **net, snare,** and being trapped in relation to **evil times** is strongly reminiscent of the description of the woman **more bitter than death** (folly?) in 7:26. This segment underscores the urgency of the preceding call to joy. The opportunity may end at any time with no warning.

9:13–18 / Qohelet tells another example story, which may be either historical or fictional. It is not clear whether the poor sage actually delivered the city or whether he only might have done so if anyone had remembered the local resource. The plight of the poor sage is even more poignant because he is forgotten in a small city with few inhabitants.

The closing verses of the segment expand themes raised earlier. The assertion that **nobody remembered** (9:15) gives a specific example of a general theme raised in 1:11 and 2:16. The limitation of the value of wisdom over strength (9:16) challenges the claim that one sage is more powerful than ten rulers (7:19). The last two verses (9:17–18) are transitional. They are linked to the preceding story because they note the potential, but not always realized, value of wisdom over weapons of war. In both theme (a little bad undoes much good) and language **(ruler, fools)**, these verses anticipate the following section.

10:1–4 / The segment is composed of traditional-sounding wisdom sayings. The first three explicitly deal with the fool or folly, the last one deals with calmness before a ruler. The reference to the **fool** in the opening verses may lead the reader to infer that the angry ruler of 10:4 is foolish; at least, one may suppose that a calm response exemplifies wisdom.

10:5–7 / Qohelet affirms the basic propriety of the social order. Situations that go against it are labeled **evil** and **error**. The contrast of **fools** with **the rich** heightens the affirmation and contrasts with Qohelet's recognition of a poor sage in 9:13–16.

10:8–11 / More sayings that sound proverbial continue the theme of reversals. Although **Whoever digs a pit may fall into it** (10:8) is reminiscent of basic retribution sayings (Prov. 26:27; 28:10), the following sayings make it clear that the danger is not limited to those who intend harm to others. Everyday life and doing one's job can be dangerous. Verse 11 recalls the snakebite of 10:8. It also qualifies **skill will bring success** (10:10): skill can bring about good results, but is worthless if not used in time.

10:12–15 / Concern with positive and negative uses of language recurs in the context of folly and wisdom (cf. especially 5:3; 6:11). The fool **consumed by his own lips** (10:12) recalls the imagery of 4:5.

10:16–11:2 / If these verses are to be read together, which is by no means certain, they have an "on the one hand . . . on the other hand" relationship. First Qohelet reaffirms the goodness of the social order, diligence, and moderate eating, while rejecting lower-class rulers, morning feasts, and laziness. The contrasting response comes in 10:19. Bread and wine are to be enjoyed. It is money (and not social standing or hard work?) that solves life's problems. The warning about propriety (10:20) sounds again like a response: it could be the one who indulges in too much feasting whose thoughtless words bring trouble.

The interpretation of 11:1–2 is disputed. If the dialogic interpretation of the context is correct, then these verses may provide a call to take risks, again in response to the warning to be careful. Others have read it as approval of international trade. The last verse may even anticipate Jesus' parable of the shrewd manager (Luke 16:1–9).

11:3–6 / This short segment, which is difficult to join with either the preceding or following verses, is a collection of sayings. They come mostly from an agricultural milieu (11:5b is the exception). They are connected by the theme of outcomes that are random or at least beyond human control. These outcomes stretch from determinism (what will happen will happen, 11:3a) to permanence (what has happened cannot be undone, 11:3b). A possible response is in 11:4 (see 3:1–17), where it is noted that one might be paralyzed by a concern with finding the proper time. But because one cannot know the work of God and God has made everything (11:5cd), it is appropriate to go ahead and act (11:6). In fact, rather than being inhibited, one ought to work harder, since it is not certain which course of action will bring success.

11:7–10 The closing segment is an extended call to joy, using imagery of light and darkness (11:7–8). Unlike the other exhortation, this one is expressly directed to the young (11:9) and cognizant of the meaninglessness (or brevity) of life (11:10) and the certainty of divine **judgment** (11:9).

Additional Notes §9

9:11 / **Time and chance happen to them all:** Cf. "there is a time for everything, and a season for every activity" (3:1) and "there is a proper time and procedure for every matter" (8:6). This verse introduces **chance** (Hb. *pega^c*) into the equation.

9:15 / **And he saved the city:** The Hb. supports the possibility that the protagonist saved the city and was later forgotten, as NIV implies. The context suggests another reading: that no one thought to consult the poor sage who could have saved the city but did not have the opportunity.

9:16 / If the causal relationship suggested by NIV **So** is correct, it is likelier that the quotation extends to the end of the verse instead of ending after "strength."

10:3 / **And shows everyone how stupid he is:** The Hb. (lit. "and tells everyone that he is a fool") is ambiguous. It could be that the the fool discloses his own folly (as NIV suggests) or that the fool calls everyone else foolish.

10:5 / **From a ruler:** The Hb. word for ruler *(šallîṭ)* is not the one used elsewhere in this section *(môšēl;* 9:17; 10:4). Given the following examples, one might wonder whether this refers to a human ruler who fails to keep social order or to God who makes the wrong people prosperous and needy.

10:6 / **Fools are put in many high positions, while the rich occupy the low ones:** The reversal of social position is here a cause for lament rather than for celebration (contrast 1 Sam. 2:4–8).

10:14 / **And the fool multiplies words:** It is possible to connect the phrase with v. 13 (as does NIV) or with the rest of v. 14. If the latter is correct, one might suspect some self-deprecation on Qohelet's part because what follows is a repetition of one of Qohelet's key claims.

10:18 / Out of context, the verse would refer to an actual physical structure. In context, one wonders whether the house is a metaphor for government that is neglected because the princes are feasting instead of governing.

11:7 / **It pleases the eye to see the sun:** Contrast the joy in seeing the sun here with the drudgery elsewhere connected with being under the sun.

11:10 / **Meaningless:** As in 9:7–10, the primary sense here is of life's brevity.

§10 The End (Eccl. 12:1–8)

The book of Ecclesiastes proper closes with a meditation on old age and death (12:1–7), followed by the concluding motto (12:8). The poem on old age balances nicely with the preceding call to joy, which emphasized the youth of the addressee. The reference to youth is picked up in 12:1 ("the days of your youth"), and the imagery of light and darkness in 12:2 ("before the sun and the light and the moon and the stars grow dark").

12:1–7 / The poem is rich with the remembrance of youthful pleasure, poignant with the gradual physical decline of old age, and relentless in its movement toward death. Decline and death are described in vivid metaphors of a decaying house. The Hebrew uses participles which are most naturally (but not necessarily) read personally (for example, **keepers, grinders**). It is a poem which seems to be slowing to a halt, but then bursts into fragments (the cut **cord**, the broken **bowl**, the **shattered pitcher**, and the **broken wheel**, 12:6). The **dust returns to the ground** and the **spirit to God** (perhaps in contrast to 3:21).

The whole poem is one long sentence. The NIV obscures this by beginning new sentences in verses 5 and 6. If read as one sentence, the reader, along with the human subject of the passage, will be "out of breath" by the end.

12:8 / The closing motto of the book matches 1:2. The use of an inclusion formula suggests completeness, and indeed Qohelet stops speaking here. The epilogue refers to Qohelet in the third person but does not adopt the persona.

Additional Notes §10

12:1 / **Your Creator:** While some emend (Qohelet never explicitly refers to God as Creator elsewhere, although the concept of God's creative role pervades the book), **your Creator** here and **God who gave it** in 12:7 form an inclusion for the poem. Thus "Creator" is the preferable meaning.

12:5 / **The almond tree blossoms and the grasshopper drags himself along and desire is no longer stirred:** There are several translation problems here. It is more likely that the correct reading is "the almond tree blossoms and the grasshopper grows fat and the caperberry bears fruit." Otherwise the blossoming almond tree has no connection with its context. By including fat and fruit, these verses provide a contrast between the decline and death of the human and the rest of the world going on and being fruitful, forming a conceptual link with 1:4.

12:6 / **Before the silver cord is severed, or the golden bowl is broken:** The images of silver cord and golden bowl are difficult. They may be images of sexual vitality or simply images of life.

§11 Epilogue (Eccl. 12:9–14)

12:9–14 / This epilogue, which refers to Qohelet in the third person, is no doubt from a later hand. But it is probably from someone who knew and appreciated Qohelet. Although many commentators suggest that the epilogist seriously misunderstood Qohelet and was trying to make the book more orthodox, the only line clearly out of keeping with the rest of the book is **Fear God and keep his commandments** (12:13), and if **keep his commandments** were altered to "enjoy life," even this line would fit nicely. It is not that Qohelet would object to keeping commandments, but commandments are nowhere else mentioned. If Qohelet believed that keeping explicit commandments would ensure God's pleasure, much of the anguish of the previous chapters would be unnecessary. The juxtaposition of a saying that values the words of the wise (12:11) with one that reminds the reader that there is no end to book-making (12:12) creates a tension which makes a fine tribute to Qohelet.

The epilogue gives some insight into the epilogist's view of both Qohelet and the book. Qohelet had a reputation both as a sage and as a teacher (12:9). The combination of finding and ordering proverbs (12:9) with meticulous writing (12:10) suggests that the book does indeed incorporate existing proverbs into Qohelet's own careful composition.

The reader may infer that the epilogist believed Qohelet's exploration had gone as far as was prudent. Such expressions as **Be warned, my son, of anything in addition** (12:12) and **Now all has been heard** (12:13) suggest that further speculation could be dangerous.

Additional Note §11

12:12   /   **My son:** This is the only occurrence in Ecclesiastes of the common wisdom address "my son."

The Song of Songs

Elizabeth Huwiler

Introduction: Song of Songs

The Song of Songs and Other Biblical Texts

The Song of Songs is the only extended corpus of love poetry in the Bible. This fact in itself makes it remarkable. The book
is also unusual in the Bible in that it mentions God directly perhaps only once (8:6), and most likely not at all. It does not refer to
most of the specifically Israelite traditions (such as Exodus, Torah,
covenant, or ancestors). Even in reference to its central concern,
sexual love, it does not mention the specific biblical regulations
regarding human sexuality or the common concern for procreation. Neither is there any clear reference to marriage between
the protagonists. Even the vocabulary is quite unusual. The book
contains nearly fifty words that do not occur elsewhere in the
Bible.[1] Finally, the Song is unusual in that it gives central place to
a woman's voice unmediated by that of a narrator.

Nonetheless, the Song is also similar to other biblical texts.
In spite of its many unique words, its vocabulary does overlap
with other biblical texts, in particular with the wisdom books and
those parts of the prophetic books that use the image of marriage.
The place name most frequently mentioned is Jerusalem and
many of the other known places are Israelite as well. The Song
also contains references to kingship and Solomon as well as one
reference to the tower of David.

Themes and Images

Several themes run through the Song. When the central
pair are apart, the woman expresses desire for her absent lover.
When they are together, they speak of delight in each other's
presence. Together or apart, each admires the other's body. There
is also the woman's sense of opposition from others (brothers
in 1:5–6 and perhaps 8:8–9; city guards in 5:7; and unnamed

persons, perhaps society in general, in 8:1). The lovers issue repeated invitations to one another. An unidentified voice warns the daughters not to "arouse or awaken love until it so desires." Finally, the lovers must often part.

Poetic images abound. There are many instances of simile and metaphor. Some of the comparisons draw attention to themselves by going beyond "you are like" to "I liken you" or "make yourself like." Out of the thirty uses of the word for "liken" or "be like" in the entire Bible, five are in the Song. This is a frequency highly disproportionate to the book's length. The poet calls attention to the lovers' imaginations and, in so doing, invites the readers to imaginative activity as well.

Metaphors in the Song can be fluid and, in a sense, disconcerting to Western ears. For example, in one descriptive passage (7:1–9), the man compares the woman's stature to that of a date palm and her breasts to date clusters. Then the speaker enters into his own private metaphor, expressing his desire to climb the tree and gain access to its fruit. The image of the date clusters transmutes into an image of grapes, then apples. The description ends with the man likening the woman's mouth to wine. The woman, who throughout the passage has been the silent object of the man's admiration, breaks in and invites him to drink the wine. I suspect that a student who produced such a chain of images in a creative writing class nowadays might well have the paper returned with "mixed metaphor" scrawled in disapproving red ink. Yet for the poet of the Song, such mixed or fluid metaphors are not a problem and, in fact, enrich the text. It is fitting that the reader may find them confusing and beguiling at the same time. With young love as the subject and wine as a recurring metaphor, heady confusion is perfectly appropriate.

The poet uses military language in relation to the woman—often in terms of likeness: her neck, nose, or breasts are "like [a] tower[s]" (4:4; 7:4; 8:10) and her eyes "majestic as troops with banners" (6:4). On the tower of David, that is like her neck, "hang a thousand shields, all of them shields of warriors" (4:4). Military language is also used in the difficult 3:6–11, explicitly in association with Solomon, but it is not clear whether this imagery is connected with one of the major characters more than the other.[2]

The woman is also associated with architectural imagery. In addition to the tower, she is also a wall (8:10). These pictures may connect with both the military and the geographical image groups. In addition, she describes herself as being in a house, apparently in a city (2:9 and probably the opening of both dream sequences, 3:1–2 and 5:2–6). She also refers to her mother's house (3:4; 8:2).

Family images are used primarily of and by the woman. She refers to both her mother and her brothers, but not to her father or her sisters. There is also one reference to the man's mother (8:5) by the woman (two references if one identifies the Solomon figure of 3:11 with the central man). The man refers once to the woman's mother and uses the language of "sister" in reference to the central woman, who is not a biological sibling.

There is a great deal of natural and agricultural imagery. Wild animal images are used for both the man and the woman. The man is a gazelle and a stag (2:9, 17; 8:14). The woman's breasts are like twin fawns of a gazelle (4:5 and 7:3) and she is associated with a lion and a leopard (4:8). Only the woman is compared with domesticated animals, including a mare (1:9), goats (4:1; 6:5), and sheep (4:2; 6:6). The principal bird image is the dove, which is used as both image and epithet of the woman as a whole and specifically as an image of her eyes (1:15; 2:14; 4:1; 5:2; 6:9). The dove is used once as an image of the man's eyes (5:12). The raven is used once as an image for the man's black hair (5:11). The (turtle)dove occurs once in reference to the season in which the Song takes place (2:12).[3]

The woman is associated particularly with specific geographical imagery. She compares her dark appearance with the tents of Kedar (and perhaps Salma, 1:5). She also compares herself to a flower in the Sharon plain (2:1). The man compares her hair to goats moving down Mount Gilead (4:1; 6:5), her beauty to Tirzah and Jerusalem (6:4), her eyes to pools in Heshbon by the gate of Bath Rabbim (7:4), her nose to the tower of Lebanon looking toward Damascus (7:4), and her head to Mount Carmel (7:5). He calls her to descend from Amana, Senir, and Hermon (4:8).

Far fewer geographical images are associated with the man. The woman compares him with henna blossoms from the En Gedi oasis (1:14) and perhaps sends him to run on the hills of Bether (see the comment on 2:17). One site (also identified separately with the woman) is associated with both of them together. The man invites the woman to come with him from Lebanon (4:8).

The woman is (or parts of her are) also associated with landscape elements—mountain, valley, garden, vineyard, orchard, spring, pool, and fountain—and with the plants in them.

Spices and incense are associated with both central characters, more frequently with the woman. The most common among them is myrrh, which is used once by the woman to describe the man (1:13), and is also clearly used once by the man to refer to the woman (4:14). In addition, myrrh is used twice by the man in contexts that make it seem symbolic of the woman (4:6; 5:1) and twice by the woman when she realizes that her lover is gone (5:5). Once it is found in an enigmatic verse in which neither speaker nor referent is clear, although the NIV assigns it to the friends (3:6). Incense is used to parallel myrrh in two of these instances (3:6; 4:6). Spices appear in the same verse with myrrh and incense once (3:6) and with perfume once (5:13, the woman speaking of the man). Spices are used alone three times (6:2, the man apparently speaking of the woman; 8:2 and 8:14, in both instances the woman is apparently inviting the man and thus perhaps speaking of herself). Perfume or oil is used three times: in 1:3 and 5:13 by the woman speaking of the man and in 1:12 where the woman speaks of herself.

Images of metals and gems are used of both characters. They appear in reference to the woman in 1:10–11; 7:1, 4; 8:9 and perhaps 8:11. In reference to the man, we see them in 5:11–12, 14–15. If he is identified with Solomon, we may add 3:10. Jewelry images refer only to the woman (1:10–11; 4:9; and hinted in 4:4). The only exception may be the crown, which is used in connection with Solomon (3:11). Fabric and garment imagery is used in connection with both the woman (1:5, 7; 2:10; 4:3, 11; 5:3, 7; 7:1, 5) and Solomon (3:10).

Wine is used by the woman speaking of the man (1:2; 2:4) and by the friends speaking of the man (1:4). It is used by the woman inviting the man (8:2) and it is used repeatedly by the man speaking of the woman (4:10; 5:1; 7:2, 9).

The interweaving of this surprising range of image groups gives the Song a complex texture. Picking one or two image groups and staying in them would inappropriately limit this relationship. While the nuances of specific images are discussed in the commentary on the relevant verses, some generalizations about the image groups can be made here. First, the number of images and image groups that are used of both characters emphasizes the mutuality of their love. The natural and agriculture images imply fertility. Geography and landscape emphasize the expansiveness of this love, while spices and incense give it an exotic aura. Metals, gems, and jewelry hint at the value the two see in one another. The frequent references to wine suggest that the relationship is intoxicating.

The images used primarily or exclusively of only one central character have an effect too. The miltary images show how awesome and frightening the woman (or falling in love with her) is. Family images situate her socially, while the man is presented as though unaffected by family and social networks. Fabrics and garments suggest both the value of the woman and her association with the domestic realm. The mix of wild and domestic animals used of the woman suggest that the man is in love with both her wildness and the hope of domesticating her.

The frequent slide between poetic imagery and descriptive language makes interpreting the imagery of the poem difficult. Ariel and Chana Bloch note that in the use of landscape imagery:

> metaphors keep shifting between the actual landscape, suffused with erotic associations, and the landscape of the body. The Shulamite waits for her lover in a garden, but she herself is a garden; the two of them go out to the fragrant vineyards to make love, but she herself is a vineyard, her breasts like clusters of grapes, and their kisses an intoxicating wine.[4]

As the quotation indicates, this shift occurs not only with landscape images but with others as well—especially wine and fruit, but also animals. The blurring of the distinction between image and association, and the confusion that a literal-minded reader may feel in trying to separate them, is part of what gives the book its particular erotic charge through delicate language. The most notable example is the second of the woman's night narratives (5:2–7). On a descriptive level, the man is without a doubt knocking on the door of the house and asking the woman to open it so that he can come in out of the heavy dew. She hesitates; then she rises to open the door for her lover. While opening it, she finds her hands slippery with myrrh on the handles of the lock. She is finally able to open for her lover, but he has left, and her heart sinks. The language allows for this strictly descriptive reading. But the poetry is also charged enough to allow for imagining that she herself is the house, ready to open for her lover. In that case, the "dew of night" and "liquid myrrh" may symbolize more erotic fluids.

Forms

If we exclude the superscription (1:1) from consideration, the whole of the Song is poetry, spoken by one or more of the characters. Almost all recent translations agree, although the NJB differs on both points, using prose for 8:8–13 and ascribing 3:6–11 and the last lines of 5:1 to the poet rather than to any of the characters in the Song.

It is often difficult to isolate specific forms and divisions between poetic units. In general, it is helpful to distinguish between soliloquies of individual characters and dialogues involving two or more characters. Yet sometimes it is difficult to be sure whether particular verses consist of two or more very short units of monologue or whether they comprise one longer unit of dialogue. I do not find it useful to ascribe formal labels to the different elements, with the exception of the descriptive motifs, narrative sequences, and refrains.

Descriptive motifs. This is a poem in which one lover describes the other from head to toe or from toe to head. The metaphors are emotive and evocative and are seemingly not designed to help us visualize the other's actual physical characteristics. This form is also called a *waṣf,* after the similar but much later Arabic poems.[5] There is an example of this form in 4:1–7, where the man describes the woman from head to breasts. In 5:10–16, the woman describes the man from head to legs, and then describes his entire appearance and mouth. Another example, where the man speaks only about parts of the woman's head, is found in 6:5–7. Finally, in 7:1–8, the man presents a graphic description of the woman: feet to head, then whole body, breasts, and mouth.

Narrative sequences. There are two sections in which the woman describes a night experience (3:1–4 and 5:2–7). These are the only passages in the Song that follow the typical pattern of Hebrew narrative: first establish a time frame, then describe, in sequence, events with an implicit relationship to one another. Ironically, these are also among the most disputed passages. Are they dream reports, descriptions of the woman's waking behavior, or fantasies expressing her hopes (3:1–4) and fears (5:2–7)? Taken together, the two narratives delimit her sense of the best and worst (whether possibility or actuality) about the relationship. Both passages end with addresses to the daughters of Jerusalem, which suggests that they have been the audience for the narratives.

Refrains. There are several refrain lines in the Song. All of them are assigned to the woman in the NIV translation. They are:

"His left arm is under my head, and his right arm embraces me" (2:6; 8:3) and "Daughters of Jerusalem, I charge you by the gazelles and by the does of the field: Do not arouse or awaken love until it so desires" (2:7 and 3:5 in full form; the beginning only in 5:8; the beginning and ending without the central section in 8:4). There is another refrain, both halves of which recur, with or without modifications: "My lover is mine and I am his; he browses among the lilies" (2:16); "I am my lover's and my lover is mine; he browses among the lilies" (6:3); "I belong to my lover, and his desire is for me" (7:10). These verses are discussed more fully below.

Repetitions and Their Function

The Song of Songs is full of repetitions—whole verses, pairs of verses, lines, images, epithets, and even the echo of an entire scene. These repetitions have the initial effect of drawing the text together into a whole and of encouraging the reader to make sense of the Song as a book. In addition, they move the reader to associate the passages in which these repetitions occur. The reader must determine when the repetition is essentially an echo of its first use and when it indicates a noticeable modification or development.

Most noticeable is the repetition of whole verses. The first of these might be translated "his left arm under my head, / his right arm embracing me" (2:6; 8:3). Although the NIV uses the present tense ("His left arm is under my head, / his right arm embraces me"), the Hebrew does not use temporal verbs, so the verse can be interpreted variously as a description of what is happening at the time, as memory, or as hope. Bloch and Bloch suggest understanding this line as embodying a combination of memory and desire,[6] but their claim may be too strong. The reader is not certain, at least in the first encounter with the verse, whether the woman lover has ever experienced what she describes. The first occurrence of this verse follows "Strengthen me with raisins, refresh me with apples, for I am faint with love," the second occurrence follows "I would give you spiced wine to drink, the nectar of my pomegranates." Both are followed by the warning, which is in full form in 2:7 and omits the gazelles and hinds in 8:4. It seems that in the first instance the woman has been speaking about the man, perhaps in his absence, while in the second she has been speaking directly to him. But in both cases the verse following, which is a warning, is addressed to the Jerusalem girls.

In the first case in particular, the verse is more likely to express desire than fulfillment. In the second, the interpretation of the verse depends on how one understands the events of the intervening chapters. In this case, a mingling of memory and desire is likely appropriate.

The second whole-verse repetition is an adjuration or warning to the woman's female companions. This verse is full and identical in 2:7 and 3:6: "Daughters of Jerusalem, I charge you / by the gazelles and by the does of the field: / Do not arouse or awaken love / until it so desires."[7] The beginning of this verse is found in 5:8, but the reference to gazelles and does is absent, and rather than being urged not to awaken love, the hearers are to tell him, if they find him, that she is faint with love (the other "faint with love" came before the first left arm/right arm refrain in 2:6). Finally, the verse occurs in 8:4, with the identical opening, but as in the third occurrence there is nothing by which to swear the oath. This last use ends with a slightly different form. In each instance, the NIV (and most versions and commentaries) assign the adjuration to the central female character—a likely but not certain ascription. A few readers have supposed that the central man is insisting that the lover be allowed to sleep until she is ready to waken. It is also possible that another voice, using the central woman's behavior as an example for good or ill, might warn the young women of Jerusalem not to be hasty in love.

This adjuration (and in the Hb., the daughters are not simply warned but asked to take an oath) always occurs after a passage of emotional and/or physical intensity between the two central characters. Is the central woman's behavior being held up as a model ("Do not stir up love until you are as certain as I am/she is") or as a negative example ("Do not stir up love too soon—see what turmoil you might experience")? This question need not be answered in the same way for each occurrence.

The third element repeated in the Song is the mutual possession formula, which is slightly different each time: "My lover is mine and I am his" (2:16a); "I am my lover's and my lover is mine" (6:3); and "I am my lover's and his desire is for me" (7:10). The first two form a complementary pair, both followed by "he browses among the lilies." The third is different, and it heightens the intensity as it moves from animal sensibilities (grazing/browsing) to a personal one (desire). There is also here the reversed echo of the Eden story and of Cain and Abel. The only three uses of the noun, meaning "desire" in the Bible, are in Genesis 3:16, 4:7, and this verse. This verse alone does not include the concept of mastery or domination of the one who is desired over the one who desires.

The three uses of the possession formula occur in strikingly different contexts. The first comes between the playful "catch the foxes" (2:15) and the ambiguous, "Until the day breaks and the shadows flee, turn, my lover, and be like a gazelle or a young stag on the rugged hills" (2:17) The formula occurs a second time after the woman tells the Jerusalem girls that her lover has gone to his garden to browse and to gather lilies, and before the abbreviated descriptive motif in 6:5–7. The third use comes after the dance *waṣf* (7:1–9a) has been transformed into wine imagery, and right before an invitation to go to the countryside and spend the night together.

There are also several repetitions within the descriptive motifs themselves, particularly in those in which the woman is described. Compare the following excerpts:

> *How beautiful you are, my darling!*
> Oh, how beautiful!
> Your eyes behind your veil are doves.
> *Your hair is like a flock of goats*
> *descending from Mount Gilead.*
> *Your teeth are like a flock of sheep just shorn,*
> *coming up from the washing.*
> *Each has its twin;*
> *not one of them is alone.*
> Your lips are like a scarlet ribbon;
> your mouth is lovely.
> *Your temples behind your veil*
> *are like the halves of a pomegranate.*
> *Your neck is* like the *tower of David,*
> built with elegance;
> on it hang a thousand shields,
> all of them shields of warriors.
> *Your two breasts are like two fawns,*
> *like twin fauns of a gazelle*
> that browse among the lilies.
> Until the day breaks
> and the shadows flee,
> I will go to the mountain of myrrh
> and to the hill of incense.
> *All beautiful you are,* my darling;
> there is no flaw in you. (4:1–7)

You are *beautiful, my darling,* as Tirzah,
     lovely as Jerusalem,
     majestic as troops with banners.
Turn your eyes from me;
     they overwhelm me.
Your hair is like a flock of goats
     descending from Gilead.
Your teeth are like a flock of sheep
     coming up from the washing.
Each has its twin,
     not one of them is alone.
Your temples behind your veil
     are like the halves of a pomegranate.
Sixty queens there may be,
     and eighty concubines,
     and virgins beyond number;
but my dove, my perfect one, is unique,
     the only daughter of her mother,
     the favorite of the one who bore her.
The maidens saw her and called her blessed;
     the queens and concubines praised her. (6:4–9)

How beautiful your sandaled feet,
     O prince's daughter!
Your graceful legs are like jewels,
     the work of a craftsman's hands.
Your navel is a rounded goblet
     that never lacks blended wine.
Your waist is a mound of wheat
     encircled by lilies.
Your breasts are like two fawns,
     twins of a gazelle.
Your neck is like an ivory *tower.*
Your eyes are the pools of Heshbon
     by the gate of Bath Rabbim.
Your nose is like the tower of Lebanon
     looking toward Damascus.
Your head crowns you like Mount Carmel.
     Your hair is like royal tapestry;
     the king is held captive by its tresses.
How beautiful you are and how pleasing,
     O love, with your delights! (7:1–6)

The first of these three descriptions consists primarily of
material that is repeated elsewhere. The elements printed in italic

occur in two or more of these three passages. In addition, the references to eyes as doves (4:1) is repeated in the woman's description of the man (5:12). The military images correspond, although without verbatim repetition, to those in the second descriptive passage. The reference to browsing among the lilies is an echo of the woman's description of the man in two of the three occurrences of the mutual possession formula (2:16; 6:3). "Until the day breaks and the shadows flee" is a precise echo of 2:17ab. "The mountain of myrrh and the hill of incense" is not a verbatim repetition but does anticipate the "spice-laden mountains" of 8:14, the last phrase in the book. Both myrrh and incense are recurring images in the Song.

It is striking that the second and third descriptive motifs contain relatively equal amounts of material that are repeated from this first description of the woman. Only the general acknowledgment of beauty links the second and third descriptions together. Likewise, only the comparison of eyes with doves links any of them with the passage describing the man (5:10–16).

Less extended repetitions also occur. In 2:9a, the woman says, "My lover is like a gazelle or a young stag"; shortly afterward, she calls to him to "turn, my lover, / and be like a gazelle / or like a young stag / on the rugged hills" (2:17c–f). The book ends with her call to him, "Come away, my lover, / and be like a gazelle / or like a young stag / on the spice-laden mountains" (8:14). The first of these (2:9a), which follows the first adjuration "by the gazelles and by the does of the field" (2:7), links the lover with that oath. The words for the animals have the same roots in both: feminine forms in the oath, masculine forms in reference to the lover. The second of these repetitions comes in a verse that can be interpreted in two opposite ways. On the one hand, the woman could be warning the man away to the distant landscape ("turn away and roam the hills") or, on the other hand, she could be inviting him to her personal landscape ("turn to me, and roam my hills"). At this point in the poem, the reader is inclined to understand it as a warning because the use of landscape imagery for the woman is not yet established. The third repetition, while also ambiguous, tends more toward the personal landscape. By this time spices and landscape images have been used of the woman frequently enough that we readers understand this as an invitation—although the wording is still ambiguous enough that bystanders (such as the brothers) who have not heard the lovers' language may well understand her to be warning him to flee.

The second of these extended repetitions described above comes in a verse (2:17) which includes yet another repetition: "Until the day breaks and the shadows flee" recurs in the man's voice in 4:6. There is some ambiguity to this line, which some interpreters understand as a reference to evening rather than morning. Like 2:17 and 8:14, 4:6 also includes a reference to mountains: "I will go to the mountain of myrrh / and to the hill of incense." At the end of a passage describing the woman, the hills certainly allude to her body. This helps to prepare us to interpret the "spice-laden mountains" of 8:14 in reference to her as well.

Twice one of the lovers speaks of going out to check on the growth of plants:

> I went down to the grove of nut trees
> to look at the new growth in the valley,
> to see if the vines had budded
> or the pomegranates were in bloom. (6:11)

> Let us go early to the vineyards
> to see if the vines have budded,
> if their blossoms have opened,
> and if the pomegranates are in bloom—
> there I will give you my love. (7:12)

The NIV assigns the former of these to the man, the latter to the woman. While 7:12 must be spoken by the woman, the speaker is less clear in 6:11, where there is no second-person pronoun. The context makes the woman a more likely speaker in 6:11. If the NIV is correct, however, this overlap of language between the two lovers serves to emphasize the correspondence between the lovers. Regardless who the speaker is, the explicit mutuality and sexual invitation of 7:12 removes any possibility of reading the curiosity of 6:11 as purely agricultural.

Repetitions also occur in the dream scenes: "I looked for him but did not find him" (3:1–2; 5:6); "The watchmen found me / as they made their rounds in the city" (3:3; 5:7). Because the outcomes of these two episodes are so different, the common language emphasizes both the risk and the opportunity that the young woman recognizes in her yearning and search for her lover.

The lovers have usual (but not invariable) names for each other. The man refers to the woman most often as "my darling" (NIV translation of Hebrew *raʿyātî*, which is the feminine form of the usual word for "friend"). The woman refers to the man most often as "my lover" (Hebrew *dôdî*), but also as "the one my heart loves." The lovers also employ similar images: preferring the other's love to wine (woman to man in 1:2; man to woman in 4:10), comparing the other's eyes to doves (man of woman in 4:1; woman of man in 5:12).

These repetitions help to establish the characters and their relationship throughout the Song. The images that both the man and the woman use in reference to each other establish a symmetry in the relationship. This symmetry is balanced by the elements of contrast between the two in other areas.

Characters

Most interpreters understand there to be two main characters actively present in the text, one woman and one man, as well as a female group (the daughters of Jerusalem), and perhaps also a male group (the woman's brothers).

Because the book is composed of direct speech, characterization is achieved through what individuals say about themselves and one another. There is no overt narrative voice intruding into the monologues and dialogues. Because the main characters are in love, their characterizations of each other are charged with emotive content. And since the language of the Song slips frequently between metaphor and description, the reader experiences occasional confusion regarding what a character is claiming about self or about another.

The central pair is quite young; indeed, some commentators refer to them as "girl" and "boy" rather than "woman" and "man."[8] Yet the two are rather sophisticated. The rustic imagery is probably just artifice. For these young lovers know about exotic spices and fine fabrics.

The lovers are single-minded in their devotion to each other and to their relationship. Both of them speak freely of invitations to romantic trysts and admire each other's physical charms. The woman speaks confidently of herself and her beauty, but the man's first-person speeches are more concerned with what he will do. As discussed above, the woman mentions family most frequently, both her own and that of her lover. We know the woman's character more fully, because we hear her not only with her lover but also in conversation with the daughters of Jerusalem, and perhaps in solitary meditation as well. The man is usually (perhaps always) in the presence of the woman when we hear his voice.

The daughters of Jerusalem are not fully developed characters and so are difficult to interpret. They function primarily as an audience for the woman's rhapsodies about her lover. They do seem willing to help her find her "missing" lover in 6:1.

The woman expresses an awareness of opposition to the relationship from others—including brothers, city watchmen, and unnamed scorners. The brothers may be guardians of their sister, and particularly of her sexuality. It is not clear whether they have a speaking part in the Song, although some ascribe 8:8–9 to them.

These characterizations are posited based on a view of the book as a unity, assuming, therefore, that there is continuity of character. Those who read the text as an anthology do not assume that "the woman" of the first poem is necessarily to be identified with the "the woman" of any of the rest of the text.

Identification of Speakers

Many translations, including the NIV, attribute each section to a given speaker. Such designations are not present in the MT or early manuscripts but are often implied by the Hebrew pronouns, verbs, and adjectives. There are, however, cases in which the identification of the speaker is not clear.

In the second person Hebrew does distinguish between masculine and feminine singular and between singular and plural forms, so it is usually possible to tell whether the central man, the central woman, or a group is being addressed. Hebrew verbs often distinguish as well between masculine and feminine plural, but in the Song of Songs the usual form used to address the "daughters of Jerusalem" is the "masculine" form. In the first person, Hebrew verbs and pronouns distinguish between singular and plural but not between masculine and feminine. It is not clear, therefore, whether the "I" speaking is masculine or feminine unless the speaker makes a self-reference using adjectives, which are inflected according to gender and number.

Passages that use the first-person plural are assigned most often to a group (usually the daughters of Jerusalem), occasionally to one of the lovers in reference to both (for example, "let us hurry" in 1:4). In passages in which an individual is speaking to or about a man, most translations assume the speaker to be the central woman. When, on the other hand, an individual is speaking to or about a woman, most assume the speaker to be the central man. Given the characters in the Song and its subject matter, this attribution of speeches is not unreasonable. Nonetheless, it it possible, especially in some passages addressed to the central woman, that her mother or one of the daughters of Jerusalem might be speaking. The terms used to address the central pair exacerbate this confusion. The most common terms in first-person singular speech for addressing the man are "my lover" (Hb. *dôdî*, twenty-seven uses) and "the one my heart loves" (Hb. *še'āhᵃbâ napšî*, five uses). Both of these terms are appropriately spoken only by one with love interest in the addressee, and are thus ascribed to the central woman. However, the term most often used in first-person speech to address the woman, although translated "my darling" by the NIV, is the Hebrew *ra'yātî* (nine uses). This is the feminine form of the common Hebrew word for "friend" or "companion." The Hebrew word *kallâ* appears six times and is translated "my bride" in the NIV and most other versions but is not in fact first-person possessive. The term next in frequency is "my sister" (Hb. *'ᵃhōtî*, five uses). None of these terms is necessarily limited to use by a person in love with the addressee. It is imaginable, then, that some passages addressed to the woman using one or more of these terms but not otherwise containing expressions of love might be spoken by someone else. There are, moreover, many passages in which the first person is not used at all. In these cases, the reader must decide whether an individual or a group is speaking.

Unity

The Song contains indications of both unity and disunity. The repetition of verses, themes, images, vocabulary, and character labels achieves a certain unity. And yet, the absence of a clear plot movement and the lack of a consistent development in the relationship between the central pair undercut this apparent unity. Overall, there are enough elements tying the text together to encourage readers to try to make sense of the Song as a whole. Nonetheless, there are enough gaps that many readers finally conclude that this is more anthology than single work.

Some interpreters, rather than seeking to discern the unity of the Song in its plot, have looked for an overall unifying structure. Several structural patterns have been proposed.[8] None of them has won widespread acceptance. The problem is that, like the metaphors, the poetic units which make up the Song flow into one another and it is very difficult to make a persuasive argument for more than a few structural divisions.

Ariel and Chana Bloch offer the most eloquent plea for understanding the Song as a unified work without denying the lack of narrative wholeness or strict structural patterning:

> The elements of a plot are available, and we can hardly help wanting to link them, although plot seems the least of our poet's concerns. The Songs of Songs is a sequence of lyric poems, episodic in its structure—not a narrative, and not a drama. The so-called gaps and discontinuities in the text are problematic only for those who attempt to read it as one or the other. . . . Because of its consistency of characterization, themes, images, and poetic voice, it asks to be read as a unified sequence. . . . It makes no sense to judge lyric poetry by the standards of logical discourse, requiring a systematic progression from A to B to C and thence to a conclusion, with every link soldered firmly into place, as some exegetes do. . . . Apparently the biblical poets had a more flexible notion of unity and structure than many scholars have recognized.[9]

This commentary takes the view that the indications of unity are sufficient to encourage reading the Song of Songs as a unified text. Thus I am assuming that the characters remain the same throughout, that there is some plot development (albeit with considerable gaps), and that it makes sense to interpret passages in reference to other passages in the Song. Unlike Bloch and Bloch, I believe that the gaps and abrupt shifts in the Song are in fact problematic for the reader—but appropriately so. The Song is about sexual desire and there is no regular linear or even concentric movement to desire. The erratic movement of the Song, the abrupt shifts of scene and audience, the difficulty in distinguishing fantasy from straightforward description—all of these are confusing, and at the same time beguiling. These idiosyncrasies draw the audience into the text and into the confusion and false confidence of young love much more effectively than a neatly wrapped-up plot or a tightly structured outline could ever do.

Genre

Over the years, commentators have produced a voluminous array of proposals to define the genre of the Song of Songs as a whole. The following list is not exhaustive, but it attempts to include those interpretations that have had significant influence. Most contemporary interpreters view the Song primarily as love poetry/songs. Depending on their view of the unity of the text, recent interpretations are most likely to fall into one of the first three categories listed here.

Collection of short love lyrics. Marcia Falk views the Song as a collection of short love lyrics: "the Song has a variety of contexts that shift frequently in no apparent dramatic sequence and within which many different kinds of voices speak. There is no reason to assume only a few fixed speakers."[10] The inclusion of many different specific forms and the absence of a clear plot all support taking the text in this way. The use of repetitions, the consistency of characters and characterization, and the presence of plot elements found in disparate sections of the text, however, undercut this view. Interpreters who see the text as a collection of short love lyrics do not agree on where one poem ends and another begins.

Sequence of related love lyrics. Ariel and Chana Bloch (see above, "Unity") see the Song as a sequence of related love lyrics. This position mediates between the view of the Song as a collection of independent texts and the view that the Song is a single unified poem. Further, it takes seriously both the text's unifying characteristics and the fact that segments of it can function as independent poems.

Another version of the "related sequence" theory sees the Song as a sequence of poems to be used in connection with a week-long wedding ceremony.[11] Parallels with much later Arabic wedding ceremonies support this idea. This is questionable not only because the parallels are late, but also because there is nothing in the text that urges marriage as a context for the Song overall.

Extended unified love poem. Michael V. Fox offers a careful evaluation of indicators of unity in the Song, particularly as compared with Egyptian love poems (see "Comparable Texts from Surrounding Cultures," below).[12] Fox considers the use of repetitions and associated sequences, together with consistency of character and narrative frame. He believes that the likeliest explanation is that the Song is one poem composed by one poet.

Nonetheless, this poet may have used earlier materials, and later hands may have made alterations. He suggests entertainment, particularly on holidays, as a possible setting for the use of such a song.[13]

Drama. The Song certainly exhibits dramatic characteristics. It consists of direct speech and presents some dramatic tension. A view of the text as a drama could also explain the lack of clarity about the plot. A dramatic presentation would resolve many of the difficulties that occur to a reader (such as identifying speakers, scene changes, and the entrance and exit of players). If the Song is only the spoken text of a play, without stage directions, it is understandable that we have these interpretive problems. Dramatic readings of the Song are quite varied. Some include two main characters and a single chorus and others have three main characters and choruses. There are also significant differences in plot and scene division.[14] Although it is possible to imagine the Song as a drama, there is not enough information in the text to make any individual dramatic interpretation convincing. The general theory is unlikely to be persuasive until a convincing dramatic presentation is developed.

Text for sacred marriage ritual. The Song contains some imagery that overlaps with sacred Mesopotamian marriage texts, which describe a marriage between male and female deities. The ritual is presumed to have included humans with royal or priestly connections playing the parts of the gods. Some interpreters have considered the Song as evidence of a parallel Israelite or Judahite ritual.[15] This theory is unlikely—partly because there is no indication that the characters are in any sense deified—but more convincingly because there is no apparent evidence of such a ritual in ancient Israel.[16]

Symbolic celebration of the divine/human relationship. These interpretations of the Song have been popular in both Christianity and Judaism. They depend on the similarity of images between the Song and prophetic texts depicting Israel as Yahweh's wife. In Christian use, such interpretations draw on the NT image of the church as the bride of Christ. In both traditions, the divine/human relationship is sometimes described as being between God/Christ and the individual soul. The text as it stands lacks reference to either God or Israel/the church as a people.

Few contemporary interpreters, therefore, are satisfied with this understanding, although some accept it as an additional meaning of the text in its canonical context.[17]

Wisdom. Several factors lead to an association of the Song with the Wisdom literature.[18] The mention of Solomon in the superscription and the tradition of composition by Solomon are primary factors. Solomon is the figure to whom wisdom texts are traditionally ascribed. The superscriptions to and within the book of Proverbs also mention Solomon, and there are hints that he is the persona for part of Ecclesiastes. The wisdom recommendation that young men enjoy sex with the proper (not "strange") woman can be connected with the presentation of sexual attraction in this text. A reference to the mother as "she who has taught me" (8:2), although this is often emended, can support association with wisdom as an educational enterprise. In addition, there is some vocabulary common to wisdom texts in the Song. The imagery of spices is similar to that in Proverbs 7 (also in connection with a sexual relationship). Finally, the wisdom sphere (especially in Egypt, but also in the traditions surrounding Solomon) is associated with compiling exhaustive lists of natural phenomena that may serve as resources for the surprising array of botanical and zoological references in the Song. These factors make an association with the wisdom tradition likely, but they do not prove that the text itself was used as a wisdom, that is, educational, text. It may prove fruitful, however, to re-examine the view of the Song as wisdom in tandem with the possibility that the text's author(s) may have been female (see "Dating and Authorship," below).

Comparable Texts from Surrounding Cultures

Although there are texts from surrounding cultures that are comparable in some ways to the Song, there is nothing connected closely enough to enable a convincing claim of literary dependence or even genre identification. The parallels are particularly helpful in establishing the common cultural milieu out of which the Song came. Parallels most frequently cited include Egyptian love poems and a variety of Mesopotamian texts. Egyptian love poems exhibit the most marked similarities with the Song of Songs.[19] Many of these poems consist primarily or exclusively of direct speech, either addressing or describing the lover. Similarly, the poems use similar images and poetic patterns, including the descriptive motif. The collection includes some multi-part poems or sequences of poems in which characters and relationships are maintained over an extended text. Finally, they do not have an overt religious function. Where the Egyptian love poems differ most sharply from the Song is in the lack of actual dialogue between the lovers.

Dating and Authorship

Dating the Song is difficult. The language (both vocabulary and syntax), the geographical references, the implicit cultural milieu, and parallels with texts from other cultures have all been used to support widely divergent dates: from the age of Solomon to the third century B.C.E.

Thus the dating is uncertain—and, of course, if the text is a composite, different segments could well have originated in different periods. It is also possible that the Song is primarily an early text to which later copyists/editors made some changes or additions. Or it could be primarily a late text which incorporated segments from earlier times or that included deliberately anachronizing elements.

Authorship is also uncertain. Solomon has been traditionally ascribed authorship by those who take the superscription "Solomon's Song of Songs" (1:1) as authorial. The Bible also refers to Solomon's wisdom as including both composition of songs and description of flora and fauna (1 Kgs. 4:32–33). Finally, Solomon is mentioned five or six times in the text of the Song (3:7, 9, 11; 8:11, 12; and possibly 1:5—see commentary) and there are additional references to a king (1:4, 12; 7:5). Finally, the Solomonic age, which saw the maximum extent of Israelite territory and active international trade, is a time in which the far-ranging geographical references would make sense and imported spices would be known.

None of these factors is conclusive, however, and there are problems with the proposal of Solomon as author. The preposition used in the superscription to the Song could indicate sponsorship or dedication instead of authorship. Solomon's reputation for womanizing does not harmonize with the apparently exclusive devotion of the lovers in this text. International trade occurred in other periods as well as Solomon's. Finally, the references to Solomon in the text are all third-person, with the exception of 8:12. In context, this latter reference is best taken as rhetorical, and in any case it is clearly not addressed to one of the central lovers.

The sages (producers of wisdom writings) are possible candidates for authorship. This text, however, contains little that is explicitly didactic. The possible exception is the refrain warning against arousing love before its time (2:7; 3:5; 8:4), but this warning is quite different in tone from the admonitions in Proverbs.

Especially in recent years, it has been suggested that a woman or group of women might be the author(s) of the Song.[20] The text's focus on the central woman supports this view. She is apparently the speaker in the majority of verses and she has the first and last words. She has striking freedom of action and she appears to be present (or within hearing distance) for all of the central man's speeches. He is notably absent for some of hers. There is great mutuality in the relationship between the central pair, with both the woman and the man issuing invitations and admiring the other's appearance. Aside from the central couple, other women (the "daughters of Jerusalem") are the most frequently addressed characters in the Song and speak most or all of the text attributed to neither of the main characters. The family member mentioned most often is the mother (3:4, 11; 6:9; 8:1, 2, 5). Brothers are mentioned ("my mother's sons," 1:6), but fathers are not. The association of women with singing in other biblical texts reinforces the possibility that they are responsible for a text labeled "Song of Songs." Although all of these factors make female authorship a likely hypothesis, it remains one that is impossible to prove.

Canonization

Rabbinic sources indicate that there was some question regarding whether the Song of Songs "defiles the hands," that is, has holy status so that after handling it one would have to wash the hands before touching profane things (mishnah Yadayim 3:5). Whether defiling the hands indicates canonicity, inspiration, or suitability for reading in the synagogue is disputed. It is in this context that Akiba made his famous comment, "all the Writings are holy, but the Song of Songs is the Holy of Holies."[21] There are no direct citations of the Song in the NT. Neither is there any indication that early Christians questioned its canonical status.

Some interpreters believe that the Song could not have been canonized before the development of the symbolic interpretation of the lovers in the Song as God and Israel. There is, however, no list of criteria for canonization that would enable us to test this theory, and other canonical texts (especially in the Writings—the poetic and wisdom books, and some of the historical ones) are also veiled in terms of their theological significance. If the symbolic understanding of the Song did not actually enable its canonization, surely canonizing it encouraged the proliferation of symbolic readings.

The Song, Theology, and Human Sexuality

The theology of the Song is implicit at most. As already mentioned, there are no clear references to the deity. In fact, the daughters of Jerusalem are asked to swear by gazelles and does—when one would expect them to swear by a deity.

The Song can be read as an extended commentary on the "very good" spoken over creation, particularly over the creation of humankind as male and female. Phyllis Trible initiated a reading of the Song as an undoing of the estrangement between men and women, as well as of the estrangement among the divine, human, and animal spheres that is described in the Eden narrative (Gen. 2–3).[22] This interpretation makes for interesting reading and there are clear vocabulary and thematic links to Eden. Most notably, "I belong to my lover, and his desire is for me" (7:10) makes a nice contrast to "your desire will be for your husband" (Gen. 3:16). Nonetheless, it is impossible either to prove or to disprove this as either an intentional parallel or as an early reading of the text.

Renita Weems goes beyond the specificity of Eden and suggests reading the Song as a corrective to an entire strain of biblical texts "which undermine human sexuality in general and female sexuality in particular."[23] As the only extended text in the Bible that focuses directly on human sexuality, the Song deserves a place in discussions of sexuality which it does not often receive. The Song presents a view of male-female sexuality which is neither exploitative or hierarchic. Both the man and the woman act on their own initiative as well as in response to one another. Neither is controlled by family or social interests. There are attempts to control the woman's sexuality by the brothers in 1:6 and the city guards in 5:7, but they do not determine the woman's action. In fact, the woman insists that she has the right to control her own sexuality, or "vineyard."

More remarkable still is that although the subject of the Song is physical attraction between the sexes, it does not speak of procreation. This may imply that, in an overall canonical scheme, childbearing is not the only legitimate aim of sexual relations. However, the lack of a reference to human procreation should not be overemphasized. Fertility abounds in the Song: it is set in springtime when flowers are budding, vines are blossoming, and both sheep and gazelles are bearing twins.

Interpreters dispute the attitude toward marriage. According to many of them, the central couple is not married. This view is supported by the fact that the lovers must part in the morning ("until the day breaks and the shadows flee," 2:17 and 4:6). The conclusion that they are not married finds further support in the difficulties the woman has with brothers and city guards (1:6; 5:7; perhaps 8:8). Also, most of the couple's lovemaking apparently takes place out of doors, in the wilds and in gardens.

Other interpreters treat the Song as a text designed for use within a marriage ritual, or at least including a marriage (usually around chapters 4–5). Although there is "bride" language in chapter 4 and a reference to Solomon's wedding in 3:11, the text otherwise does not explicitly relate sexuality to marriage and overall it does not seem to insist that the appropriate expression of sexuality is necessarily limited to marriage. Neither does it claim that marriage is insignificant. Marriage is simply not an overt concern in the text.

If this text were taken seriously, it would complicate discussion of "the biblical view" of human sexuality. In the Bible, as in the contemporary world, the sexual dimension of human life is multifaceted, involving more than legal prescriptions and proscriptions.

Notes

A note on the NIV translation. The NIV designation of speakers has in two instances changed in the years since its first publication. Both 1:8 and 6:10 are assigned to the "Lover" in early editions of the NIV, more recently to the "Friends." This commentary uses the character designations in more recent printings of the NIV.

The only group to which the NIV assigns speech is designated "Friends." In most cases, this group can be identified with the daughters of Jerusalem, but in a few instances (e.g., 8:8–9) it is possible that another group (such as the woman's brothers) might be the speakers.

The NIV label for the central male character is "Lover," and for the central female character "Beloved." It seems singularly infelicitous to use a passive form in reference to the woman who is the most active character in the Song. I will generally refer to these characters as "central woman" and "central man," and when context makes it clear I will simply say "lover" (that is, "her lover," "his lover"). References to verse segments (e.g., 2:1b) are to lines as divided by the NIV.

1. M. H. Pope, *Song of Songs: A New Translation with Introduction and Commentary* (AB 7C; Garden City, N.Y.: Doubleday, 1977), p. 34.

2. C. Meyers considers the military images as "strong and innovative metaphors." This is particularly appropriate for a popular work "arising from the non-official and non-public arena of daily life," where women did in fact wield considerable power ("Gender Imagery in the Song of Songs," in *A Feminist Companion to the Song of Songs* [ed. A. Brenner; Sheffield: Sheffield Academic Press, 1993], pp. 211–12).

3. The word translated here as "dove" (Hb. *tôr*) is a different word from that rendered "dove" elsewhere in the text (Hb. *yônâ*).

4. A. Bloch and C. Bloch, *The Song of Songs: A New Translation with an Introduction and Commentary* (New York: Random House, 1995), p. 9.

5. This form was also known in ancient Egypt; see #31 in M. V. Fox, *The Song of Songs and the Ancient Egyptian Love Songs* (Madison: University of Wisconsin Press, 1985), p. 52. The *waṣf* is one of the genres used in Syro-Palestinian wedding ceremonies; see discussion of wedding week under "sequence of related love lyric," p. 237.

6. Bloch and Bloch, *Song*, p. 17.

7. Throughout this commentary, slash marks indicate the poetic line divisions of the NIV.

8. M. V. Fox argues for an age of between 13 and 16 for the girl and not much older for the boy (*The Song of Songs and the Ancient Egyptian Love Poems*, p. xii).

9. Perhaps the best known is J. C. Exum's division of the Song into six poems: 1:2–2:6; 2:7–3:5; 3:6–5:1; 5:2–6:3; 6:4–8:3; and 8:4–14, in which the first is paired with the last, the second with the fourth, and the third with the fifth, "A Literary and Structural Analysis of the Song of Songs," *ZAW* 85 (1973), p. 49.

10. Bloch and Bloch, *Song*, pp. 18–20.

11. M. Falk, *The Song of Songs: A New Translation and Commentary* (San Francisco: Harper & Row, 1990), p. xiii.

12. Pope cites a number of variations on this theory, which originated in the late seventeenth century and was most popular during the

late nineteenth and early twentieth centuries (*Song,* pp. 141–45). He also cites quotations from a number of these poems, pp. 56–65.

13. Fox, *Song,* pp. 209–26.

14. Fox, *Song,* p. 247.

15. Pope discusses various dramatic theories in *Song,* pp. 34–36.

16. See especially S. N. Kramer, *The Sacred Marriage Rite: Aspects of Faith, Myth, and Ritual in Ancient Sumer* (Bloomington: Indiana University Press, 1969), pp. 85–106.

17. "One is, of course, at liberty to assume that our book represents a secular reworking of a no longer extant litany of an assumed Israelite cult which has left no record of its existence behind it. Such a complex of unsubstantiated hypotheses recalled the argument that the ancient Hebrews must have known of wireless telegraphy, because archaeologists in Palestine have found no wires in their excavations," R. Gordis, *The Song of Songs and Lamentations* (New York: Ktav, 1974), p. 8.

18. R. E. Murphy offers a detailed and appreciative summary of these interpretations over the centuries in his discussion of the history of interpretation (*The Song of Songs: A Commentary on the Book of Canticles or the Song of Songs* [Hermeneia; Minneapolis: Fortress, 1990], pp. 11–41).

19. One of few recent writers to suggest wisdom as an interpretive matrix for the Song is B. S. Childs, *Introduction to the Old Testament as Scripture* (Philadelphia: Fortress, 1979), pp. 569–79.

20. Fox *(Song)* provides the most thorough treatment of the Egyptian love poems, including literary analysis and discussion of similarities with the Song of Songs.

21. A particularly detailed argument is put forth by S. D. Gotein, "The Song of Songs: A Female Composition," trans. A. Brenner, in A. Brenner, *A Feminist Companion to the Song of Songs* (Sheffield: Sheffield Academic Press, 1993), pp. 58–66.

22. Mishnah Yadayim 3:5 as translated by S. Z. Leiman in *The Canonization of Hebrew Scripture: The Talmudic and Midrashic Evidence* (2d ed.; New Haven: Transaction of the Connecticut Academy of Arts and Sciences, 1991), p. 121.

23. P. Trible, "Love's Lyrics Redeemed," in *God and the Rhetoric of Sexuality* (OBT; Philadelphia: Fortress, 1978), pp. 144–65.

24. R. Weems, "The Song of Songs," in *The Women's Bible Commentary* (ed. C. A. Newsom and S. H. Ringe; London: SPCK and Louisville: Westminster/John Knox, 1992), p. 160.

§1 Introducing the Characters (Song 1:1–6)

The opening verses of the Song give the title and introduce the characters. The central woman (identified in the NIV as "Beloved") and a group (NIV "Friends") both speak. The central man (NIV "Lover") is addressed in the second person and mentioned in the third person. He does not speak here, although admiration of him by both the individual woman and the group forms the core of this section. Both sensory images and royal language are used to describe him.

1:1 / The first verse is a superscription for the entire Song, no doubt affixed to the otherwise completed work. Within both Jewish and Christian traditions, **Solomon's** has been understood to ascribe authorship, although it could also indicate dedication or association (see "Dating and Authorship" in introduction). **Song of Songs** is a superlative and might be translated "supreme song" (cf. "king of kings" or "holy of holies").

1:2–4 / The book proper opens with some disconcerting shifts between both speaker and addressee. A reader who is able to set aside the NIV's designations of speakers and simply read these verses is likely to be confused. After the superscription labeling the Song as Solomon's, one might expect to hear his voice. Yet the first poetic line is, **Let him kiss me with the kisses of his mouth.** This cannot be the Solomon of biblical tradition, who would hardly wish to be kissed on the mouth by anyone identified as "him." Within the social world constructed by biblical texts, this must be a woman's voice.

The as-yet-unnamed speaker is direct in expressing her desire ("let him kiss me"), but her speech darts about at a tempo that is difficult to follow. She talks first about the man, then to him. She speaks of his kisses, his **love,** and **wine.** Perfume seems to be in the air. Then suddenly the **perfume** is his **name.** Then she calls him "king" and she is again speaking about rather than to him.

The celebration of him becomes clamorous: **we rejoice and delight; we praise.**

By this time the reader suspects that identifying the speaker as "she" is too simple. Rather, a collective voice has spoken at least these last lines. It is not clear, however, exactly which lines belong to the central woman and which lines to the group. The NIV's assignment of speakers is likely but not certain, especially for those lines that lack a first-person reference that would ascribe them to either an individual or a group.

There is equal ambiguity about what characters are addressed or even present. The most straightforward reading is that the central pair and chorus are present throughout these first verses. The man does not speak, but is addressed in second-person references to him. References to the man in the third person indicate either conversation between the woman and the group or asides to the audience.

This reading of the text, however, is not certain. The group could be present throughout, although **your love is more delightful than wine** sounds more appropriate for a couple alone. Alternatively, the group might appear only when the collective voice speaks, or perhaps they are to be an off-scene chorus that is never present with the couple.

Although it is very easy to imagine that the man is present at least for the lines addressed directly to him, do we imagine him entering the scene after the first line of verse 2, as the fulfillment of the woman's wish? Or is he present throughout? If the latter, the woman might speak the first line as an aside to the audience or chorus, or directly to him with a mock formality that she cannot maintain. The entire scene could even consist of the woman's private musings—with her friends or alone. In this case, the man would be present only in the imagination of the speaker(s). The shift to direct address then indicates a growing vividness of imagination.

It is not only the characters that are uncertain. The text also evokes confusion about what is image and what is description (see "Themes and Images" in the introduction). Is there perfume in the air? Or is there only the sound, or the thought, of the man's name? Perhaps there is confusion even about why we are hearing this woman's intimate musings.

Though the text is confusing, it is not badly written romantic drivel. Its ambiguity functions in multiple ways. First, it demands involvement with the text from the outset. The reader is forced to pay attention and to make decisions to make sense of it. The Song of Songs is not to be absorbed passively. The blurring of identifications also invites readers to imagine possible speakers and addressees, and thus to explore potential meanings of the text rather than to settle on a single determined meaning. The urgency of the voices, together with the lack of clarity about their identity, encourages the reader to try to make sense of what is on the page. This combination of attraction and confusion is entirely appropriate to the subject matter. The swirl and rush of image and description, together with the alternation of presence and desire, aptly express the riotous flow of emotions in the young lovers. Something new, powerful, and disconcerting is happening to the characters in the Song. We will understand them a bit better if we too feel the interpretive ground shifting beneath us.

In view of these points of ambiguity, it is not surprising that interpreters do not all agree about who is speaking and who is present in these verses. The understanding expressed by the NIV assignment of speakers makes good sense. The central woman is speaking in 1:2–4b, a group in verse 4cd, and the central woman again in verse 4e. And yet, it is also possible that the central woman is the speaker throughout these verses (as in NJB) or that a group speaks the second half of verse 4a (as in NAB).

The imagery of these verses evokes the senses of touch ("kiss"), taste ("wine"), and smell ("perfume"). The double mention of wine (vv. 2b and 4d) may evoke a sense of headiness which is replicated in the readers who struggle to make sense of the shifting linguistic landscape.

1:5–6 / A woman is speaking to other women. The speaker refers to herself with feminine adjectives and the addressees are labeled **daughters of Jerusalem.** The imagery shifts to an emphasis on the visual **(dark, lovely),** although the reference to **the sun,** from which one can almost feel the heat, maintains the sense of the tactile.

The speaker is apparently darker-skinned than the other characters; **darkened by the sun** may suggest either a light-skinned person with suntanned skin or someone naturally dark-skinned who comes from a sunny region. Interpreters disagree on whether the woman is speaking defensively to a hostile audience (as implied by the NIV's **dark . . . yet lovely**) or whether she is celebrating her beauty, including her dark skin. The conjunction translated **yet** in NIV can be either conjunctive ("and") or

disjunctive ("but"). The speaker realizes, or imagines, that her lis-
teners are staring at her dark skin. It is not clear whether they
stare out of admiration for her exotic beauty, scorn at her need to
work out of doors, or simple curiosity at her difference.

The brothers are introduced on a negative note. They were
angry and assigned the woman to take care of the vineyards. Although the Song is primarily an idealization of young love, there
is this recurrent note of opposition not only from the brothers but
also from the city guards (5:7) and unnamed others (8:1).

Vineyards (v. 6) is a loaded term. In the simplest, most literal, sense of verse 6d, the woman claims that she was engaged in
agricultural work. But the term can also be symbolic of female
sexuality (see Isa. 5:1), and verse 6e, **my own vineyard I have neglected,** raises this association. If the latter is a correct reading, the
woman acknowledges that, in an unspecified way, she has neglected her own sexuality.

Additional Notes §1

1:1 / The relative pronoun used here is the fuller form, Hb.
ʾăšer, distinguishing this verse from the rest of the book, which uses pre-
fixed *šᵉ*.

1:2 / **Your love:** The Hb. word used here, *dōdêkā*, is not the
usual word for "love," which is *ʾahăbâ*. However, throughout the Song
the female speaker uses this unusual term to refer to her lover. The
grammatically plural form is used a total of only ten times in the Bible,
of which six are in the Song of Songs. (By contrast, *ʾahăbâ* is used forty
times in the Bible, eleven in the Song.) A. and C. Bloch argue convincingly that this form refers to a range of activities associated with lovemaking rather than to the emotion of love (*Song*, p. 137).
Your name is like perfume: The association of "name" (Hb. *šēm*)
with perfumed oil (Hb. *šemen*) also occurs in Eccl. 7:1. J. Kristeva notes
the fusion of the sensory and the significant (*Tales of Love* [trans. L. S.
Roudiez; New York: Columbia University Press, 1987], p. 90).

1:4 / **Let the king bring me:** The Hb. is most naturally translated by simple past narration ("the king brought me"), although the
NIV translation as a wish is possible and makes a nice inclusion with v.
2a (older editions of the NIV read: "The king has brought me").
The king: The use of royal language is taken by some to indicate
that the male lover (or, alternatively, a rival to the central man) is to be
identified with Solomon. It is more likely that "king" is an image used to

express the woman's esteem for her lover (compare the English "Prince Charming").

1:5 / Tents of Kedar: Kedar is an Arabic tribe. The simile refers to their use of black goat hair to weave their tents (see references in Pope, *Song,* p. 319).

Tent curtains of Solomon: The word translated "tent curtains" indicates some kind of curtain of hanging fabric. "Solomon" is often emended to "Salma" (as in NIV note), another Arabic tribe, to provide a closer parallel with "Kedar."

1:6 / My mother's sons: This expression for "brothers" is taken by Falk as an indication of distancing (*Song,* p. 159), by Bloch and Bloch to indicate a special closeness (*Song,* p. 141). In a society that allowed one man to have several wives but did not allow a woman to have more than one husband, the latter is more likely.

§2 The Lovers Together (Song 1:7–2:7)

As this section opens, the two lovers are clearly together: they become partners in dialogue. The woman and the man first exchange playful banter, then admiring comments. The admiration closes with the woman speaking to or about the man. She then speaks for the first time a verse which will recur. This verse is clear in imagery although not in time (2:6). Then there follows the first instance of another recurring verse, the adjuration to the daughters of Jerusalem (2:7).

1:7–8 / These two verses are most likely a teasing exchange between the two central characters, with the woman speaking in 1:7 and the man replying in 1:8 (although recent versions of the NIV, along with many interpreters, assign 1:8 to the friends instead of to the male lover). There is a double-entendre in 7a–b. Although the NIV adds **your flock** and **your sheep,** these expressions are not in the Hebrew. The second of the verbs (NIV **rest**) is a form ordinarily used with a direct object, although the Hebrew does not include one. Thus, the woman's speech is halfway between asking the man where *he* grazes and rests, and asking him where he takes *his flocks* to graze and rest.

The central characters tease each other in these verses. The woman pretends that she does not know where to find the man. The man plays hard to get. There is also an intimation that the woman is testing the man for jealousy as she hints that she may lurk around the tents of his companions if he does not answer her questions. Rather than objecting, he is secure enough to tease back. Thus her confidence in approving of "the maidens" loving him (1:3c, 4d) is matched by his, as he invites her to approach the shepherds' **tents.**

1:9–11 / **Mare harnessed to one of the chariots of Pharaoh** (1:9) is more accurately translated "mare among the chariots." There is no indication in the Hebrew that the mare is harnessed. The sense of this image is made clear by Pope, who notes that Egyptian practice was to use only stallions for royal chariots. He cites a text that describes setting a mare loose among the chariots to distract the stallions (*Song,* pp. 336–40). There would be a comparable result, the male speaker implies, if the woman were to appear at the shepherds' tents. The reference to chariots sounds the first note of military imagery used in connection with the woman.

Verse 10 is transitional. When read in connection with the previous verse, its image of jewelry implies a comparison of the woman's adornments with those of royal horses. The verse also points forward to verse 11, which continues the jewelry image. On first reading, it is natural to assume (as do the NIV translators) that the man, who is the likely speaker in 1:9, now describes the loveliness of the woman when wearing jewelry and continues his speech in verse 11. In that case, the first-person plural of verse 11 ("we") may suggest that the two lovers together will make jewelry. It may just imply that the man will do so as part of a group (perhaps with the friends/shepherds of verses 7 and 8). Or it may simply be that the man refers to himself with a majestic plural.

It is also possible that the plural "we" indicates that a group is speaking in verse 11. The shared imagery might suggest the same speakers in verse 10. In this case, we might imagine the Jerusalem women, the only group that has spoken so far, helping the central woman prepare her toilette for a rendezvous with her lover. If one takes literally the banter in verses 7–8, at this point the woman might have actually or imaginatively gone out to the shepherds' tents, and the shephards are the ones speaking of making jewelry for her. The sensory images in this passage are primarily visual **(earrings, jewels, gold,** and **silver).**

1:12–14 / The central woman is the speaker in these verses where she refers to **the king** and **my lover.** It is possible that she is speaking to the Jerusalem women, especially if they are the ones who offered to make earrings for her in 1:11. It is also possible that she is addressing her lover in the third person to create a playful distance between them. She could also be talking to herself or making an aside to the audience. "King" creates an association with verse 4.

On first reading verse 12, one imagines the lover ("king") reclining, whether at table or in bed, and the woman's scent reaching him. But in verses 13 and 14, the man himself is identified with myrrh and henna blossoms. Thus **my perfume** in the preceding verse suggests mutual fragrant attraction between the two central characters.

The primary physical sense here is that of smell: **perfume, myrrh,** and **henna blossoms.** The vineyard image (v. 14), resumed from verse 6, again creates a loose allusion to female sexuality.

1:15–17 / The lovers express their mutual admiration. First the man, then the woman, admires the other's appearance. The words translated **beautiful** and **handsome** are the feminine and masculine forms of the same adjective. The whole of verse 15 is repeated in 4:1 in reference to the woman. The comparison of **eyes** with **doves** also recurs in 5:12 in reference to the man. The woman is called **my dove** in 5:2 and 6:9. The image incorporates softness, color, and an association of doves with love.

In verses 16c–17, the lovers are in a natural setting, which raises the possibility that they do not have a house of their own. The **verdant** bed pushes interpretation in this direction, as does the fact that the Hebrew uses the plural "houses" (rather than singular **house** in NIV). It is not clear who is speaking and who is addressed in these lines. Dividing them between the two lovers, as the NIV does, is plausible as a resumption of the playful banter between them. It is also possible that all three lines belong to the same speaker, who could be either of the lovers.

This section combines a variety of sensory imagery. Sight predominates, particularly in the lovers' references to each other's attractiveness. The presence of **cedars** and **firs** suggests the sense of smell.

2:1–7 / Again (or still), the lovers are together. The woman, perhaps remaining in the verdant setting of 1:16–17, proclaims her own loveliness. Interpreters disagree over whether her comparison of herself to flowers is modest (she is a simple wild flower, not a cultivated hybrid) or extravagant (the flowers named are significant in biblical floral imagery). In either case, her reference to herself as a flower recalls her metaphorical identification of her lover with myrrh and henna blossoms. In 2:2, the man affirms and heightens her claim. She is indeed a **lily.** What is more, she is **a lily among thorns,** beauty amidst plainness, softness among prickly things, and uniquely fragrant. The woman responds in kind in 2:3. She says he is like a fruit tree, fruitful among trees that are not. In 2:4 the woman extends the image of the fruit tree by referring to both **shade** and **fruit.** The image of the man's "sweet fruit" shading her is erotic, but not explicitly so.

Verse 4 initially seems to be an interruption. The couple has moved from the shade of the tree to a banquet hall, resuming the imagery of 1:12. However, the phrase which the NIV renders **banquet hall** (literally "house of wine") is not used elsewhere in the Bible and the language is less concrete than the NIV translation suggests. It is unlikely that we are to imagine the lovers at a formal dinner. Some have suggested that "house of wine" is a tavern, but it is better not to be too specific. The lovers' houses are referred to as verdant places and wine is an image that they use both for one another and for their lovemaking. If the woman's sexuality is associated with a vineyard, the "house of wine" might be any place where her sexuality is brought to intoxicating fruition.

Verse 5 maintains the fruit imagery while shifting the mood. The woman calls out to (unnamed, but plural) others to nourish her. **Faint with love,** as the NIV translates, is preferable to the traditional "sick with love." This expression recurs in 5:8. The context hints that the lover is the source of this sweet, sustaining fruit.

There are no verbs in verse 6, and thus no tense. It is most accurately translated as an ambiguous, fragmentary exclamation: "His left arm under my head, his right arm embracing me." By using present tense *is,* the NIV interprets this as a description of what is taking place as the verse is spoken. It is equally possible to understand it as remembrance of a past event: "His left arm *was* under my head, and his right embracing me." Or it may be anticipation of a future or possible event: "Oh, *that* his left arm *were* under my head, and his right arm embracing me." This is a refrain line, also occurring in 8:3.

Verse 7 is another refrain line that is repeated exactly in 3:5 and with modifications in 5:8 and 8:4 (see discussion under "Repetitions and Their Function" in the introduction). The verse identifies the daughters of Jerusalem as the addressees. The speaker is not named, but is usually understood to be the central woman. All that is textually clear is that an individual ("I") is speaking. **Charge** is the causative form of the verb for "swear," so the speaker is at least figuratively asking the daughters of Jerusalem to take an oath. The use of an oath formula gives this verse a sense of urgency and gravity unusual in the Song.

Like every other refrain in the Song, this one is open to multiple interpretations. Most readings fall into two groups: either the daughters of Jerusalem are not to stimulate love artificially but are to wait for its proper time or they are not to disturb the lovers until they have finished their lovemaking. The NIV translation follows the former understanding of the verse. At least in isolation, this is the most natural understanding of the Hebrew. In support of the alternate reading, one might observe that this sense of warning sounds a bit out of character coming from the central woman, and that the adjuration always occurs after references to the lovers together and touching, often embracing. It is almost impossible to translate the verse into English without choosing between these understandings, but maintaining both possibilities is preferable. An ambiguous sense in a grammatical framework that suggests urgency gives the Hebrew a powerful tension that is maintained throughout the book.

These verses contain a combination of sensory images. The lilies evoke both sight and scent, the **apple tree** sight and taste, and the reference to **shade** has a tactile sense. **Raisins** and **apples** suggest taste. The man's arms under the woman's head and embracing her are tactile for the central pair, but evoke a visual image for the audience.

The use of double refrain lines in verses 6 and 7 suggests to those who divide the book into major sections that this is the end of one of them. This division is likely and is reinforced by the fact that while the central man was apparently present at least through verse 5 and possibly throughout the section, in verse 8 he is apparently coming onto the scene from elsewhere.

Additional Notes §2

1:7 / **You whom I love:** This is the same expression translated "the one my heart loves" in 3:1, 2, 3, 4. The central woman identifies the man as one whom she loves with her whole being.

Veiled woman: This expression is sometimes interpreted as suggesting a prostitute on the basis of Gen. 38:14–15, but the idea that the veil implies prostitution is disputed by interpreters of the Gen. text. Thus it is unwise to use that reading to establish meaning here. The word translated **veiled** is an unusual one and may mean "covered" in some way; just how is not clear. Some interpreters make a slight change in the text which allows the translation "lost" or "wandering."

1:10 / **Earrings:** The Hb. indicates a kind of circular jewelry. Some interpreters suppose bangles or nose rings, but the precise referent is not important to the image.

1:12 / **At his table:** The Hb. indicates a place of reclining. Interpreters are divided as to whether it implies a place for eating, for sleeping, or for sexual activity. The language is open and permits ambiguity. In light of the amount of sexually allusive language in the Song and the frequent use of eating and drinking images to suggest sexual encounter, it is probably better to accept the ambiguity in this verse than to insist on a single meaning.

1:14 / **En Gedi:** This is an oasis on the Dead Sea.

2:1 / **Rose of Sharon . . . lily of the valleys:** The identity of these flowers is disputed. As Bloch and Bloch note, their precise botanical identification is less important than their symbolic value. Isa. 35:1–2 and Hos. 14:5–8 show that these are the "two flowers that are the very epitome of blossoming" in biblical imagery (*Song*, pp. 148–49). The word used for lily, Hb. *šôšannâ*, is cognate with the Egyptian word for lotus. In any event, the lily is not what we think of as a "lily of the valley."

2:3 / **Apple tree:** Many interpreters believe that apricot or quince is more likely—at any rate, a kind of fruit tree native to Israel.

2:4 / **His banner over me is love:** The sense of this verse is unclear. The word for **banner** (Hb. *degel*) is used only here and in Numbers, where it is used in connection with different tribal groups apparently bearing their standards.

2:5 / **Raisins:** The precise meaning is unclear, although the reference is to some kind of delicacy.

2:7 / **By the gazelles and by the does of the field:** Gordis ingeniously suggests that these animals are chosen not only because they have associations with fertility but also because in Hb. the sounds of their names come close to the sounds of epithets of Yahweh (*Song*, pp. 26–28). The text uses a feminine plural of gazelle (Hb. *ṣᵉbāôt*) that is the same as the word for "Almighty" or "hosts" in the expression "Lord Almighty" or "Lord of hosts" (used hundreds of times in the Bible, of which the most familiar may be Isa. 6:3). The expression translated "does of the field" (Hb. *ᶜalôt haśśādeh*) sounds similar to another Hb. expression for God Almighty (Hb. *ʾel šadday;* Gen. 17:1; 35:11; 28:3; 43:14). Thus the verse contains a "fractured" oath, something like modern people saying "Jiminy Christmas" to avoid saying "Jesus Christ." This is both charming and plausible but cannot be proved.

§3 Hope and Invitation (Song 2:8–17)

As this section opens, we attend to the voice of the central woman (2:8–13), who hears and sees (or does she only imagine?) her lover approaching, and who then remembers or anticipates him speaking to her (2:10–13). Then we hear the actual voice of the central man (2:14), asking to see and hear her.

The relationship of the three following verses to one another and to what precedes them is unclear. There is an enigmatic verse about catching foxes that are spoiling budding vineyards (2:15), the first instance of the mutual possession formula (2:16), and a verse urging the central man to spend the night (day?) on the mountains (2:17).

Throughout, the tone is one of breathless urgency. The Hb. particle *hinnēh* ("Hey!" "Notice this!") is used three times (twice by the woman, in 2:8 and 2:9, and once by the man as quoted by the woman in 2:11). The NIV translates "Look! and "See!" Although the Hebrew word is not exclusively visual, it does describe an immediate and noteworthy perception.

The section is structured with multiple inclusions. The reference to mountains and hills (2:8) combines with the comparison of the man to a gazelle or stag (2:9) to form a link with the call to the man to be like a gazelle or stag on the hills (2:17). Thus it is appropriate to read the entire passage as a unit. The woman's version of the man's speech begins and ends with "Arise, my darling, my beautiful one, [and] come with me" (2:10, 13). The man's reference to his lover's "voice" (Hb. *qôl*, 2:14) recalls her reference to his voice/sound (NIV "Hark!" Hb. *qôl*, 2:8). The blooming vineyards (2:15) recollect the image of blossoming vines (2:13). "Browses among the lilies" (2:16), suggestive of the man as a grazing animal, both recalls and anticipates the comparison of him with a gazelle or stag (2:10, 17).

2:8–13 / In a soliloquy, the central woman describes the approach of her lover in both visual and auditory images. Because she is not directly addressing anyone in these verses, it is not certain whether other characters are present or whether we are eavesdropping on her solitary musing.

Leaping across the mountains, bounding over the hills (2:8) gives the impression of an animal seen from the distance. **Like a gazelle or a young stag** in the following verse reinforces this picture. The Hebrew words for these animals are the masculine equivalents of the words for the creatures mentioned in feminine form in the adjuration (2:7 and repetitions). **Gazing through the windows, peering through the lattice** (2:9) continues the image of a wild animal, which is now tame or courageous enough to approach human dwellings.

The woman announces the man's speech: **My lover spoke and said to me.** The inference is that in verses 10–13 we are hearing her voice imagining what she wants or expects him to say. Perhaps she is remembering things he has said before. Images of springtime suffuse the invitation to come away. This quoted speech ends with verse 13, where the repetition of **Arise, come, my darling, my beautiful one, come with me** forms an *inclusio* with verse 10.

The physical senses are intertwined in this section, with the woman both seeing and hearing her lover. The references to figs and vine blossoms hint of taste and smell. Only the sense of touch is lacking, as is natural if the lovers are parted.

2:14 / In this verse we hear the voice of the central man himself. Although the woman had described herself as being in a house, he refers to her being **in the clefts of the rock, / in the hiding places of the mountainside.** His language suggests that she has been difficult for him to find. This elusive quality corresponds with her playful difficulty in finding him (1:7). The actual request **(show me your face, / let me hear your voice)** asks considerably less of her than the invitation as she imagined it **(arise . . . and come with me).** His references to seeing and hearing, the same senses she used to describe his approach, underscore the mutuality of their relationship.

2:15 / The verse is very difficult, not in translation but in interpretation in context. The literal sense is of **vineyards** in spring, when they are **in bloom** and have not yet set fruit. Into this scene young **foxes** or perhaps jackals appear who run through the vineyard in a disruptive and destructive fashion.

The imagery of the verse connects with that of other parts of the Song. The vineyards, again, allude to female sexuality. The foxes—grammatically masculine—suggest a threat from males (or perhaps male sexuality) to not-yet-fruitful female sexuality. A group (or an individual speaking for more than one: **for us; our vineyards**) urges another group (plural imperative: [all of you] **catch**) to catch the foxes that are spoiling the vineyards.

But what is the sense of this verse in context? Does "for us" suggest that the verse belongs to both lovers, or to one of them speaking on behalf of both? Does the verse urge an audience to leave the two so that they can be alone? Might the foxes then be those who pose a threat to the fruition of their sexual relationship (brothers, city guards)? Or does the first-person plural suggest that a group is speaking, perhaps to the lovers? If so, why would the lovers be expected to safeguard more than one vineyard? Might the chorus be the brothers, urging another group (perhaps the city guards, who will appear in chapters 3 and 5) to safeguard the central woman, whose sexuality they consider their property? Or might it be the Jerusalem women, warning the central pair not to risk the potential fruitfulness of the vineyard/woman by letting foxes/the man into it/her?

Murphy suggests that the verse is sung by the woman: in response to the man's request, **let me hear your voice,** she teasingly sings a fragment of a popular ditty (*Song,* p. 141). This interpretation has the advantage of making the plurals irrelevant. If this is a popular ditty, the number of speakers and hearers need not match up with any numbers in the text. But there is nothing in the text itself that makes this reading compelling.

The verse sounds playful. These are, after all, **little** foxes and, if symbolic of males, they are more naughty boys than wicked men. The playful tone makes the brothers unlikely as speakers. And yet, the sense of threat, however playfully presented in this verse, foreshadows the violence of the city guards in 5:7.

2:16 / Verse 16a is another refrain line, containing the mutual possession formula. This particular refrain is always modified slightly when repeated (6:3; 7:10). It emphasizes the mutuality of the relationship between the lovers both by its content and by the variations in its several uses. **Browses among the lilies** (v. 16b) is suggestive, and recurs after this same refrain in 6:3 (although it does not appear in 7:10). The woman (or perhaps part of her body) is symbolically identified with lilies or lotus blossoms.

2:17 / The segments of verse 17 are all repeated (exactly or with modification) in other verses: a–b in 4:6; d–e in 8:14. The literal sense can be interpreted in two very different ways. On the one hand, the woman may be telling the man to turn away or go away from her and roam the hills until dawn (or nightfall). Or on the other hand she may be inviting him to herself (with **hills** as a reference to her body) for the night (or day).

It is the ambiguity of key verses such as this one that makes it possible for some interpreters to read the Song of Songs as a celebration of premarital chastity while others find in it a description of fulfilled sexuality. The text makes sense both ways; neither side can justly accuse the other of willful misreading. The reader's confusion about just what is happening is entirely appropriate.

Is this the end of another section? The double use of refrains suggests that it is. Yet the reference to the time of day creates a link with the beginning of the following chapter.

Additional Notes §3

2:8 / **Listen! . . . Look!** The imperatives, while not present in the Hb., give a good approximation of the exclamatory force of the woman's dawning awareness (or developing fantasy) that her lover is approaching.

2:9 / **My lover is like a gazelle or a young stag:** The woman uses the verb for "be like" rather than a simple preposition. This verb draws attention to the act of making a comparison.

Our wall: "Our" has been taken variously to refer to the woman and her mother (the man is visiting her at her family home) or, more playfully, to the woman and the lover (in which case the house language may be used in reference to a natural setting, as in 1:16c–17).

2:10 / **My lover spoke and said to me:** This introductory line marks what follows as the woman's rendition of the man's speech; thus NIV is correct in keeping her as the speaker through verse 13.

With me: There is no equivalent of this phrase in the Hb.; it is supplied from the LXX.

2:11 / **Winter . . . rains:** The lyrical description of springtime begins with an awareness of the previous season. Winter is the only time when there is significant rainfall in Israel/Palestine.

2:12 / **The season of singing:** The Hb. carries an ambiguity unavailable in English. The word translated "singing" (Hb. *zāmîr*) can also mean "pruning." C. Gordon calls this an instance of "Janus parallelism," or parallelism which points both backward and forward. In the sense of "pruning," the verb faces back to the blossoms of the previous line, and in the sense of "singing" it faces forward to the turtledove of the following line ("New Directions," *BASP* 15 [1978], p. 59).

2:13 / **The fig tree forms its early fruit:** It is not clear exactly what the fig tree is doing. The verb is used only here and in Gen., where it refers to the Egyptian practice of embalming human bodies. The reference is probably to the addition of fluid or the change in color that takes place in both the ripening of fruit and the embalming process.

2:14 / **Show me your face:** The word translated "your face" (*marʾayik*) is plural in Hb.; Bloch and Bloch take this usage to mean something like "every aspect of you" (*Song,* p. 156).

2:15 / **Catch for us the foxes:** Gordis translates, "Little foxes have seized us," and notes that some commentators read "Take us, you little foxes" (*Song,* p. 83). Although the line is admittedly difficult to interpret, these alternate translations are not much help. The most natural reading is that of the NIV.

2:17 / **Until the day breaks / and the shadows flee:** Pope notes that it is difficult to decide between "until" and "while" for the opening Hb. expression *ʿad še* (*Song,* p. 408), but this is the least of the ambiguities in this verse. The verb translated "breaks" (*yāpûaḥ*) is lit. "breathes." The reference seems to be to a breezy time of day, which could be late afternoon or early morning. Some interpreters understand "shadows flee" to mean the shadows are disappearing, others that they are lengthening. Again, it is best to maintain the ambiguity.

Turn, my lover: The root used here, Hb. *sbb,* means "turn around" in the sense of circling, not necessarily reversing direction. It is difficult, then, to know whether the woman is inviting the man to come to her or warning him away from her.

On the rugged hills: "Rugged" (Hb. *bāter,* non-pausal form *beter*) is an unknown word. The NIV note gives an alternate reading, in which the Hb. is simply transliterated as a place name, although the site cannot be identified with any certainty. Whether one reads the word as a place name or a descriptive term, the hills may be identified either with the ones from which the woman perceived the man approaching in v. 8, or with the woman herself.

§4 Dream and Vision (Song 3:1–11)

This chapter presents a surprising mix, unlike what has come before, although it is clearly linked with the context. The opening section (3:1–4) apparently reports a dream in which the woman seeks her lover and finds him, followed by another instance of the adjuration to the daughters of Jerusalem (3:5). The next verse (3:6) is an enigmatic question or exclamation, perhaps functioning as a transition from the adjuration to the following section. The closing verses form a descriptive passage which mentions Solomon three times (at least half the total references to him in the book) and refers to his wedding—the only clear wedding reference in the Song.

3:1–4 / A temporal reference links this section to the preceding one. The preceding section ended with the woman telling the man to roam the mountains until daybreak or nightfall. This section opens with her in her **bed** at **night**. Such temporal markers are rare in the Song and are lacking in the section corresponding to this one, 5:2–8. The temporal link suggests a conceptual one as well. If in 2:17 the woman invited the man to stay until daybreak or warned him not to go away until nightfall, it makes sense that she is surprised and disappointed to find him absent in the night. If, on the other hand, one takes verse 17 as a request for the man to stay until evening or to leave only until morning, she should not have expected to find him with her at night. In this case, her distress may signal a change of mind.

This passage (like the corresponding section in 5:2–7) is most likely the description of a dream, or perhaps of a half-waking reverie. The central woman dreams that her lover is not with her in bed and resolves to scour the city **streets and squares** to **find him.** There is an urgency to her quest that is not foreshadowed earlier in the text, except perhaps in the adjuration of 2:7 and parallels. The lovers had been secure enough in their affection to simply play hide-and-seek games. Nor has anything in the preceding chapters prepared us for the idea that a **city** is a reasonable place to search for the man, who is elsewhere connected with pastoral and mountainside locations. In fact, if 2:17 provides narrative context, the woman has sent the man to the rugged hills, not to the streets and squares of 3:2.

The narrow city streets, however, provide labyrinthine imagery appropriate to a dream quest. In her conscious mind, the woman would not be likely to identify the man to the city guards only as **the one my heart loves**—and if she did, one can hardly imagine the conversation ending without follow-up questions to further identify him. In this encounter, however, the city guards are merely a distraction. They ask no questions and do not accost the woman. Neither are they helpful. She finds her lover without their assistance (as might happen in a wish-fulfillment dream). It makes dreamlike sense that when she finds him she takes him to her mother's house. But at this point in the Song it could not have happened, because in 8:2 she is still wishing for the opportunity to take him there. The passage closes with the woman bringing the man to her mother's house, to a room associated with her conception. There is no image of sexual fulfillment, although the woman's reference to her own conception suggests a sexual encounter as her intention. One of the charmingly ambiguous refrains would provide closure here (the left arm/right arm embrace, for example, or "he browses among the lilies")—but the narration is over. Suddenly the woman is speaking to the daughters of Jerusalem. If the passage is a dream, one might assume that the woman wakes up before the sexual encounter she has been seeking.

All of these factors point toward the interpretation of this passage as a dream, and yet the text does not identify it as such (a simple "I dreamed" would suffice). So the reader must be content with likelihood. We are left wondering whether the woman has described a dream, reported what she did in the night after waking, or told us her fantasy.

O. Keel connects the language of this passage with imagery of a goddess searching for a dying and rising god. Therefore he finds strong evidence in this passage for a cultic origin for the Song (*The Song of Songs* [trans. F. J. Gaiser; CC; Minneapolis: Fortress, 1994], pp. 121–22). The very human terms of this passage, though, combined with the fact that longing for an absent lover is hardly limited to deities, makes his claim less than certain.

According to some interpreters, the imagery of seeking and finding in this passage connects it with wisdom. While seeking and finding is a wisdom motif, this activity is not unusual else-where in the Bible or more generally in human behavior. There-fore the connection, while possible, cannot be certain.

3:5 / The adjuration of 2:7 is repeated (and will recur with modification in 8:4 and 5:8). The other occurrences of the ad-juration follow descriptions of the male lover's embrace. Murphy notes that **I held him and would not let him go** provides a corre-sponding image and further observes that the context both here and in 8:4 mentions finding the lover and bringing him to the mother's house (*Song,* p. 146).

3:6 / Like 2:15, this verse is not difficult to translate but is difficult to understand in context. Neither the speaker nor the addressee is clear. The speaker perceives a figure, taken to be fe-male, **coming up from the desert** like a puff of **smoke** in the dis-tance. The speaker describes this figure with references to exotic perfumes. Most interpreters understand the verse as a question, which is answered in the description in 3:7–11. Other uses of the question "Who is this?" in the Song (6:10 and 8:5) call for the answer "the central woman." If the NIV's ascription of the line to her is correct (which is not certain), it would preclude this understanding here. Perhaps it is appropriate that the first in-stance of "who is this?" leaves many interpreters asking the same question.

3:7–11 / This segment describes an item connected with Solomon, perhaps a couch or litter (NIV **carriage**). Most interpret-ers take 3:7 as a response to 3:6, and the NIV translation reflects this assumption. It is easy to imagine a carriage coming up from the wilderness. It is not clear whether we are to imagine this as **Solomon's wedding** day or whether at a later date he is once again wearing the **crown** that his mother used on his (previous) wedding day.

There are several links in both vocabulary and image to other passages of the Song. The **sixty warriors** here anticipate the sixty queens of 6:8, as well as the thousand shields of warriors as-sociated with the woman lover's neck (4:4). The **terrors of the night** call to mind the behavior of the guards in 5:7. **Lebanon,** pedestals, and **gold** occur together here and in the description of the central man in 5:14–16.

There are also some linguistic connections between this passage and Psalm 45, which is a royal wedding psalm:

references to wearing swords (Ps. 45:3), myrrh (Ps. 45:8), and gold (Ps. 45:13). In addition, the accompanying warriors here might have some counterpart in the virgin companions of Psalm 45:14. Unfortunately, we do not know enough about Israelite wedding customs, royal or otherwise, to make sense of these images in connection with a wedding.

For those who understand Solomon to be the male protagonist in the text, the references to him are expected (although he is not the speaker here, as all the "Solomon" references are in the third person). For others, it is possible to imagine that "Solomon" is an image of the male lover, who was described as "king" in 1:4 and 1:12. It is also possible that Solomon is mentioned because he is identified with luxury and wealth.

The function of the passage, either in its immediate context or in the Song of Songs overall, is not clear. Interpreters who believe that the Song's context is a wedding see the wedding procession happening here. Some believe the groom to be King Solomon, whereas others interpret the image of Israel's wealthiest and most extravagant king as honoring the more modest festivities of a non-royal couple. Interpreters who see the Song as an anthology understand this passage as an independent poem that happened to be included, perhaps because it mentions a wedding and shares some images with other poems in the Song. However, if the Song is a unified work about young lovers and their dreams, it is most likely that this passage is to be understood in the context of their delight in one another and their longing to be together. If firs and cedars could become the beams and rafters of their "house" in 1:17, then it is not too much to suppose that whatever the setting for their lovemaking, to them it was a royal structure of precious metals and luxurious appointments. The reference to Solomon's wedding might well express their longing for public affirmation of their own life together.

Additional Notes §4

3:1 / **All night long:** The Hb. uses the plural form of "night"; this might give the sense of the NIV or might simply mean "during the night." The form can also suggest repeated or habitual action, as Fox suggests (*Song*, p. 118).

I looked for . . . did not find: Or "longed for." The repetition of seeking and not finding sharpens the urgency of the woman's quest.

The one my heart loves: The expression is in each of the first four verses of this chapter, otherwise only in 1:7 (where NIV has "you whom I love").

3:3 / The watchmen: Although the presence of the guards is benign in this passage, Keel appropriately notes that they represent the interests and laws of society. These are in tension with the interests and laws of love's passion which sent the woman out on her search (*Song*, p. 124).

"Have you seen": The woman quotes herself without introducing the quotation with an expression such as "I asked them." As Bloch and Bloch note, the abbreviated narrative style combines with unusual word order (lit. "The one my heart loves—you've seen him?") to heighten the urgency of the woman's search (*Song*, p. 158).

3:4 / I held him and would not let him go / till I had brought him: Fox argues that the tenses are ambiguous here. Most of the verbs in this section are perfect forms (indicating completed action), but "let him go" is imperfect (suggesting incomplete action). Fox believes that the form signals a change in time: "she took hold of him in the recent past and is now holding on to him, but she has not yet brought him home . . . It is unclear whether she intends to bring him to her mother's house right then and there or is resolving not to lose sight of him until she brings him home and makes their love public sometime in the future" (*Song*, p. 118).

The room of the one who conceived me: The woman stops just short of saying that this is the room where she was conceived; the wording raises the association without making a claim.

3:6 / Who is this: The Hb. expression is *mî zōʾt*. Ordinarily *mî* is the interrogative personal pronoun "who," although it can also be used in exclamations and there are a few instances where it is used of inanimate objects. The pronoun *zōʾt* is feminine singular. What creates a problem for interpreters is that if this is a question answered in 3:7–11, the answer is not obvious. No female person is mentioned in the following verses, although some interpreters infer the presence of the bride. Others translate "what" instead of "who," which makes it possible for the answer to be the carriage or couch, which is grammatically feminine—but ordinarily the interrogative pronoun used for "what" is *mâ*. One might also conclude that, seeing a figure approaching like a smoky mist, the speaker assumed it to be a woman—although it turned out to be a Solomon figure instead.

3:7 / Look! It is Solomon's carriage: The NIV translation heightens the relationship between 3:6 and 3:7. If 3:7 occurred in isolation, this line would most naturally be translated, "Look! Solomon's bed!" "It is" is not necessary in the translation, and the word translated "[his] carriage" is Hb. *miṭṭātô*, normally a bed. The translation "carriage" reflects an attempt to describe something that might be seen coming up from the wilderness.

3:9 / **Carriage:** The Hb. word here is ʿappiryôn, a word of uncertain meaning occurring only here in the Bible. If it is related to the Gk. *phoreion,* "carriage" or "pavilion" might be an appropriate translation, but the connection is not certain. The meaning of the word must be inferred from context, which is far from clear.

3:10 / **Its interior lovingly inlaid:** The word translated "lovingly" in NIV is the noun "love." Its syntactic relationship to its context is uncertain. Most interpreters understand it as an adverbial accusative of some sort; "lovingly" is possible but hardly certain.

By the daughters of Jerusalem: "Daughters of Jerusalem" is difficult in context (the Hb. preposition is *min,* often "from") and many remove it. Some connect the remaining phrase with the following verse ("Daughters of Jerusalem, go out; / and see, daughters of Zion").

§5 Admiration and Invitation (Song 4:1–5:1)

This is the only section in which the central man's voice is more prominent than that of the central woman. He speaks in every verse but one (4:16) and is the only speaker in all of these but the last (5:1). This section also contains the formal center of the book. The man begins by describing the woman's beauty from the head downward in the first of the Song's descriptive motifs (4:1–7). Then he speaks to her directly (4:8–15). He invites her to come with him, telling her that she has captivated him and describing her with garden and nature images. The woman responds with an indirect (third-person) invitation that maintains the garden imagery. In his reply he claims that he has already entered and enjoyed the garden. The section closes as what is most likely a chorus (NIV "Friends") invites the lovers to indulge in "eating" and "drinking."

4:1–7 / This is the first of four descriptive motifs in the Song. The descriptive motif consists of a description of the admired person part by part (see "Forms" in the introduction). The speaker here is no doubt the central man, as indicated by the NIV. The extent of the passage is marked by *inclusio:* **How beautiful you are, my darling!** (v. 1) corresponds with **All beautiful you are, my darling** (v. 7).

In this motif, the description begins at the top of the woman's body and specifically mentions **eyes, hair, teeth, lips, mouth, temples** (or cheeks), **neck,** and **breasts.** Given this sequence, it is likely that **mountain of myrrh** and **hill of incense** (v. 6) allude to parts of the woman's torso, perhaps the genital area, unless they are summary images referring to the woman's entire body.

Individual elements of comparison may sound odd to Western ears, but they were no doubt more natural to the ancient audience. The images are emotive and evocative, although many have visual or other sensory associations as well. Most of the images are drawn from the natural and agricultural world. Parts of the woman are compared to animals **(doves, goats, sheep, fawns of a gazelle)**, plants **(pomegranate, lilies)**, or spices **(myrrh, incense)**. There is also a military image **(tower of David** hung with **shields of warriors)**.

The passage begins with relatively detached, although admiring, observation, but ends with involvement: the speaker resolves to **go to** the mountain of myrrh and the hill of incense. This verse is reminiscent of 2:17; both have the same temporal marker **(until the days breaks and the shadows flee)** and a reference to mountains. The latter part of the verse also anticipates the "spice-laden mountains" of 8:14.

Verse 7 is a summary statement. The descriptive motif is over, although it ended before treating the woman's legs and feet.

4:8–15 / The central man invites the woman to come with him, then addresses her with a series of admiring exclamations. The structure of the verses from 8 to 12 is fairly regular. Each begins with a line addressing the woman as **bride** and in the central verses, 9 to 11, **my sister** is added. This pattern has the effect of making each verse a separate stanza of a love poem. Although each of the verses from 8 to 12 would be intelligible independently, the combination provides a coherent movement from invitation through captivation to celebration.

The invitation itself (v. 8) is tersely worded (lit. "With me from Lebanon, bride; with me from Lebanon come"). The mountain names associate the woman with areas in and to the north of Israel. These suggest not only the woman's inaccessibility (as did the imagery of 2:14) but also that there is danger in her environment. The reference to predatory beasts **(lions, leopards)** relates loosely to the foxes in 2:15.

After verse 9, in which he describes the woman's effect on his **heart**, the man focuses exclusively on her. He does not mention himself again until 5:1, after she has spoken.

The man's celebration of the woman in verses 10 and 11 recalls her similar praise of him at the beginning of the Song. Both 4:10 and 1:2–3 contain the expressions **your love, better than wine,** and **the fragrance of your perfume.** There is an additional similarity in sound: the word translated "spices" in NIV (Hb. *bᵉśāmîm*) sounds much like the preposition *b* plus the word for oil (Hb. *šemen*), which occurs in 4:10 and 1:3. The association with 1:3 associates another similar-sounding word, "name" (Hb. *šēm*).

Verse 11, with its reference to the **sweetness** of her **lips** and the **milk and honey** under her **tongue,** is reminiscent of the woman's wish for the man's kiss at the beginning of 1:2. The language also anticipates 5:1.

Verse 12 closes this group of "my sister, bride" verses while opening an extended celebration of the woman as a garden. Verses 12 and 15 give two contrasting images of the water sources in the garden, while verses 13 and 14 list the plants contained in it. The list includes many plants that are not native to Israel, suggesting an exotic (or even fantasy) garden. It is as though the catalogue of fruits and spices itself alters the man's perception of his lover's accessibility. Before the listing, she is a **locked garden, enclosed spring,** and **sealed fountain;** following the catalog she has become a **garden fountain** and a **well of flowing water streaming down** from the north country. Many interpreters believe that verse 12 suggests that the woman is a private garden for her lover alone, and not that she is closed off from him. However, the distant and dangerous wilderness in which he imagines her in verse 8 suggests that she is not as accessible as he wishes her to be.

4:16–5:1 / The woman is the speaker in 4:16. She develops the **garden** imagery that the man has used of her. She wishes that the **wind** would **spread** the **fragrance** of "her" garden so that the man would enter "his" garden and enjoy its **fruits.**

The man's response in 5:1a–d suggests that he has already come into the garden and has enjoyed its fruits and spices, **wine** and **milk.** The wine and milk recall 4:11, where he located them under her tongue. The difference in perspective between the woman's invitation and the man's claim need not be resolved. As at many other points in the Song, the text points toward both anticipation and fulfillment.

According to most interpreters (and the NIV assignment of speakers), 5:1d–e is a blessing by an external voice or voices (probably a chorus) in which the lovers are invited to **eat** and **drink.** As elsewhere in the Song, especially in the context of the preceding verses, the language of eating and drinking is associated with lovemaking. Others (reflected among recent translations by the REB) understand the lines to be spoken by the central man, perhaps as host of a wedding banquet, to his guests. The NJB follows yet another line of interpretation which understands the speaker to be the poet.

Additional Notes §5

4:1 / **Your eyes behind your veil are doves:** The image of eyes as doves has appeared already in 1:15 in reference to the woman; it will recur in 5:12 referring to the man. Bloch and Bloch argue strenuously that the Hb. *ṣammātēk* here and in v. 3 should be translated "your hair" instead of "your veil" (*Song*, pp. 166–68).

4:2 / **Each has its twin; / not one of them is alone:** The NIV's translation is preferable to the common translation "each bearing twins" and "none barren." The literal implication is that the woman has no teeth missing and that they are well placed; the affective impact of the verse is of freshness, bounty, and symmetry.

4:4 / **Your neck is like the tower of David, / built with elegance:** This is one of the more difficult images, but probably describes a confident woman, one who holds her head high. The word translated "elegance" is uncertain. The reference to the tower reintroduces military imagery, which is developed in the remaining lines of this verse.
On it hang a thousand shields, / all of them shields of warriors: Taken visually, the image suggests a necklace hung with many metal plates. The only previous reference to warriors is in 3:7, where sixty of them surround Solomon's carriage. Thus the woman metaphorically outdoes Solomon's splendor, a thousand as opposed to sixty.

4:5 / **Twin fawns of a gazelle:** The gazelle is the animal referred to in the oath in 2:7 and 3:5.
Browse among the lilies: Usually it is the man who browses among the lilies, implying an enjoyment of the woman's physical charms. Thus the image is allusive to sexuality although not directly indicative of it.

4:9 / **You have stolen my heart:** Exactly what the woman has done to the speaker's heart is not clear. The rare verb is derived from the noun "heart." Interpreters disagree on whether it means "hearten" or "steal/ravish the heart"; either is possible in context.
My sister: "Sister" is apparently a term of endearment. The equivalent is also used in Egyptian love poetry. The corresponding "brother" is expressed in the Egyptian poems. In the Song, the woman wishes to relate to her lover as a brother (8:1)

4:12 / **A garden locked up:** The man perceives the woman as unavailable, as in 2:14. (This seems to reverse the woman's claim in 1:6 that she did not keep her own vineyard.) The verse intimates wasted potential and may be something of a taunt. One thinks of Robert Herrick's seventeenth-century poem "To the Virgins, to Make Much of Time" (in *The New Oxford Book of English Verse 1250–1950* [ed. Helen Gardner; New York: Oxford University Press, 1972], p. 243), which begins, "Gather ye rose-buds while ye may" and reminds the virgins that they, like flowers, are at their peak for only a short time.

4:13 / **An orchard:** With the following list of fruits and spices, there is a sense that the woman is overwhelmingly fruitful, fragrant, and luxuriant. The sense of bounty is emphasized by the variety of plants listed in vv. 13–14. With a realization that the list is inadequate, a kind of "etc." is placed at the end **(all the finest spices).**

5:1 / **I have come . . . I have gathered . . . I have eaten . . . I have drunk:** These lines provide the clearest claim of sexual fulfillment in the Song—and even here the claim is couched in very indirect language.

§6 Dream and Search (Song 5:2–6:3)

A new scene opens with 5:2. The central man, who was the principal speaker throughout the fourth chapter, is no longer present. Now the woman's voice predominates, occasionally punctuated by a question from the daughters of Jerusalem. The structure of the section is much like that of 3:1–11. It opens with an apparent dream report (5:2–7; compare 3:1–4), followed by an address to the daughters of Jerusalem (5:8; compare 3:5), a transitional question (5:9; compare 3:6), and a descriptive passage (5:10–16; compare 3:7–11). The latter is a standard descriptive motif treating the central man. It is reminiscent of the description in chapter 3 only because of the dominant imagery of precious materials. The section closes with an exchange between the daughters of Jerusalem and the central woman and a second version of the mutual possession formula.

5:2–7 / The central woman speaks in this, the second of two apparent dream narratives. She hears her lover at the door, asking her to **open** to him and complaining about **the dampness of the night.** To the woman (whether in her dream state or still groggy because just awakened), getting up and opening the door seems like an impossible task. She has already locked the door and washed her feet. Or perhaps she is teasing her lover, pretending that he is not worth the bother. In any case, she does finally rise, but when she opens (the door?) the man is gone. She goes out into the city looking for him, although a moment ago it had been too much work to put on a robe. The city guards find her, as they did in 3:3. This time they are not so benign. They beat her and take her garment. Many interpreters suppose that they assume her to be a prostitute. There is no explicit claim of rape. In a culture that keeps tight reins on female sexuality, perhaps their response is not unusual.

What is problematic in this narrative is not primarily the fact that an assault is described. After all, there are other negative notes in the Song. In a culture in which male control of female sexuality is the norm, the guards' response may be seen as a heightened version of the brothers' angry insistence that the woman be keeper of the vineyards (1:6) and the brothers' desire to board up the woman's budding sexuality should she prove to be a "door" (8:9). The problem with understanding the episode as a straightforward narration rather than an anxious dream or fantasy is that there is no aftermath. There is no indication later in the text that the woman has been physically or psychologically traumatized by this assault. No one offers her comfort and her lover does not ever demonstrate awareness that anything untoward has happened to her. The lack of follow-up of any sort may be the strongest indication that the passage narrates a dream or fear fantasy. And yet, since in this passage as in 3:1–4 there is no explicit statement that it is a dream, other possibilities remain.

This section corresponds and contrasts with 3:1–4. Common elements in the two sections include an urban nighttime setting, one of the lovers seeking the other at the outset, the woman rising, and the woman looking for the man but not finding him. Both include the lines, **I looked for him but did not find him** and **The watchmen found me as they made their rounds in the city.** Both passages end without resolution. The points of contrast are equally important. In 3:1, it is the woman who seeks the man; in 5:2, it is the man who knocks and calls to the woman. The woman rises for a different reason in each of the two sections: in 3:2 it is to look for her lover, in 5:5 to open for him. The encounter with the city guards is innocuous in 3:3 but concludes with violence in 5:7. The first episode ends before describing the anticipated sexual fulfillment; the second ends before potential sexual violation. In addition, in the first the woman refers to her lover as **the one my heart loves** (3:1, 2, 3, 4), while in the second she calls him **my lover** (5:2, 4, 5, 6, 8). If these are indeed dream narratives, one might describe the first as a wish-fulfillment dream, the second as a nightmare. This passage (5:2–7) overlaps in other ways with 2:8–14. In both the woman hears her lover coming and in both he issues a request to her.

Verses 2–7 are charged with sexual innuendo. The man's request is **Open to me**—not specifically "open the door." The woman complains that she has already **washed** her **feet.** In the Bible feet are occasionally a euphemism for genitals. The man **thrust his hand** into the opening (**latch** in the NIV is not in the Hb.) and the woman's insides leaped. "Hand" is another euphemism for phallus. The woman's **hands** drip liquid **myrrh.** This recalls the **mountain of myrrh** in 4:6, which may have alluded to her genital area. The indications of moisture—the man's hair **drenched with dew** and the woman's hands dripping liquid myrrh—recall the water images used to describe the woman and the drinking images associated with their lovemaking. These are evocative of the body fluids associated with sexual arousal. She finally opens for her lover (again, no door is mentioned). But all of this is in the realm of double entendre. Contrary to the claims of some interpreters, on a descriptive level the passage narrates the man's visit to the woman's house. Yet the language raises sexual associations in every line.

5:8 / The beginning of the refrain from 2:7 and 3:5 recurs in 5:8, but there is a break after the first line, **I charge you, daughters of Jerusalem.** This time the woman haltingly asks them to tell her lover, if they find him, that she is faint with love.

5:9 / This transitional verse provides the occasion for the descriptive motif that follows. The apparent speakers are the Jerusalem women mentioned in the previous verse. There are two ways to read this verse: as a challenge or as a request for information. The women could be asking "What makes your lover so special that we should bother helping you to find him?" Or they may be asking, "What are his identifying characteristics, so that we will know whom to seek?" The central woman's response suggests the former.

5:10–16 / This descriptive motif, or *waṣf,* is the only one in the Song spoken by the woman about the man. The imagery here is largely visual and the references to precious metals and stones are evocative of sculpture. The movement is from the **head** down to the **legs** and perhaps the feet **(bases).** Both of these extremes are described as **gold,** which suggests that the man is gold from head to toe, or thoroughly gold. After a summary statement, the speaker refers back to the **mouth,** as though she cannot resist kissing him. At the conclusion, the woman addresses the **daughters of Jerusalem;** they are presumed to be the audience throughout.

6:1–3 / These verses contain innocent, playful dialogue between the daughters of Jerusalem and the central woman character. They ask the woman where her lover has gone. This seems like a foolish question, because if she knew she would not need help finding him. But the question provides the opportunity for the central woman to respond that she knows quite well where her lover has gone (6:2). The implication of **to his garden,** which resumes the image last used in 5:1, implies that in some sense the lovers are still together.

In 6:3, we find the second version of the mutual possession formula (2:16; 7:10). **Browses among the lilies** is a sexual allusion. The same expression occurred in 2:16 after the mutual possession formula and in a *waṣf* describing the woman's breasts in 4:5. Both principal words are also used in 6:2, although not together.

Additional Notes §6

5:2 / **I slept but my heart was awake:** The heart is the equivalent of the mind. This line suggests dreaming more than anything in 3:1–4 but stops short of labeling the experience a dream.

My sister, my darling, / **my dove, my flawless one:** The verse combines four epithets from various parts of the book: "my sister" occurs in 4:9, 10, 12, and 5:1; "my darling" (or "friend") is the man's usual address to her; "my dove" is used in 2:14 (see also 1:15; 4:1); "my flawless one" is used in 6:9 (with similar concept in 4:7).

5:4 / **My heart began to pound for him:** The NIV provides a good cultural equivalent of the Hb. "my insides leaped toward him," although the Hb. expression allows for association with a specifically sexual response.

5:6 / **My heart sank:** With this expression (Hb. *nepeš*), this section comes closest to using the favorite phrase of the corresponding dream passage (**the one my heart loves** in 3:1–4). The association of the expression with death (Gen. 35:18), noted by some commentators, is probably not relevant here.

At his departure: The NIV provides the likeliest reading for Hb. *bᵉdabbᵉrô* in this verse. The expression would more commonly mean "when he spoke." There are two Semitic roots with the letters *dbr*. Although "speak" is used more often, it is not likely in this verse. Recent translations are almost equally divided in choosing between them, but what dismayed the woman was not his speech in 5:2 but his departure, discovered in 5:6.

5:7 / **They took away my cloak:** The Hb. word translated "cloak" is used only here and in Isa. 3:23, where it refers to a kind of feminine finery worn by women to whom the prophet objects. Some commentators speculate that it may be significantly lighter than a normal outer garment.

5:8 / What will you tell him? / Tell him I am faint with love:
Although the NIV has the simplest and most likely reading, Fox points
out that it is possible to read this verse as an actual adjuration. If so, the
meaning of these lines would be "Do not tell him that I am sick with
love" (*Song*, pp. 141–42). This reading is possible because the verse begins as a call to take an oath ("I charge you" = "I have you swear"). As
oaths are typically formulated, a word that is conditional in other circumstances (Hb. ʿim) is used with negative force (as in 2:7; 3:5). Instead
of the conditional, occasionally the oath formula uses a word that normally is the interrogative "what" (Hb. mâ). The interrogative acquires
strong prohibitive force in this specific context (as in 8:4). Most interpreters and translations assume that although the verse begins with the
language of taking an oath and uses both of these Hb. particles, there is
a break after the opening line. With this break, the particles have their
usual force ("*if* you find my lover" and "*what* will you tell him"). Fox's
suggestion is that mâ here actually does function as a prohibition in continuity with the opening line. His argument has not been found persuasive by most interpreters, but this may be another instance of the (often
deliberate) ambiguity found throughout the Song.

5:9 / Most beautiful of women: The daughters of Jerusalem
address the central woman with this label, with which the central man
also addressed her in 1:8.

5:10 / Outstanding: The Hb. dāgûl is derived from the word
translated "banner" in 2:4. Another variant of this root is used in 6:4 and
6:10. Its meaning here is uncertain, but "outstanding" is likely.

**5:12 / His eyes are like doves / by the water streams, / washed
in milk, / mounted like jewels:** The image of eyes as doves is used only
here of the man, but of the woman in 1:15; 4:3. If the Hb. is correct, this
is the most extended simile of the waṣf. "Washed in milk" could refer to
the whites of the eyes or to a glistening quality. It evokes a sense of luxury. The phrase "mounted like jewels" could be an image of a statue
with jewels inlaid for eyes. Murphy suggests that only the first half of
the verse is about eyes, and that the word for "teeth" has dropped out of
the second half (*Song*, p. 166). Indeed, it makes sense to think of milky
white teeth and their careful placement. It would be natural also to discuss teeth with other parts of the face. There is, however, no external
evidence for this reading.

5:16 / This is my lover, this is my friend: In addition to her
usual label for him ("my lover"), this is the one time when the woman
uses the masculine form of the word that the man customarily uses in
reference to her ("my friend").

§7 Admiration and Desire (Song 6:4–8:4)

The section begins with the man admiring the woman in the beginning of another descriptive motif (6:4–9) that does not go below the neck. This description is followed by another "who is this?" verse (6:10; see 3:6; 8:5). The following verse (6:11) does not answer the question: rather, an unidentified speaker (NIV "Lover") tells of going to the nut orchard. Both the speaker and the sense of 6:12 is unclear. The next verse (6:13) contains an exchange about the Shulammite (apparently the central woman). There follows another descriptive motif about her, which develops into a poem of admiration and desire and is concluded by her interruption. Another version of the mutual possession formula follows, this one reminiscent of (and contrasting with) Genesis 3:16. The woman then issues an invitation to the man to go out to the countryside for a night of love. Finally, the woman tells her lover of her fantasy that that he is her brother, and she issues a modified version of the adjuration to the daughters of Jerusalem.

6:4–10 / Beginning with a partial descriptive motif or *waṣf* (see 4:1–7; 5:10–16; 7:1–7), this passage describes the central woman's head, including her **eyes, hair, teeth,** and **temples.** Concluding the motif, or directly following it in 6:8, is general admiration of her in comparison with other women, who are described in 6:9d–e as praising her. It may be that the admiring question/exclamation in 6:10 is the praise described in the preceding verse.

The first and last verses of the passage conclude with the same line in Hebrew, although the NIV translates the two lines quite differently: **majestic as troops with banners; majestic as the stars in procession.** This repetition, like that in 2:10 and 2:13, functions as a framing device which pushes the reader to read the passage as a unity. Thus it is possible that 6:10, although quoting the actual or imagined praise of the women mentioned in verse 9d–e, is actually spoken by the central man. In similar fashion, the central woman quotes the central man in 2:10–13.

The combination of images in this description is striking. Pastoral and agricultural images of **goats, sheep,** and **pomegranate** are repeated almost verbatim from 4:1–3. The comparison of the woman's beauty with that of cities puzzles many interpreters; it is a reversal of the common personification of cities as women. Military imagery is likely in verses 4 and 10. It is possible that awe comparable to that inspired by military pageantry lies behind the surprising request in verse 5, **Turn your eyes from me; / they overwhelm me.** The **queens, concubines,** and **virgins/maidens** (6:8–9) suggest an image of the lovers as royalty. Some find images of deities in the references to heavenly bodies in 6:10.

The sense of the reference to multiple queens and concubines depends on whether, with most interpreters, one understands the central couple to be commoners, or whether one believes that Solomon is the central man. If a commoner, the man, as the lover of only one woman, claims that he would rather have her than the many that are available for a king. If Solomon, he may be saying that of all the women in his harem, this one is uniquely lovely.

The admiration of the maidens for the central woman here corresponds to their admiration for the central man in 1:3–4. The use of royal imagery creates a connection with the other passages that mention Solomon or describe the man as king.

6:11–12 / These verses break with their context. Although the NIV identifies the central man as the speaker here, it is as easy to imagine that the central woman is speaking. In fact, there is nothing that precludes a different speaker for each verse.

The meaning depends on the speaker(s). If the woman speaks both, the sense may be: "I meant to go to the orchard. I don't know what I'm doing among the royal chariots with this admiring throng." She could also be using the orchard and the vineyard as images for her own sexuality, so that in taking a walk to the budding vineyards she is also exploring her own developing sexuality. If the man is speaking in both lines, they suggest, "I wanted to go and check on the fruitfulness of my orchards and vineyards"—again alluding to the woman's sexual ripeness— "but instead find myself among these chariots." If there are two different speakers, the exchange could suggest a missed connection. One of the lovers went to a nut grove, hoping for a rendezvous with the other, who then replies, "I didn't know" and makes an obscure reference to chariots. Verse 12 is the most difficult verse to translate in the entire book and its meaning must remain uncertain.

6:13 / Some group ("we") wants the woman, here called the Shulammite, to return (or do something again). If this verse belongs with the preceding verses, perhaps they call her to return because she has started for the orchards or because she is being whisked away on the chariots. In either case, they do not want her to leave. The Jerusalem women may be speaking here, but it may also be a group of men.

The second half of the verse seems to be a response. The woman may be speaking of herself in the third person. It is also possible that the man (as the NIV reads) or another character is speaking of her. The exchange can be read as playful banter, along the lines of 1:7–8.

7:1–6 / This is another descriptive motif, spoken about the central woman and apparently by the man. It moves up from the feet instead of from the head down. This arrangement may be related to the reference to dancing in the previous verse. If a woman is dancing, her moving feet may be the initial focus of attention. The imagery is wide-ranging, but interconnected. The opening image of **jewels** mentions a **craftsman.** The reference to the **goblet** being rounded also suggests the work of an artisan. Wine connects with the image of **wheat** in the following line, which suggests not only food but also agriculture. This progresses into the reference to lilies and fawns of a gazelle.

The reference to a dance in a simile in 6:13 is too obscure to conclude that this passage describes the woman dancing. In any case, the Hebrew particle *k* makes this a comparison: "*as* on the dance of Mahanaim." It is not to be read as straightforward description, as if it said, "while she performs the dance of Mahanaim." The reference to the woman's "steps" rather than "feet" in 7:1 may suggest movement, but this is not certain either. Nonetheless, these two elements together make a dance possible and perhaps likely. This would be the case especially if 6:13, in which a group is calling for the woman to do something that they may watch, is part of the context.

7:7–9 / The banter in these verses between the lovers takes off from the descriptive motif. In verses 7–9a, the speaker compares the woman's **stature** with that of a date palm and her

breasts with its clusters. Then the image seems to run away from him. What does one do with a tree? Climb it, of course! So he resolves to do so. But by the time he gets to the breasts they have changed from dates to grapes **(clusters of the vine)**, perhaps in keeping with the more usual image of grapevines and vineyards for her sexuality. Then he moves to another fruit image, the apple (or apricot), which has alluded to his own sexuality; we have already seen the association of grapes/raisins and apples in 2:5. By the time he speaks of her **mouth**, he has moved to another grape image, **wine.** Halfway through the verse, the woman interrupts by offering the wine in/of her mouth to her lover.

This is a passage rich in sensory imagery. The man moves from sight to touch to smell to taste. The woman picks up the images of taste and touch. The abrupt change of speakers also implies the sense of hearing.

7:10–13 / The segment opens with another variation on the mutual possession formula (2:16; 6:3). Verse 10b is a counterpart to (or even a reversal of) Genesis 3:16, where the woman's desire is for her man.

In verse 11, the woman is speaking to the man. She suggests that they spend the night together in the countryside. This is the first direct invitation from the woman to the man. In 2:10–13 and 4:8, the invitation is from the man to the woman—whether in her imagination or in reality. We might, however, infer an invitation in 3:4 when she (again, actually or in imagination/dream) speaks of taking him to her mother's house.

Verse 12 is reminiscent of 6:11 (**to see if the vines have budded** is repeated), but in chapter 6 it seemed as though the speaker was alone while here the two will go together. This time there is also the addition of a promise: **there I will give you my love.** The fruit imagery in verse 13 enriches the sexual implications of the invitation.

8:1–4 / The woman fantasizes about making her relationship with her lover public, then again describes or remembers or imagines his left arm under her head, his right embracing her. In this case, since the woman has been expressing a wish in verses 1–2, it is best to understand verse 3 as anticipatory as well. Finally, she repeats the adjuration to the daughters of Jerusalem in a slightly modified version. The use of double refrains indicates that this is the close of the main body of the book; the rest is epilogue.

Additional Notes §7

6:4 / Beautiful . . . as Tirzah, lovely as Jerusalem: The pairing of Tirzah and Jerusalem in parallel has led some to suppose that the Song, or at least this part of it, dates from the brief period after the breakdown of the federated kingdom and before Omri's establishment of Samaria. At this time, Tirzah was the capital of the northern kingdom. This hypothesis has not been found generally convincing.
Majestic as troops with banners: The Hb. *ʾᵃyummâ* suggests something more terrifying than "majestic." The only other use of the adjective is in Hab. 1:7 where it is used to describe an invading army. "Troops with banners" is literally "bannered ones." Throughout the Song (2:4; 5:10; 6:10), as here, the exact meaning of the Hb. root for "banner," *dgl*, is difficult to determine.

6:10 / Who is this that appears like the dawn / fair as the moon, bright as the sun: The usual words for "sun" and "moon" are not used here; the second line is lit. "fair as the white, bright as the hot." Using the word "white" for "moon" raises the association of "blackness" with "dawn." Although the two words ("blackness" and "dawn") are not etymologically related, they share the same root letters (Hb. *šḥr*). The central woman refers to her own blackness in 1:5–6 with words using these root letters (Hb. *šᵉḥôrâ* and *šᵉḥarḥoret*).
Majestic as the stars in procession: The Hb. wording is identical to 6:4c, which was translated "majestic as troops with banners." "Bannered ones" seems to have become "stars in procession" in the NIV by association with the sun and moon. Indeed when "sun" and "moon" in the Bible are followed by a third term, it is typically "stars," "hosts of heaven," or a similar term, as Bloch and Bloch note (*Song*, p. 191).

6:12 / Before I realized it, / my desire set me among the royal chariots of my people: This verse is so difficult to understand that a few commentators refuse even to translate it. A very literal rendering is:

> I did not know
> my desire–being–soul
> it–you–she set me
> chariots of Ammi-Nadib

The first problem is whether to relate Hb. *nepeš*, the word for "desire" or "self" or "soul" with what follows (as does the NIV) or with what precedes. If the latter, the speaker could be saying "I did not know myself," with the probable sense, "I was beside myself." The second problem is the Hb. verb *śmtny*. It can be read with a third-person feminine subject: "she" or "it" set me. Since *nepeš* is a feminine noun, it can be the subject. But the central woman could equally well be the subject of this verb, if she is not speaking this verse. Different vocalizations of the same consonants give masculine and feminine forms of "you set me," in which case it is most likely that one central character is speaking to the other. The third problem is the syntactic relationship between the last phrase (NIV **the royal chariots of my people**) and the rest of the verse. No preposition is used, and it is difficult to make sense of the verse without inferring one. Finally, is the last element (Hb. *ʿammî-nādîb*) a proper name (as read by early versions) or not? There are several biblical characters named Amminadab, but none of them would make particular sense in this verse.

6:13–7:13 / The versification in the Hb. text differs from that of the English translations by one verse throughout this section. Thus 6:13 is in fact 7:1 in the Hb. text, 7:1 is 7:2, and so on.

6:13 / **Come back, come back, O Shulammite:** "Come back" is Hb. *šûbî;* it might also be translated "again." "Shulammite" is a problem term. It may be a feminine form of Solomon, with which it shares root consonants. Or it could be a variation of Shunammite, in which case it may refer to the beauty of Abishag the Shunammite. Finally, the Hb. root *šlm,* in addition to being the root of Solomon and Shunammite, has the meaning of "completion" or "peace," so the epithet could imply that the woman is complete or brings peace. Equally likely is that it is a reference to something else, the meaning of which has been lost over the centuries.

As on the dance of Mahanaim: This is another uncertain term. It could be translated "two camps," as in army camp, so that the sense of this would be: "Why stare at her as if she were putting on a show for soldiers?" Mahanaim is a known place but not known to be identified with a dance. Some suppose that the dual is used to refer to a line dance or even an antiphonal call. As Murphy notes, it is not certain that the passage describes the woman dancing ("Dance and Death in the Song of Songs," in *Love and Death in the Ancient Near East: Essays in Honor of Marvin H. Pope* [ed. J. H. Marks and R. M. Good; Guilford: Four Quarters, 1987], pp. 117–19).

7:1 / **Prince's daughter:** It is not clear whether to take this literally or as a way of honoring the woman. The word for "prince" is also used in the enigmatic 6:12.

7:2 / **Navel:** Although the word used means "navel" or "umbilical cord" in Ezek. 16:4, some interpreters suppose that it means "vulva" here. There are several reasons for this. The description comes between legs and waist and the vulva is more likely than the navel to be wet **(never lacks blended wine).** On the other hand, if this is indeed a description of the woman dancing, it is more likely that her navel rather than her vulva would be visible. On the basis of iconographic finds, Keel argues that there is evidence that the navel and the vulva were interchangeable symbolically (*Song,* p. 234). It seems best to translate "navel" but recognize that this is a more strongly sexual image than it would be in our culture.

Your waist is a mound of wheat / encircled by lilies: Numerous commentators observe that it was common to surround cut wheat with a hedge of thorns or brambles to discourage foraging or theft. If it can be assumed that readers would associate a hedge with thorns, then the verse associates with 2:2, where the woman is described as a lily among thorns or brambles.

7:4 / Your neck is like an ivory tower: Cf. 4:4 and the image of the nose later in this verse. The tower is a military image. This is a proud woman, well defended, even awe-inspiring.

Your eyes are the pools of Heshbon: This image represents a shift in the development of imagery about the woman's eyes. They were doves in 1:15 and 4:1. In 4:9, something about the woman's eyes (perhaps a glance from them) is enthralling, and even captivating. In 6:5, her eyes were so disturbing that the speaker asked her to turn them away. Now her eyes are like pools. This is a peaceful image and is reminiscent of the doves, especially of the woman's own use of "eyes as doves" imagery in reference to the man.

7:5 / Your hair is like royal tapestry: The word translated "tapestry" (Hb. *ʿargāmān*) is lit. "purple." Maybe her hair is dyed, but maybe she is simply majestic.

The king is held captive: If the speaker is not using royal language of himself, he is probably making a comparison: "if a king would be held captive, how much more am I." If bystanders are speaking, they are acknowledging that the male lover (actually or symbolically a king) is captivated. "Held captive" resumes the military imagery and is also reminiscent of **stolen my heart** in 4:9. In a culture in which women were quite literally taken as spoils of war, a reference to the male lover being taken captive is another element of the Song's gender equality.

7:6 / O love: The word for "love" (*ʾahᵃbâ*) is generally used for the abstraction, rather than for a person. Perhaps it tends in both directions here.

7:13 / Every delicacy / both new and old: The word for delicacy, Hb. *mᵉgādîm,* is used with the word for "fruit" in 4:13, 16, and may have the same implication here. "New and old" is a merism (a use of extremes to imply an entire range). It seems odd to some commentators to refer to new and old fruit. Given the emphasis on exotic imports in the Song, the reference to "new and old" delicacies might mean both old-fashioned fruits and those newly available as imports. It could also mean fresh and preserved, whether by drying or fermenting (as wine). In any case, the delicacies at the door are suggestive of erotic pleasures, perhaps both those the lovers have already shared and those with which the woman promises to experiment with the man.

8:1 / If only you were to me like a brother: Although the woman has been addressed as "sister" in 4:9, 10, and 12, this is the first hint of corresponding language for the man, and it is a wish rather than an address to him. The use of brother/sister language for romantic attachment is also found in Egyptian texts.

8:2 / My mother's house: The woman's desire to bring the lover to the mother's house has appeared before (3:4).

She who has taught me: This expression is often emended to "she who bore me" to correspond with 8:5. This emendation, however, involves both a change of a consonant and its transposition (Hb. *lmd,* "teach" to *yld,* "give birth"). The use of the verb for teaching may suggest a wisdom connection.

8:4 / **Daughters of Jerusalem, I charge you: / Do not arouse or awaken love / until it so desires:** In this rendition of the adjuration, the gazelles and does are missing and the particle used to express the negative is Hb. *mâ.* This makes the verse a stronger prohibition than the versions in 2:7 and 3:5.

§8 Loose Ends (Song 8:5–14)

Corresponding to the opening section of the book (1:2–6) which introduced the characters (the lovers, the daughters of Jerusalem, and the brothers), the closing verses include all of them as speakers. As usual, the focus is on the central woman. This inclusion does not mean, however, that the book ends with all the loose ends neatly tied. The daughters of Jerusalem ask a question that is not clearly answered. The central woman solemnly announces the seriousness of love. The brothers reveal a breathtaking blindness to the fact that their little sister has grown up. The central woman declares her independence. The central man calls for her to speak. She issues an invitation framed as a warning. The book may end, but the relationship that it describes is open-ended. As the Song began in the middle of things, with the woman wishing for a kiss from a lover already familiar, so it ends with an invitation to one who has already accepted.

This final section problematizes the book as a whole. While there is much overlap in both vocabulary and syntax with the rest of the book and most of the refrain lines occur here in one form or another, this ending seems to demand a plot, yet the book as a whole does not provide one. In effect, the ending is as destabilizing for plot development as the opening was for characters.

8:5 / The first two lines of the verse are another "who is this" question or exclamation (see 3:6; 6:10). No speaker is identified; the daughters of Jerusalem are likely, as the NIV indicates. The two lovers are coming toward the speakers from an unpopulated area (NIV **desert**). The fact that the woman and her lover are together as they approach may hint that the invitation in 7:11–12 was accepted.

The last lines of the verse resume the image of the fruit tree first mentioned in 2:3. In the NIV as in the majority of translations, the woman is speaking to the man. In 2:3 the man was the apple tree, but now it is the place where she arouses him and where his

mother conceived and perhaps gave birth to him. Although there have been several references to the central woman's mother and conception, this is the first set of corresponding references for the man.

8:6–7 / This segment, in which the woman is still speaking (as the NIV indicates), is remarkable in both tone and vocabulary. Throughout the book, love has been celebrated exuberantly. Occasionally there have been hints of danger: the resistance of the brothers, repeated warnings about arousing love before its time, the beating by the city guards, and even the use of military imagery. Yet throughout the rest of the book, to celebrate love is to celebrate life. Only here is the strength of love compared with **death** and Sheol and raging flames. This is not to suggest that love is no longer celebrated; but the fierceness of love is recognized as being deadly serious.

8:8–10 / The speakers in verses 8–9 are most likely the brothers (in the NIV, the designation "Friends" is used for any group), and the **young sister** is most likely the central woman. If so, the brothers' perception of the woman's physical maturity is different from that of both the central man and the woman herself. The speakers here claim that their sister's **breasts** have **not yet grown,** while the central man has compared her breasts to date clusters (7:7) and the woman will claim that her **breasts are like towers** (8:10). The speakers express a desire both to protect and to decorate the woman, by building silver towers (from which to watch out for predatory males?) and cedar door panels (to keep those males out?). The apparent assumption is that a woman needs to be protected by men, and implicitly she needs to be protected from other men. The image of foxes in the vineyard in 2:15 may fit into the same conceptual framework.

Some read these lines as contrasting rather than synonymous. If the woman is **a wall** (that is, well defended), then we will reward her with decorations; but if she is **a door** (that is, too easy to enter), then we will punish her with enclosures. This interpretation underestimates the similarity between the two lines. In both, the images are of defenses that are made of valuable materials. The brothers do not indicate that they will choose between decorating and defending the woman; rather, they will build decorative defenses.

The brothers then intend to increase the woman's value in two ways: first by adorning her with **silver** and **cedar,** and second by ensuring her inviolability. The brothers here, like Solomon (and the tenants?) in the next subsection, are set up to be "utterly scorned" in the terms of verse 7. All of these men suggest thinking in terms of the wealth of the household/kingdom, rather than in terms of love.

Others read verses 8 and 9 as spoken by the central woman about her own little sister. There is no textual motivation for doing so. The use of "we" makes it most natural to understand a group as speakers and there has been no indication that the central woman has a little sister.

The central woman does, however, speak in verse 10. She uses the imagery of the preceding verses to protest their assumptions. She resists both the claim that she is still a child and the suggestion that she is in need of male protection. The contrast between this verse and 1:6 is strong. There the woman acknowledged that she did not keep her vineyard; here she claims that she does keep herself.

8:11–12 / It is not clear who is speaking here. Most likely, this is a continuation of the woman's response to her brothers. Especially when her response is read in counterpoint to 1:6, the use of vineyard imagery is appropriate for the woman speaking to or about her brothers. **My own vineyard is mine** expresses a claim over against the brothers, who think they own the woman as they would a vineyard. Another possibility is that the man is speaking, claiming that the woman is his vineyard and expressing his preference for his only one over Solomon's thousand.

8:13–14 / These verses constitute another exchange between the central couple. Verse 13 is reminiscent of 2:14 and repeats **let me hear your voice.** The problem in this verse is identifying the **friends,** grammatically masculine in Hebrew. Perhaps they are the brothers who are still striving to keep the lovers apart. It is also possible that, since grammatically masculine verbs are frequently used to address the daughters of Jerusalem, the grammatically masculine noun here refers to them as well.

The response in verse 14 uses language and imagery from 2:17. The central woman is speaking. It sounds as though she is warning her lover away; yet given the previous use of geographical imagery, **mountains** is best understood as self-referential. Most likely, she is using the language of warning to invite her lover to herself and assumes that he will understand the import of her words—and any listening "companions" will take her warning at face value. If this is correct, the book ends with the central characters again waiting for a reunion.

Additional Notes §8

8:5 / **I roused you:** "Roused" is appropriately ambiguous here: it is a word typically used of awakening someone from sleep, but is also the verb used in the adjuration, where it may well refer to sexual arousal.

8:6 / **Place me like a seal over your heart, / like a seal on your arm:** The seal is the primary means of identification by which the individual leaves his or her mark on items and documents. The woman here is asking to be that identification for the man, either a cylinder seal worn on a cord around the neck ("over your heart") or a ring seal ("over your arm").

Its jealousy unyielding as the grave: "Its" is not in the Hb. This is the only indication of jealousy in the entire Song, which leads some commentators and translators to substitute "passion." The Hb. word translated "grave" is *šeʾôl* (Sheol), the abode of the dead.

Like a mighty flame: The word here is a normal word for fire but with the suffix *yâ*, a shortened form of Yahweh, God's proper name in Hb. The translation problem (indicated in NIV note) is whether the suffix signifies God's name or is used as an intensifier. Either is possible.

8:9–10 / **We will build towers ... my breasts are like towers:** Two different words for "towers" are used in the two verses. The word in 8:9, not used elsewhere in the Song, refers to defensive military structures. That in 8:10 is not a purely military term and emphasizes elevation and grandeur rather than defense; it is used of the woman in 4:4; 5:13; 7:5. Thus, the group proposes defending the woman, while she insists on displaying her magnificence.

8:10 / **Thus I have become in his eyes / like one bringing contentment:** No referent for "his" is expressed, but the central man can be assumed. The Hb. for "contentment" is *šālôm*, which has the same root as both Solomon and Shulammite.

8:12 / **My own vineyard is mine to give:** The Hb. structure is emphatic, with three first-person suffixes in three words: "my vineyard, which is mine, is before me." "To give" in NIV expresses one possible reason for the speaker's emphasis on her ownership, but does not directly reflect anything in the Hb.

8:14 / **Come away:** The word that is used here suggests flight more than invitation.

For Further Reading

General Treatments of Wisdom

Bergant, Dianne. *Israel's Wisdom Literature: A Liberation-Critical Reading*. Minneapolis: Fortress, 1997.

Brown, William P. *Character in Crisis: A Fresh Approach to the Wisdom Literature of the Old Testament*. Grand Rapids: Eerdmans, 1996.

Clements, Ronald E. *Wisdom in Theology*. Grand Rapids: Eerdmans, 1992.

Murphy, Roland E. *The Tree of Life: An Exploration of Biblical Wisdom Literature*. 2d rev. ed. Grand Rapids: Eerdmans, 1996.

Perdue, Leo G. *Wisdom and Creation: The Theology of Wisdom Literature*. Nashville: Abingdon, 1994.

Perdue, Leo G., Bernard B. Scott, and William J. Wiseman, eds. *In Search of Wisdom: Essays in Memory of John G. Gammie*. Louisville: Westminster/John Knox, 1993.

Rad, Gerhard von. *Wisdom in Israel*. Trans. James D. Martin. Nashville: Abingdon, 1972.

Sheppard, Gerald T. *Wisdom as a Hermeneutical Construct: A Study in the Sapientializing of the Old Testament*. BZAW 151. Berlin: de Gruyter, 1980.

Whybray, R. N. *The Intellectual Tradition in the Old Testament*. BZAW 135. Berlin: de Gruyter, 1974.

Commentaries on Proverbs

For a recent summary of publications on Proverbs, see Roland E. Murphy, "Recent Research on Proverbs and Qoheleth," in *CurBS* 1 (1993), pp. 118–40. The most complete survey of studies on Proverbs in the twentieth century is done by R. N. Whybray, *The Book of Proverbs: A Survey of Modern Study* (HBIS 1; Leiden: Brill, 1995).

Aitken, Kenneth T. *Proverbs*. DSB. Philadelphia: Westminster, 1986.

Alonso Schökel, Luis. *Proverbios*. NBE. Madrid: Ediciones Cristiandad, 1984.

Barucq, André. *Le livre des Proverbes*. SB. Paris: Librairie Lecoffre, 1964.

Boadt, Lawrence. "Proverbs." Pages 644–74 in vol. 1 of *The Collegeville Bible Commentary: Based on the New American Bible*. Ed. Dianne Bergant and Robert J. Karris. Collegeville, Minn.: Liturgical, 1989.

Clifford, Richard J. *Proverbs*. OTL. Philadelphia: Westminster/ John Knox, 1999.

Collins, John J. *Proverbs, Ecclesiastes*. KPG. Atlanta: John Knox, 1980.

Cox, Dermot. *Proverbs: With an Introduction to Sapiential Books*. OTM 17. Wilmington, Del.: Glazier, 1982.

Delitzsch, Franz. *The Book of Proverbs*. Trans. M. G. Easton; 1874–75; repr., Peabody, Mass.: Hendrickson, 1996.

Fontaine, Carole R. "Proverbs." Pages 495–517 in *HBC*. Ed. J. L. Mays. San Francisco: Harper & Row, 1988.

Fox, Michael V. *Proverbs*. AB. New York: Doubleday, forthcoming.

Garrett, Duane A. *Proverbs, Ecclesiastes, Song of Songs*. NAC 14. Nashville: Broadman, 1993.

Gemser, Berend. *Sprüche Salomos*. HAT 16. Tübingen: J. C. B. Mohr (Paul Siebeck), 1963.

Hubbard, David A. *The Communicator's Commentary: Proverbs*. ComC 15A. Dallas: Word, 1989.

Jones, Edgar. *Proverbs and Ecclesiastes: Introduction and Commentary*. TBC. London: SCM, 1961.

Kidner, Derek. *The Proverbs: An Introduction and Commentary*. TOTC. Downers Grove: InterVarsity, 1964.

Mouser, W. *Walking in Wisdom: Studying the Proverbs of Solomon*. Downers Grove: InterVarsity, 1983.

McCreesh, Thomas P. "Proverbs." Pages 453–61 in *NJBC*. Ed. Raymond E. Brown, Joseph A. Fitzmyer, and Roland E. Murphy. Englewood Cliffs, N.J.: Prentice-Hall, 1990.

McKane, William. *Proverbs: A New Approach*. OTL. Philadelphia: Westminster, 1970.

Meinhold, Arndt. *Die Sprüche*. 2 vols. ZBk 16. Zürich: Theologischer Verlag, 1991.

Murphy, Roland E. *Proverbs*. WBC 22. Nashville: Nelson, 1998.

Oesterley, W. O. E. *The Book of Proverbs: With Introduction and Notes*. WC. London: Methuen, 1929.

Perowne, Thomas T. *The Proverbs*. CBSC. Cambridge: Cambridge University Press, 1916.

Plöger, Otto. *Sprüche Salomos (Proverbia)*. BKAT 17. Neukirchen-Vluyn: Neukirchener, 1981–84.

Ringgren, H. *Sprüche. ATD* 16/1. Göttingen: Vandenhoeck & Ruprecht, 1962.

Ross, Allen P. "Proverbs." Pages 833–1134 in vol. 5 of *EBC*. Ed. Frank E. Gaebelein. Grand Rapids: Zondervan, 1991.

Rylaarsdam, John C. *The Proverbs; Ecclesiastes; The Song of Solomon.* LBC 10. London: SCM, 1964.

Scott, R. B. Y. *Proverbs, Ecclesiastes: Introduction, Translation, and Notes.* AB 18. Garden City, N.Y.: Doubleday, 1965.

Toy, Crawford H. *A Critical and Exegetical Commentary on the Book of Proverbs.* ICC. Edinburgh: T & T Clark, 1899.

Van Leeuwen, Raymond C. "Proverbs." Pages 19–264 in vol. 5 of *The New Interpreter's Bible.* Nashville: Abingdon, 1997.

Whybray, R. N. *Proverbs: Based on the Revised Standard Version.* NCBC. Grand Rapids: Eerdmans, 1994.

Special Studies of Proverbs

Alter, Robert. "The Poetry of Wit." Pages 163–84 in *The Art of Biblical Poetry.* New York: Basic Books, 1985.

Bauer-Kayatz, Christa. *Studien zu Proverbien 1–9. Eine form- und motivgeschichtliche Untersuchung unter Einbeziehung ägyptischen Vergleichmaterials.* WMANT 22. Neukirchen-Vluyn: Neukirchener, 1966.

Boström, Gustav. *Proverbiastudien: die Weisheit und das fremde Weib in Spr. 1–9.* Lund: C. W. K. Gleerup, 1935.

Brown, William P. *Character in Crisis: A Fresh Approach to the Wisdom Literature of the Old Testament.* Grand Rapids: Eerdmans, 1996.

Bryce, Glendon E. *A Legacy of Wisdom: The Egyptian Contribution to the Wisdom of Israel.* Lewisburg: Bucknell University Press, 1979.

Bühlmann, Walter. *Vom rechten Reden und Schweigen: Studien zu Proverbien 10–31.* OBO 12. Freiburg/Schweiz: Universitätsverlag, 1976.

Camp, Claudia V. *Wisdom and the Feminine in the Book of Proverbs.* BLS 11. Sheffield: Almond, 1985.

Clifford, Richard J. *The Book of Proverbs and Our Search for Wisdom.* The Père Marquette Lecture in Theology. Milwaukee: Marquette University Press, 1995.

Crenshaw, James L. "Education in Ancient Israel." *JBL* 104 (1985), pp. 601–15.

Emerton, John A. "Note on Proverbs 12:26." *ZAW* 76 (1964), pp. 191–93.

_____. "Note on the Hebrew Text of Proverbs 1:22–3." *JTS* 19 (1968), pp. 609–14.

Fontaine, Carole R. *Traditional Sayings in the Old Testament: A Contextual Study.* BLS 5. Sheffield: Almond, 1989.

Gammie, John G. and Leo G. Perdue, eds. *The Sage in Israel and the Ancient Near East.* Winona Lake, Ind.: Eisenbrauns, 1990.

Gilbert, M., ed. *La Sagesse de l'Ancien Testament.* BETL 51. Leuven: University Press, 1971.

Grollenberg, Lucas H. "A propos de Prov 8:6 et Prov 17:27." *RB* 59 (1952), pp. 40–43.

Habel, Norman C. "Symbolism of Wisdom in Proverbs 1–9," *Int* 26 (1972), pp. 131–57.

Hausmann, Jutta. *Studien zum Menschenbild der älteren Weisheit (Spr 10ff.).* Tübingen: J. C. B. Mohr (Paul Siebeck), 1995.

Hermisson, Hans-Jürgen. *Studien zur israelitischen Spruchweisheit.* WMANT 28. Neukirchen-Vluyn: Neukirchener, 1968.

Hoglund, Kenneth G. "The Fool and the Wise in Dialogue." Pages 161–80 in *The Listening Heart.* Ed. Kenneth G. Hoglund et al. JSOTSup 58. Sheffield: JSOT Press, 1987.

Huwiler, Elizabeth. "Control of Reality in Israelite Wisdom." Ph.D. diss., Duke University, 1988.

Lang, Bernhard. *Die weisheitliche Lehrrede: eine Untersuchung von Sprüche 1–7.* SBS 54. Stuttgart: KBW, 1972.

_____. *Wisdom and the Book of Proverbs: A Hebrew Goddess Redefined.* New York: Pilgrim, 1986.

McCreesh, Thomas P. *Biblical Sound and Sense: Poetic Sound Patterns in Proverbs 10–29.* JSOTSup 128. Sheffield: JSOT Press, 1991.

_____. "Wisdom as Wife: Proverbs 31:10–31." *RB* 92 (1985), pp. 25–46.

Murphy, Roland E. "The Kerygma of the Book of Proverbs." *Int* 20 (1966), pp. 3–14.

_____. "Wisdom and Eros in Proverbs 1–9." *CBQ* 50 (1988), pp. 600–603.

_____. *Wisdom Literature: Job, Proverbs, Ruth, Canticles, Ecclesiastes, and Esther.* FOTL 13. Grand Rapids: Eerdmans, 1981.

_____. " 'Wisdom's Song:' Proverbs 1:20–33." *CBQ* 48 (1986), pp. 456–60.

Nel, Philip J. *The Structure and Ethos of the Wisdom Admonitions in Proverbs.* BZAW 159. Berlin: de Gruyter, 1982.

Preuss, Horst D. *Einführung in die alttestamentliche Weisheitsliteratur.* Kohlhammer Urban-Taschenbücher 383. Stuttgart: Kohlhammer, 1987.

Rad, Gerhard von. *Old Testament Theology.* Trans. D. M. G. Stalker. 2 vols. New York: Harper & Row, 1962.

_____. *Wisdom in Israel.* Trans. James D. Martin. Nashville: Abingdon, 1972.

Rüger, Hans P. "ʾAmôn—Pflegekind: zur Auslegungsgeschichte von Prv 8:30a." Pages 154–63 in *Übersetzung und Deutung: Studien zu dem Alten Testament und seiner Umwelt.* Nijkerk: Callenbach, 1977.

Skehan, Patrick W. *Studies in Israelite Poetry and Wisdom.* CBQMS 1. Washington: Catholic Biblical Association, 1971.

Snell, Daniel C. *Twice-Told Proverbs and the Composition of the Book of Proverbs.* Winona Lake, Ind.: Eisenbrauns, 1993.

Trible, Phyllis. "Wisdom Builds a House: The Architecture of Proverbs 1:20–33." *JBL* 94 (1975), pp. 509–19.

Van Leeuwen, Raymond C. *Context and Meaning in Proverbs 25–27.* SBLDS 96. Atlanta: Scholars Press, 1988.

_____. "Proverbs 25:27 Once Again." *VT* 36 (1986), pp. 105–14.

_____. "Proverbs 30:21–23 and the Biblical World Upside Down." *JBL* 105 (1986), pp. 599–610.

Washington, Harold C. *Wealth and Poverty in the Instruction of Amenemope and the Hebrew Proverbs.* SBLDS 142. Atlanta: Scholars Press, 1994.

Westermann, Claus. *Roots of Wisdom: The Oldest Proverbs of Israel and Other Peoples.* Trans. J. Daryl Charles. Louisville: Westminster/John Knox, 1995.

Whybray, R. N. *The Book of Proverbs: A Survey of Modern Study.* HBIS 1. Leiden: Brill, 1995.

_____. *The Composition of the Book of Proverbs.* JSOTSup 168. Sheffield: JSOT Press, 1994.

_____. *Wealth and Poverty in the Book of Proverbs.* JSOTSup 99. Sheffield: JSOT Press, 1990.

Williams, James G. "The Power of Form: A Study of Biblical Proverbs." Pages 35–58 in *Gnomic Wisdom.* Ed. J. D. Crossan. Semeia 17. Chico, Calif.: Scholars Press, 1980.

Commentaries on Ecclesiastes

Collins, John J. *Proverbs, Ecclesiastes.* KPG. Atlanta: John Knox, 1980.

Crenshaw, James L. *Ecclesiastes: A Commentary.* OTL. Philadelphia: Westminster, 1987.

Gordis, Robert. *Koheleth: The Man and His World, A Study of Ecclesiastes.* 3d ed. New York: Schocken, 1968.

Murphy, Roland E. *Ecclesiastes.* WBC 23. Waco: Word, 1992.

Ogden, Graham. *Qoheleth.* Sheffield: JSOT Press, 1987.

Scott, R. B. Y. *Proverbs; Ecclesiastes: Introduction, Translation, and Notes.* AB 18. Garden City: Doubleday, 1965.

Seow, Choon-Leong. *Ecclesiastes: A New Translation with Introduction and Commentary.* AB 18C. Garden City: Doubleday, 1997.

Towner, W. Sibley. "The Book of Ecclesiastes: Introduction, Commentary, and Reflections." Pages 265–360 in vol. 5 of *The New Interpreter's Bible.* Nashville: Abingdon, 1997.

Whybray, R. N. *Ecclesiastes: Based on the Revised Standard Version.* NCBC. Grand Rapids: Eerdmans, 1989.

Wright, Addison G. "Ecclesiastes (Qoheleth)." Pages 489–95 in *NJBC.* Ed. Raymond E. Brown, Joseph A. Fitzmyer, and Roland E. Murphy. Englewood Cliffs, N.J.: Prentice-Hall, 1990.

Wright, J. Stafford. "Ecclesiastes." Pages 1135–97 in vol. 5 of *EBC.* Ed. Frank E. Gaebelein. Grand Rapids: Zondervan, 1991.

Special Studies of Ecclesiastes

Ellul, Jacques. *The Reason for Being: A Meditation on Ecclesiastes.* Trans. Joyce Main Hanks. Grand Rapids: Eerdmans, 1990.

Fox, Michael V. *Qohelet and His Contradictions.* JSOTSup 71. Sheffield: Almond, 1989.

Loader, J. A. *Polar Structures in the Book of Qoheleth.* BZAW 152. Berlin: de Gruyter, 1979.

Murphy, Roland E. "Qohelet Interpreted: The Bearing of the Past on the Present." *VT* 32 (1982), pp. 331–37.

_____. "Qohelet's 'Quarrel' with the Fathers." Pages 235–45 in *From Faith to Faith.* Ed. D. Y. Hadidian. Pittsburgh: Pickwick, 1981.

Wright, Addison G. "The Riddle of the Sphinx: The Structure of the Book of Qoheleth," *CBQ* 30 (1968), pp. 313–34.

_____. "The Riddle of the Sphinx Revisited: Numerical Patterns in the Book of Qoheleth," *CBQ* 42 (1980), pp. 38–51.

_____. "Additional Numerical Patterns in Qoheleth," *CBQ* 45 (1983), pp. 32–43.

Commentaries on the Song of Songs

Bloch, Ariel and Chana Bloch. *The Song of Songs: A New Translation with an Introduction and Commentary.* New York: Random House, 1995.

Falk, Marcia. *The Song of Songs: A New Translation and Commentary.* San Francisco: Harper & Row, 1990.

Gordis, Robert. *The Song of Songs and Lamentations.* Rev. and aug. ed. New York: Ktav, 1974.

Keel, Othmar. *The Song of Songs.* Trans. F. J. Gaiser. CC. Minneapolis: Fortress, 1994.

Kinlaw, Dennis F. "Song of Songs." Pages 1199–244 in vol. 5 of *EBC.* Ed. Frank E. Gaebelein. Grand Rapids: Zondervan, 1991.

Murphy, Roland E. *The Song of Songs: A Commentary on the Book of Canticles or the Song of Songs.* Hermeneia. Minneapolis: Fortress, 1990.

Pope, Marvin H. *Song of Songs: A New Translation with Introduction and Commentary.* AB 7C. Garden City, N.Y.: Doubleday, 1977.

Weems, Renita J. "The Song of Songs." Pages 361–434 in vol. 5 of *The New Interpreter's Bible.* Nashville: Abingdon, 1997.

_____. "The Song of Songs." Pages 156–60 in *The Women's Bible Commentary.* Ed. Carol A. Newsom and Sharon H. Ringe. London: SPCK and Louisville: Westminster/John Knox, 1992.

Special Studies of the Song of Songs

Brenner, Athalya. *The Song of Songs.* OTG. Sheffield: Sheffield Academic Press, 1989.

_____, ed. *A Feminist Companion to the Song of Songs.* FCB 1. Sheffield: Sheffield Academic Press, 1993.

Dorsey, David A. "Literary Structuring in the Song of Songs." *JSOT* 46 (1990), pp. 81–96.

Exum, J. Cheryl. "A Literary and Structural Analysis of the Song of Songs." *ZAW* 85 (1973), pp. 47–79.

Fox, Michael V. *The Song of Songs and the Ancient Egyptian Love Poems*. Madison: University of Wisconsin Press, 1985.

Gotein, S. D. "The Song of Songs: A Female Composition," trans. Athalya Brenner. Pages 58–66 in *A Feminist Companion to the Song of Songs*. Ed. Athalya Brenner. FCB 1. Sheffield: Sheffield Academic Press, 1993.

Landy, Francis. *Paradoxes of Paradise: Identity and Difference in the Song of Songs*. Sheffield: Almond, 1983.

Meyers, Carol. "Gender Imagery in the Song of Songs." Pages 197–212 in *A Feminist Companion to the Song of Songs*. Ed. Athalya Brenner. FCB 1. Sheffield: Sheffield Academic Press, 1993.

Murphy, Roland E. "Dance and Death in the Song of Songs." Pages 117–19 in *Love and Death in the Ancient Near East: Essays in Honor of Marvin H. Pope*. Ed. John H. Marks and Robert M. Good. Guilford: Four Quarters, 1987.

Trible, Phyllis. "Love's Lyrics Redeemed." Pages 144–65 in *God and the Rhetoric of Sexuality*. OBT [2]. Philadelphia: Fortress, 1978.

Webster, Edwin C. "Pattern in the Song of Songs." *JSOT* 22 (1982), pp. 73–93.

Other Works Cited

Albright, William F. "Some Canaanite-Phoenician Sources of Hebrew Wisdom." VTSup 3 (1955), pp. 1–15.

Berlin, Adele. *The Dynamics of Biblical Parallelism*. Bloomington: Indiana University Press, 1985.

Childs, Brevard S. *Introduction to the Old Testament as Scripture*. Philadelphia: Fortress, 1979.

Crenshaw, James L. *A Whirlpool of Torment: Israelite Traditions of God as an Oppressive Presence*. OBT 12. Philadelphia: Fortress, 1984.

Dietrich, Manfried and Oswald Loretz. "Die angebliche Ug.-He. Parallele SPSB//SPS(J)G(JM)." *UF* 8 (1976), pp. 37–40.

Humphreys, W. Lee. *The Tragic Vision and the Hebrew Tradition*. OBT 18. Philadelphia: Fortress, 1985.

Koch, Klaus. "Is There a Doctrine of Retribution in the Old Testament?" Pages 57–87 in *Theodicy in the Old Testament*. Ed. James L. Crenshaw. Issues in Religion and Theology 4. Philadelphia: Fortress, 1983.

Kramer, Samuel Noah. *The Sacred Marriage Rite: Aspects of Faith, Myth, and Ritual in Ancient Sumer.* Bloomington: Indiana University Press, 1969.

Lambert, W. G. *Babylonian Wisdom Literature.* Oxford: Clarendon, 1960.

Leiman, Sid Z. *The Canonization of Hebrew Scripture: The Talmudic and Midrashic Evidence.* 2d ed. New Haven: Transaction of the Connecticut Academy of Arts and Sciences, 1991.

Lichtheim, Miriam. *Ancient Egyptian Literature.* 3 vols. Berkeley: University of California Press, 1971–80.

Morenz, Siegfried. "Feurige Kohlen auf dem Haupt." *TLZ* 78 (1953), pp. 187–92.

O'Connor, Michael P. *Hebrew Verse Structure.* Winona Lake, Ind.: Eisenbrauns, 1997.

Pritchard, James B., ed. *Ancient Near Eastern Texts Relating to the Old Testament.* 3d ed. Princeton: Princeton University Press, 1969.

Williams, James G. *Those Who Ponder Proverbs: Aphoristic Thinking and Biblical Literature.* BLS 2. Sheffield: Almond, 1981.

Subject Index

Scripture Index

NEW TESTAMENT

APOCRYPHAL/DEUTERO-CANONICAL BOOKS